MANAGING PROFESSIONAL PEOPLE

MANAGING PROFESSIONAL PEOPLE

Understanding Creative Performance

Albert Shapero

The Free Press
A Division of Macmillan, Inc.
NEW YORK

Collier Macmillan Publishers
LONDON

The Free Press
A Division of Macmillan, Inc.
866 Third Avenue, New York, N.Y. 10022

Collier Macmillan Canada, Inc.

First Free Press Paperback Edition 1989

Printed in the United States of America

printing number

1 2 3 4 5 6 7 8 9 10

Library of Congress Cataloging in Publication Data

Shapero, Albert.
  Managing professional people.

  Bibliography: p.
  Includes index.
  1. Professions.   2. Personnel management.   I. Title.
HD8038.A1S53   1985   658.3′044   84-18728
ISBN 0-02-929360-X

To Gitel

Contents

Introduction

THE MANAGEMENT of creative workers has become the most critical area faced by managements in both the private and public sectors. Without a great deal of fanfare, creative workers, or, more strictly, professionals, have come center stage in the United States and in the rest of the developed world. Quantitatively, professionals now surpass all other categories in the work force of the United States. Qualitatively, professionals have a disproportionate effect on all aspects of our society, as the researchers, designers, decision makers, and managers who define and direct much of what is done in society. The quality and extent of what is accomplished in the foreseeable future have become a function of the ability of managements to harness and channel the efforts of creative workers. The difference in success between one effort and another, one organization and another, increasingly depends on whether management understands the differences between the management of professional activities and the management relevant to the assembly line.

An early definition of the term *profession* was "a particular order of monks, nuns or other professed persons" (compact edition of the *Oxford English Dictionary*, 1971). More recent is the definition "a vocation in which a professed knowledge of some department of learning or science is used in its application to the affairs of others or used in the practice of an art founded upon it" (ibid.), and a *professional* is one who "belongs to one of the learned or skilled professions" (ibid.). Social scientists use the term profession to denote "occupations which demand a highly specialized knowledge and skill acquired at least in part by courses of more or less theoretical nature and not by practice alone, tested by some form of examination either at a university or some other unauthorized institution, and conveying to the persons who possess them considerable authority in relation to 'clients.' . . . Such authority is carefully maintained . . . by guildlike associations of the practitioners . . . which lay down rules of entry, training, and behavior in relation to the public . . . and watch over their professional status" (J. Gould and William A. Kolb, eds., *A Dictionary of the Social Sciences*, New York: The Free Press, 1964).

In modern society a professional is usually someone who has completed the equivalent of at least a baccalaureate degree that has the number and mix of courses certified by some professional society. The members of the profession identify themselves in terms of their profession and have expectations of status and treatment on the job that are clearly different from those of people in skilled and unskilled trades and blue-collar and white-collar work. Because of the status attributed to the professions, occupations constantly attempt to be identified as professions by restricting entry through special educational requirements, examinations, licensing, and the establishment of a code of ethics. Furthermore, would-be professions are marked by calling for "more professionalism" and institutionalizing what is considered professional and nonprofessional behavior in the occupation.

To be a professional has very positive social connotations, and members of a profession identify strongly with their profession even when there is an apparent conflict between employer and profession. It is quite in character to call on professionals to "blow the whistle" on an employer when the employer is seen as doing something in conflict with the standards of the profession or contrary to the public good. The word *profession* still carries something of its earlier definition as a religious "order," and the more narrow definitions used today of clergy, medical doctors, and lawyers (the so-called free professions) characterize what all professions reach for.

Where once professionals were few in number relative to the total working population, today they are far more numerous relatively and absolutely. The proportion of the work force that can be designated as professionals is steadily increasing. In 1979 (*Statistical Abstract of the United States*, 1979), over fifteen million workers were classified as professional and technical workers as compared with a little over eleven million in 1970 and approximately seven and a half million in 1960. In 1979, professional and technical workers constituted just under 16% of the total work force as compared with 14% in 1970 and a little over 11% in 1960. If we admit managers and administrators to the ranks of professionals, the numbers go up to twenty-five and a half million and 27% in 1979 as compared with nineteen and a half million and 25% in 1970 and fourteen and a half million and 22% in 1960.

By all measures professionals make up the largest single category in the work force of the United States, surpassing those classified as "craft and kindred workers," "operatives" of all kinds, "service workers," and "clerical workers." Further, the numbers shown above refer only to those employed in industry and do not include the substantial number of professional workers to be found among the self-employed, who numbered over six million in 1979. The self-employed include those physicians, lawyers, other health professionals, and consultants of all kinds who work by themselves or in group practices. The list of those classifiable as professionals includes architects, accountants, engineers, scientists of all kinds, doctors, dentists, nurses, pharmacists, lawyers, designers, librarians, computer specialists, editors, journalists, managers, clergy, dieticians, advertising specialists, statisticians, and on and on.

There are many reasons for the growth in the professional

work force, among which are (1) the steep growth in technology requiring specialists, (2) the growth in large organizations requiring the services of many technical specialists, and (3) the sharp increase in the number of educated people who generate a demand for professional status.

Ours is the era of the "knowledge society" or of the "information revolution." Increasingly our society and economy are shaped by special bodies of knowledge, and by those who possess them—these are the professionals, and their management is the subject of this book.

HOW PROFESSIONAL ACTIVITIES DIFFER FROM OTHER ACTIVITIES

Mapping the world of work in terms of the types of activity carried out and the types of human resources required, the results can be roughly depicted as in Figure I–1. Work activities can be distributed along a dimension of increasing uncertainty. At one extreme are those activities that are denoted by being essentially routine. They are predictable, stable, and specifiable. Consequently, they are relatively easy to plan and budget. They lend themselves to long-run operations. All of the conditions describing routine activities tend to make them process-dominated. To meet the conditions of predictability, stability and specifiability over time managers must understand and control the process.

At the other extreme of the dimension are the activities that are most unpredictable, those that can be described as one-of-a-kind. One-of-a-kind activities are essentially unspecifiable or predictable and are least amenable to the arts of estimation and budgeting. Such activities are inherently human-dominated, for when one is unable to predict the nature of a process one inserts a human, a substitute for oneself, to do what is needed within the unpredictable context. If it is to be done at all, a one-of-a-kind activity will be dominated by a human.

The types of human resources required by different kinds of work activity are distributed along a dimension of knowledge

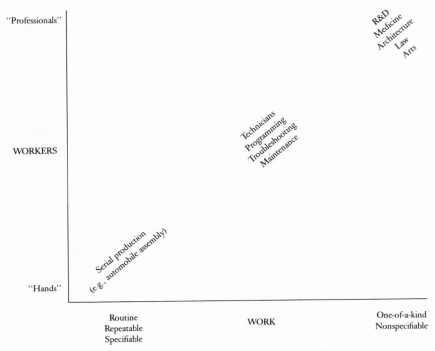

FIGURE I–1. A Map of the World of Work

required and decision-making. At one extreme of the dimension are found those referred to as "hands," those who essentially perform motor activities with a minimum of autonomous decision-making. At the other extreme of the dimension are those referred to as "professionals," who have a special body of knowledge and who are called upon for significant judgment and decision-making in carrying out their work.

Exploring the map, it is easy to locate all work activities and the kinds of management they require. In the corner of the map, where routine activities performed by "hands" are located, we find serial production activities typified by the automobile assembly line, parodied by Charlie Chaplin in the classic movie *Modern Times*. At the other extreme corner of the map, where one-of-a-kind activities performed by "professionals" are located, are a host of diagnostic, consultative, prescriptive activities characterized by the knowledgeable transformation of information from one form into another. In the center of the map are those activities clustered under such terms as "semi-professional" or "technician activities"; these include equipment maintenance, trouble-shooting, programming, and other jobs combining high motor skills with special knowledge.

There is an implicit assumption in most writing on management that management is the same for all activities. However, any close examination of both successful and failed managerial practices quickly establishes the fact that the management appropriate for assembly line operations is inappropriate to professional activities, if not downright harmful. Managing the routine activities exemplified by an automobile assembly line includes:

1. The layout of the entire process before beginning operations with all subprocesses specified
2. Decision as to how each part of the process is to be done, including all input and output characteristics
3. Where humans are to be used in the process, the requisite human and physical characteristics are specified and distributed, including dexterity levels, non-color blindness, physical size restrictions—for example, during World War II, the Douglas Aircraft Company used human midgets to work on aircraft nose-wheel assembly and inspection operations because they were of a size to ride the wheel up into the fuselage conveniently
4. The development of very explicit job descriptions in which the requisite human activities are distributed and clustered into human-sized packages to which are assigned titles, compensation levels, and positions in the organizational hierarchy
5. The hiring of people with the requisite skill and physical characteristics and in appropriate numbers to operate the process—testing and other forms of measurement are used in this step to make sure that those hired "fill the bill" of specifications
6. Training those hired to perform the work required to the specified standards

7. Developing and applying incentives of various kinds to assure performance of the work required by the process in the appropriate time
8. Continuing supervision of the process to assure that it is being performed as specified; the techniques that fill management magazines are clustered here, including flextime, suggestion systems, piece rates, production prizes, quality circles, and foreman training in interpersonal skills; production line quality control is dedicated to measuring and taking steps to assure that the process works within the prespecified limits. Personnel practices are used to assure that the assemblers will maintain their quantitative and qualitative production within prespecified limits.

The qualities that are most desired in assembly line activities are dependability, predictability, and steadiness. About the last quality desired is creativity. The creative assembler is the person who puts the proverbial soda bottle in the automobile door to rattle and tantalize the owner. The creative operator in the middle of a petroleum refinery can be a dangerous person if the urge to try out something new finds expression in new valve settings.

By contrast, when it comes to the one-of-a-kind activities performed by professionals, the management described for assembly line activities is clearly inappropriate. First of all the process cannot be specified. Any professional who has taken over a project or patient or operation in mid-stream knows that the first thing to be done is to change the way the process is conducted. Changing the process is not a product of the perversity and egotism of individuals. It is simply that to reach a specified output from a specified starting point each professional carries out the process differently. After the desired results and the general kind of human capabilities required are given by the manager, the professional doing the job is in control of the specifics. To intervene is to slow and confound the process.

For professional work, management must hire someone

with the requisite general capabilities, and then let go of the details of the process. Anyone who has had experience as a professional or manager of professionals has heard the exasperated response given to detailed supervision, "Look! Either you're going to do it or let me do it!" There is really no way successfully to apply the personnel practices appropriate to mass production to the management of professionals. As long as the process cannot be specified in detail it is not possible to spell out the specific requisite skills and to train people for them. In the context of professional work, job descriptions are at best glittering generalities; "Do science in a scientific manner, and answer the phone in the absence of the boss."

All routine, specifiable tasks are theoretically automatable, and it is no accident that robots are replacing people on the automobile assembly line. On the other hand professional work is unspecifiable, it is dependent on situation and problem, and requires the judgment, ingenuity, and creativity of an individual possessing a particular body of knowledge. Whenever a professional is doing routine and specifiable work you can be sure that it is nonprofessional work, e.g., the physician giving shots, the engineer doing routine testing, the professor administering multiple-choice tests, the accountant doing set-piece bookkeeping.

The techniques developed for managing assembly lines are not appropriate to the management of professional activities. Most management literature is written to explain and advise on the management of routine and specifiable jobs, and is consequently inappropriate to the management of professional activities. In their efforts to improve performance, professional societies often advocate the use of so-called modern management techniques by their membership, and many consultants with business administration backgrounds have sincerely sold their repertoires of techniques appropriate to General Motors to organizations concerned with professional activities. In most cases, the attempts to apply techniques developed for the routine and specifiable to professional activities make little difference since, according to Shapero's Second Law, "No matter how you design a system, humans make it work anyway." Elaborate job description systems are devised that have little effect except to encourage political skirmishing. "New" organizational structures are elaborately installed, such as Matrix organization. ZBB, MBO, OR, Quality Circles, and Theory Z (courtesy of the Japanese who learned their management techniques from the Americans), are sold, installed, modified, and forgotten in rapid sequence. In some cases the application of inappropriate management techniques to professional firms has been disastrous, particularly for smaller firms that lack the resources to survive large perturbations.

If professional activities are not specifiable and humans make all systems work anyway, why should we even bother to talk about "management" of professional activities? The foregoing is a good question, and the answer is definite: we can do far better than chance, and we can do far better than depending on the natural skills and expensively acquired lessons of experience. A better understanding of what is known about the nature and management of professional activities can provide us with the knowledge and tools to do more than cut and try, and systematically to improve the overall performance of the professional activities for which we are responsible.

The available literature is scattered throughout several fields under a variety of classifications. It is the purpose of this book to bring the available data together and to organize it in terms of the processes and structures critical to this particular world of management. The information used here is drawn from such diverse areas as information science, the diffusion of innovations literature, personnel research, advertising research, the history of science and technology, the psychology and sociology of creativity, the history of art, the physiology and sociology of age and aging, labor economics, organization behavior, and the psychology of work, as well as the traditional fields of business administration and the occasional offerings to be found in trade and professional journals of the professions.

This book is concerned with the management of professional activities in organizational contexts. It is intended for use by those charged with managing professional activities in large and small firms, whether they are primarily concerned with professional outputs (as is true of architectural and other design-related firms, advertising, consulting, the health professions, and the like), or serve as functional parts of organizations delivering non-professional products and services (such as the R & D, design, and advertising functions in an industrial or consumer products company). The book is also aimed at that broader category of professional activities called "management," and is concerned with providing useful information for the management of managers.

1

Hiring: The Most Important Management Decision

THE PROFESSIONAL WORKER is *the* critical resource in any professional activity. All other resources, without exception, are far down the list in terms of importance in the achievement of professional outputs. Further, the most important management decision in the conduct of professional activities is hiring. All other decisions have far less effect in determining the capabilities, productivity, quality, and quantity of output achieved by a professional organization than the apparently simple task of hiring.

The importance of the hiring decision cannot be overemphasized. Professional activities are person-dependent, and consequently the quality of the work produced is dependent on the qualities of those hired. It is possible for management to influence the quality and quantity of output of those hired, but management is severely constrained by the capabilities and outlooks of those hired. If one hires well, the chances are that the organizational output will be more than satisfactory. If one hires badly, no matter what management techniques are used

I

(aside from early firing), chances are the output will be less than desired.

Professionals are not "replaceable" in the interchangeable-parts sense of the word. Though two professionals may have the requisite professional capabilities to accomplish a particular task successfully, each will perform that task with a different style and approach. Two physicians treating a patient with a given disease will each go about it differently. Two actors playing the same role or two musicians playing the same composition can each produce satisfactory but different interpretations. Two professors teaching the same course from the same textbook and syllabus will produce different experiences though both meet all criteria for acceptance. Anyone who has had to take over a project from someone else has gone through the painful process of realizing that one cannot just continue one's predecessor's work but must restructure the approach to fit one's own style.

The importance of hiring is further amplified by the evidence that (1) quality of performance persists through time, and (2) a relatively small percentage of those hired are responsible for a disproportionately large percentage of both the best and worst performance.

The Persistence of High and Low Performance

A demonstrated persistence in high and low performance on the part of professionals underlines the relative importance of the hiring decision. What you hire in the way of performance quality essentially determines the level of performance you will have to reckon with in the absence of heroic management efforts. If you hire carelessly or poorly the probability is low that you will be able to "correct" the situation by professional development programs, management techniques, or on-the-job therapy. In a rare longitudinal study of the job performance of professionals, Price, Thompson, and Dalton (1975) measured the performance of technical professionals in an industrial laboratory at two points in time separated by nine years. They

TABLE 1–1
Performance Ratings of Professionals in an Industrial Laboratory
at Two Points in Time Nine Years Apart

AGE IN SECOND ROUND (1960)	NUMBER IN GROUP	1960 RANKING	1968 RANKING High	Medium	Low
31–40	124	High	63%	28%	9%
		Medium	20	45	35
		Low	10	35	55
41–50	129	High	45	45	10
		Medium	45	37	18
		Low	9	24	67
50+	58	High	55	35	10
		Medium	33	33	33
		Low	60	30	10

SOURCE: From Price, Thompson, and Dalton, 1975.

found a strong tendency for those judged "high" performers in the first round to be "high" performers in the second round, and those judged "low" performers tended to persist as "low" performers (see Table 1–1). There was little migration from the "low" to the "high" category or from the "high" to the "low" category over time. Only those judged to be "medium" performers in the first round showed any progression or retrogression, with one-third moving up and one-third moving down in the second round.

A Few Account for a Lot

Small percentages of the work force account for the best and worst performance. This is an example of Pareto's law, or Pareto's principle, which holds that, in social and economic affairs, many relationships can be expressed as a straight line on a double-log diagram; or, simply, a few of the x's account for a large percentage of the y's. Among some management practitioners it is known as the "eighty-twenty" or "ninety-ten" rule. Typically, 80% of an inventory's costs are attributable

3

to 20% of the items, or 12% of the Californians account for 75% of the alcohol drunk in that state.

Interviews with managers in the fields of R & D, architecture, publishing, academia, engineering, and the performing arts provide evidence of Pareto's law. Those interviewed state that 80–90% of the best output of their organizations can be attributed to 10–20% of their people, and, conversely, 80–90% of the disasters to another 10–20%. Any manager can name the people in each extreme category and remember the former employees, by name and accomplishment, who were at the extremes. A manager of one of the best industrial R & D organizations in the world told me that over half of the laboratory's successful developments were attributable to one of the twelve hundred fifty members of the laboratory.

The Pareto law effect in professional activities provides an opportunity to achieve powerful leverage on the quality and productivity of an organization. Relatively small improvements in hiring can achieve very large improvements in performance. If 80% of the outstanding work accomplishments are attributable to 20% of the workers, and 80% of the disasters are, similarly, attributable to 20% of the workers, a systematic improvement in the numbers in either limited category can have a disproportionate impact on the organization's performance. The trick is to identify and hire in the high-performing category and to identify and make sure not to hire those in the other extreme. To overcome hiring mistakes always takes too long and is too expensive in terms of damge caused, managerial time lost, and feelings hurt.

Hiring Can Be Systematically Improved

Since hiring is the most important management decision in professional work, anything that improves the quality of hiring can determine whether professional efforts succeed or fail, clients and customers are satisfied, the organization is exposed to liability suits, and whether managers' jobs are fun or are miserable chores.

Is it possible to do any better than we are doing at the present time just using our instincts and our experience as guides? The data available from a variety of sources leads to the unequivocal conclusion that it is possible to achieve significant qualitative and quantitative improvements in the hiring of professionals. The evidence, however, brings conventional hiring practices into serious question, and a manager who wants to improve hiring must be ready to challenge many popular and cherished personnel practices.

CRITERIA FOR HIRING OF PROFESSIONALS

What does a manager explicitly or implicitly look for in a professional being considered for hire? What should guide how he or she seeks potential hires? What should he or she expect of them? Any group of experienced managers can easily reach a consensus on two or three obvious criteria, but other criteria are relevant:

1. Capability for high technical performance
2. Ability to enhance group performance
3. Initiative-taking capability
4. Potential for development and renewal over time
5. High probability for retention
6. Creativity

Capability for High Technical Performance

Technical capability is the *sine qua non* when hiring professionals. The ability of a professional to perform the job competently comes before all other considerations in hiring, and much of the hiring process is taken up with efforts to determine a potential hire's professional competence. To demonstrate their abilities, architects, artists, and advertising professionals maintain a portfolio of paintings and drawings. Academics list their publications by title and publication to establish their research

5

competence. Other professionals list patents, projects, descriptions of positions attained, and places of employment (a matter of competence by association).

From the evidence provided by a potential hire a manager attempts to deduce something of the qualitative and quantitative professional output to be expected from the candidate. Given a choice among apparently competent professionals the tendency is to hire the person one "likes" in terms of some gestalt or overall judgment. Given the pressures of a tight labor market the tendency is to hire whoever comes through the door, despite personal likes or dislikes, as long as the individual is above some minimal threshold of technical capability. Civil services attempt to hire on "objective" grounds of technical merit as a matter of principle, implying that this is the only way to obtain equity. Unfortunately, in many cases the criterion of technical competence is the only one applied, and it is too limited a basis for so important a decision as hiring.

Ability to Enhance Group Performance

Experienced managers worry about the interactions of a potential hire with the rest of the work group, the net impact of the potential hire on the overall performance of the organization and on the energy and time of the manager. Experienced managers often cite "the potential effect of an individual on group performance" as an even more important criterion than that of technical competence.

On the negative side, a candidate may be considered in terms of potential for causing interpersonal problems within the group. A frequent question in the mind of an employer is, "Will this person be a problem?" A technical genius who manages to enrage the clients, insult colleagues, and make disproportionate demands on the time of management can generate a net loss for an organization. A potential hire with two doctorates and a distinguished list of publications whose behavior on the job may cause an exodus of other competent people is a threat rather than a find.

6

Initiative-Taking

Almost by definition, a professional is someone who can act independently while bringing a body of special knowledge to bear in a work situation. "We would like someone who is a 'self-starter,'" is the common way managers describe this initiative-taking capability. Professional work depends to a great extent on the self-direction of its workers, unlike the world of routine work.

The notion of "the span-of-control," developed in the context of production management, refers to the number of subordinates a manager can supervise directly. Traditionally, management authorities held a span-of-control of five to eight subordinates as the number that could be effectively managed. For routine production tasks the number was increased to ten or fifteen. When it comes to professional activities the concept does not make the same kind of sense. In production work the process dominates, and the manager can be aware of the entire process and specify the tasks of each subordinate. The manager deals with a relatively small set of circumstances, the only limit being the capacity of the manager to observe and keep track of operations.

In professional work the process is in the heads of the professionals, each of whom, legitimately, approaches the task somewhat differently. In professional work, the manager cannot directly control the details of the process. Control of professional activities depends on the capabilities and motivation of the professionals carrying out the work. Consequently, control consists in eliciting from employees a propensity to initiate requisite actions without their being constantly directed by a manager who cannot know whether the professional sitting with feet on desk is loafing or doing the kind of thinking that makes the difference between success and failure. Given competent, initiative-taking professionals, a manager's span-of-control in professional work can be as high as fifty. With one incompetent professional the span-of-control quickly becomes one, since the manager will have to do the job of that individual until he is replaced by someone else who is competent.

7

Potential for Development and Renewal Over Time

Managers often forget when hiring that beyond current needs and conditions will be future projects and changing technology and environments. It is expensive to hire and integrate new professionals into an organization, and it is difficult to fire old employees. Furthermore, among the most painful problems faced by a manager of professionals is the so-called plateaued or burnt-out individual: the person who has contributed well for years, has reached a high salary level, but who is not performing adequately anymore. The thoughtful manager considers what will happen beyond the current set of tasks when considering a potential hire. It makes good sense to hire those most likely both to maintain their current capabilities and to develop new capabilities to match new needs.

Retainability

"What is a good turnover rate?" is a question managers frequently ask. The only sensible answer is, "It all depends." If you have technically competent professionals who are good to work with, who are initiative-takers, and who develop themselves to meet new demands, the answer is, "A turnover rate of zero is just fine." However, if your professionals are incompetent, miserable as colleagues, inactive, and resistant to change the answer could be, "A turnover rate of 100% is called for."

If you have hired a desirable professional who meets all the criteria for hiring, you should want to keep that desirable worker in the organization. At the time of hiring it is useful to consider the likelihood of retaining the promising candidate.

Creativity

In some professional fields such as advertising, R & D, the performing arts, the plastic arts and architecture, employers consciously seek out people who are "creative" in the belief that such individuals will give their organization a competitive advantage.

MEETING THE CRITERIA FOR HIRING

It is possible to identify and rank a set of criteria for hiring professionals that describes what is wanted in terms of work behavior, but the key difficulty is to know if a candidate for hire meets any or all of the stated criteria for hiring. Experienced managers often express reluctance to go through the hiring process because of past unhappy experiences. Typical comments are, "The best interviewee I ever encountered turned out to be the worst paranoid I ever had to deal with. It was only after the fact that I learned an intelligent paranoid will give you all the responses you want in the interview situation," and "I look upon each candidate for hire as a potential disaster, a destroyer of my peace of mind, a disrupter of my department."

How can you determine whether someone has the desired capabilities and characteristics? In an assembly line situation, it is possible to determine quickly, through straightforward testing, whether an individual has the necessary motor skills and intellectual capacity. In the case of a professional, determination of the requisite capacities is far less straightforward. The high turnover rates for professionals indicate the difficulties encountered.

Hiring the Experienced Professional

When hiring an experienced professional some formal and informal record is available on which to base judgement. Sometimes there is physical evidence in the form of a portfolio, a listing of publications, citations, or news items. Witnesses of the past work of the potential hire such as employers, co-workers, or clients might be contacted for evaluations. The data on the application form can be checked for accuracy and evaluated. Interview information, and sometimes test results, are also available.

9

Despite the abundance of conventional wisdom on hiring, there is relatively little useful data on the relationship between information available at time of entry and subsequent performance on the job. It is common for an experienced manager to state that after many years of hiring he can determine who is going to do well on the job. The available data suggest that the confidence expressed is misplaced. How then can a manager tell what he is getting in the way of potential performance? What is the relative utility of the various kinds of information available at the time of hire? What specific information relates to work performance identified as desirable?

Information available at the time of hire. Typically, at the time of hire, managers make use of a variety of sources of information about the candidate. The data in the resumé and application forms, the portfolio of past work, and references show something about the demonstrated performance of the potential hire. Testing, interviews, and references reveal applicant characteristics considered relevant to the work situation.

The interview. The available data on interviewing throw doubt on the validity and reliability of interview information as an indicator of how an individual will perform on the job. Interviewing can be improved somewhat by training interviewers, by clearly structuring the questions to be asked, and by using a series of different interviewers. Nevertheless, the results of these improvements are minimal, and their implementation tends to trap the interviewer into justifying personal judgments and strongly held biases.

Despite research demonstrating the low validity and reliability of the interview in hiring, it remains the dominant method for evaluating candidates. The dominance of the interview in hiring decisions is remarkable in view of its limitations. If only one hiring tool could be used, 80% of those hiring would choose the interview (Martin et al., 1971). According to the same study, 90% would hire individuals on the basis of an interview even if negative information was received from other sources.

Authorities on interviewing consider the interview to be a social situation affected by the nature of the transaction, and the perceptions the two actors in the situation have of each other and of the task at hand. The interview is an obtrusive process in which the interviewee is a conscious part of the game. The interviewee's responses are affected by embarrassment at ignorance, fear of consequences, liking for the interviewer, physical condition (a severe cold can make a significant difference), and self-perception (we prefer to see ourselves in ways that may not represent the way we really are).

Different interviewers get different responses from an interviewee. Interviewers unconsciously indicate which responses are more acceptable to them, and the interviewee is likely to try to provide these responses. If the interviewer, just to make conversation, mentions having been an athlete in college, the respondent will attribute a constellation of values and preferences to the interviewer and respond accordingly. In the interview process managers tend to identify with interviewees who are most like themselves. Several studies have found that the decision to hire is made very early in the selection interview.

In effect, the interview, usually a matter of an hour or less, is like the passing of two ships at sea. Each ship presents its best side and all of its flags. Friendly signals are exchanged. Little is learned about the cargos buried in the hold, possible destinations, changes of course, responses to emergencies, or past engagements.

The application form and the resumé. The application form and the resumé are intended to provide an employer with enough biographical information to (1) determine whether an individual meets the minimum, formal requirements for hiring (e.g., a degree in the appropriate discipline or the requisite license), (2) provide the interviewer with indicators worth following up, and, less frequently but more importantly, (3) provide biographical data and experience data that might be used to predict performance on the job. The forms used by different organizations ask very similar questions and in recent years have been modified to remove data concerning race, sex, age, and religious and sexual preferences.

Since biographical data shown in the application form or resumé is important to whether an individual is even considered, the validity and relevance of the information found in these biographical forms should be evaluated in relationship to potential performance on the job.

In the instances where they have been systematically used, biographical data have been found to be of greater validity than those obtained by other carefully constructed selection procedures. It is reasonable to infer that if an individual has succeeded in the past in a work situation similar to the one being applied for, he or she will most likely do well in the future. The behavior of an individual is reliable over time, and past performance is the best predictor of future performance. The question to be asked is whether the past situations are those the individual will encounter in the future. The less variation between past and predicted situations the easier it is to predict. With the inherent variation in professional work, good matches between past and present are hard to come by, and only an ability to deal with variation may be relevant.

There is a question of whether applicants lie in presenting their biographical data. One study of 112 applicants for jobs in a police department (Cascio, 1975) found a high correlationship between the application information provided and fact. Another study found significant distortions in both biographical data and in responses to a standard personality test, the MMPI, on the part of respondents. In a study using the application forms of aerospace scientists and engineers, my colleagues and I were informed by personnel people that they found differences between application forms data and data provided by the same applicants in security forms serious enough for termination of individuals already hired.

Testing. A potential hire's characteristics and skills are tested to predict work-related behavior. Thus, for a mechanical assembly job, a mechanical aptitude test might accurately predict how an individual will do on the assembly line. A test is essentially a sample of a person's behavior under particular, and inevitably limited conditions, and the test situation hardly represents the real work context. Consequently, the art of testing is to identify critical behavior patterns and to develop probes that might validly and reliably predict them on the job.

First, for a test to be useful, it is necessary to develop a clear understanding of the requirements of the job. Without clear-cut criteria against which to match test results it is not possible to construct a relevant test or to determine what the test results mean. Second, tests must be selected or developed that can be related to the job criteria. Third, the tests must be shown to be valid and reliable. Finally, any program of testing must avoid violations of privacy, feelings of equity, and legality.

Tests used in hiring can be broadly classified as aptitude tests, achievement tests, and motivation tests. Aptitude tests attempt to measure general intelligence, job-related intellectual aptitudes, motor skills, and personal decision-making competence and interpersonal skills. Achievement tests essentially measure what the individual has learned, as compared with the aptitude test which measures the individual's ability to learn (Schneider, 1976), and includes performance tests for craftsmen, paper and pencil tests on occupational knowledge, and behavior in simulations (e.g., the in-basket test for managers). Motivation tests include personality tests and measures of interests. Personality tests operate on the premise that certain personality variables differentiate successful from unsuccessful work behavior. Interest tests compare the interests of the candidate with the measured interests of successful performers in the field.

Tests can be valuable in the hiring process when done carefully with due regard to their relevance and with a clear understanding of their limitations. Every serious review of the testing literature underlines the limitations of applying generalized tests to specific situations and the consequent need for tailoring a test to the specific job and organization. The great majority of work on testing has been done with clerical and blue-collar occupations where the work varies little compared with professional occupations. To develop valid and reliable tests is an expensive process, and, if undertaken, it must be assumed that the jobs will remain relatively unchanged over time. Consequently, we find that most of the testing data available refer to large and relatively stable corporations such as Sears, Standard Oil of New Jersey, AT&T, and 3M.

Testing often reflects the biases of personnel departments and managers. For example, there is the strong feeling that "general intelligence" is somehow related to job performance (Landy & Trumbo, 1980). However, the only proven utility of such tests has been to predict the success of young children in school work (Schneider, 1976). There is no real agreement on what general intelligence is and whether what is measured by general intelligence tests is related to specific occupations.

The one developed area of testing relevant to professional work is that concerned with managerial performance. Managers are professionals, and managerial activities share the unpredictability and variation typical of other professional activities. One review of work on prediction of managerial performance from aptitude test results (Campbell et al., 1979) concludes from work done in the largest corporations that some very specific aptitude tests, such as those for verbal and abstract reasoning, do provide useful predictors, and that even general intelligence tests predict performance in forecasting and budgeting but not in sales or interpersonal relations. A great deal of work has been done with the in-basket test, in which a series of simulated job situations are presented to the person tested, who is then judged by a panel of managers and/or personnel professionals. Though good results have been obtained with this test, questions have been raised about the difficulty of obtaining reliable results with different panels of observers and about the expense and time required for the process. Questions remain concerning the relevance of the exercises to the particular jobs for which they are used as predictors.

References, formal and informal. References are usually required in the hiring process. Written references and letters of recommendation are hardly worth the paper they are written on. One study of written references found they tended to leave out any negative information. A study of the validity of different types of references found some correlation between references from supervisors and acquaintances and subsequent performance and absolutely none between recommendations from personnel officers, co-workers, and relatives and subsequent performance (Mosel & Goheen, 1959).

Recent court cases have even made a request for references a question of invasion of privacy, and many organizations (including universities) will not give any kind of reference without written permission from the concerned person. Some organizations will not take the chance of a lawsuit and will not give any kind of recommendation even with the express permission of the person being considered.

Informal references made face-to-face or over the telephone are far more productive of relevant information, bringing closer the connection between requester and provider and minimizing the threat of loss of confidentiality which is inherent in a formal document. More importantly, spoken communications are orders of magnitude richer than the written language. Because of hesitation, emphasis, and intonation, it is almost impossible not to provide significant information in spoken language (see Chapter 4, "Managing Information"). If someone writes, "This man is a good worker," the message seems clear. The same individual, over the phone, might respond with a long hesitation, followed by a rather toneless, "This man is a good worker." The phone response alerts the listener, and all kinds of suspicions fill the mind. The same words produce different messages in the two forms used.

Technical Competence

Technical competence in a professional may be associated with degrees received, years of experience, nature of experience, promotions, honors, salary level, and evidence of specific outputs. The resumé and application blank are useful in identifying these quantitative extrinsics, but less useful in providing qualitative information, except in the case of honors. Even "portfolios" may be of questionable value. As one newspaper editor put it, "A sheaf of articles in a portfolio may mask the extent to which the applicant's writing was improved by a good editor."

In large organizations, structured wage and salary rules make it difficult to differentiate between the average and the very competent. Promotion policies are such that rank cannot generally be assumed to be directly related to technical competence. It is hard to know from the record whether two parallel "one year" experiences are equal: did one consist of forty hours a week of routine activities while a second was sixty hours a week of diversified, developing experiences?

To obtain some notion of the qualitative aspects of an individual's technical abilities requires combining the information found in the resumé and application blank with that obtained through conversations with people who have had the opportunity to see the applicant's work, such as former employers, colleagues, clients, and professors. It is necessary both to evaluate the source of the reference to determine if it is to be taken seriously, and to go into enough detail and depth to get a rounded idea of the applicant's ability to respond to a variety of problems and situations.

Other considerations related to technical competence are encompassed in the questions, "Is it better to hire a generalist or a specialist?" and "What is the relationship of age to performance?"

The generalist versus the specialist. Unless a specialty is defined very broadly (a contradiction in terms) it has a limited lifetime. A tidal wave of new information floods each profession every year. New techniques, new concepts, new data, new equipment, and new interpretations are the norm in medicine, engineering, management, advertising, and social work. Specialties are quickly made obsolete by technical events—anyone practicing a profession for more than five years need only think back to what was central in the practice five years ago compared with the present. Note a few of the changes: the impact of the small computer and the silicon chip, of new drugs, and of recent environmental concerns.

There is nothing sadder than professionals in a specialty that has been abruptly made obsolete. What happened to electronic tube specialists once semiconductors took over? The narrow specialist is most valuable in the short run, saving much time and uncertainty, but who can predict that current specialties will accommodate to new technology and problems? A survey of industrial R & D groups found that one-half of them were engaged in fields of research different from 10 years ago and that over a fourth had changed from five years ago (*Industry Week*, 1982).

Though any specialist can retrain for another field, there is a very human resistance to change from a field in which one has made a large investment. One study found that Ph.D.'s were least amenable to shifts to new enterprises or fields while those with the master's degree were the easiest to transfer and had the best record of success. The resistance of those with Ph.D.'s was attributed to their personal investment and to a socialization process they go through in a particular narrow slice of a technology which makes it difficult for them to transfer to another field. Anyone with a Ph.D. is as able as (if not more able than) a master's degree holder to learn and do new and different technical work. Yet the generalist may be a far better bet in the long run.

Age and technical competence. (See Chapter 5, "Technical Obsolescence, Burnout, and Staying Alive.") In general, professional competence increases with age. Measures of performance used in the relevant studies included annual order-of-merit rankings used for salary evaluations, unpublished reports, published papers, scientific contributions, and overall helpfulness as judged by peers and supervisors and patients. On the average, performance increased with age, peaking in the mid and late fifties. The probable explanation for the decline after age fifty is social-psychological rather than a matter of technical know-how, and is probably a manifestation of what is now referred to as the "middle-age" or "mid life" crisis.

The evidence clearly shows a gain in contribution and utility with age and experience. With a few exceptions, such as in the field of mathematics and in some areas of basic research, competence persists and is enhanced by experience. With experience, competent individuals gain in knowledge and ability. For example, creative people tend to remain creative throughout their careers. If the employer can find someone who has demonstrated creativity in the past, the likelihood is high that the individual will be creative in the future. Despite a general tendency to assume that a recent university graduate has command of "the latest," the evidence is that the competent older worker is more useful than the competent younger worker, and certainly a better bet than the unproven younger person.

Ability to Enhance Group Performance

An individual can substantially affect the way a group operates and the subsequent quality and quantity of the group's professional output. In terms of technical contribution, in addition to direct labor, an individual brings access to an "extended family" of information sources that are part of his or her personal professional network outside the organization.

Beyond the strictly technical professional aspects of work an individual professional can make a substantial contribution through many kinds of social and professional interactions that include: helping new and younger people; helping to create a positive atmosphere during tough or pressure-filled times; a willingness to work through the night to finish something on time without being asked; dealing well with clients or other groups; and, not least, making only limited demands on managerial time.

Information. The information made available by an individual is a function of (1) what is "in the head" of that individual, (2) what can be obtained by that individual through interaction with others within the organization or through social and professional circles to which he or she belongs, and (3) that individual's ability and willingness to communicate with others.

Some idea of an individual's information potential can be gathered from the number and variety of the candidate's personal periodical subscriptions and book buying habits, and the interest the candidate takes in company information offerings and facilities, and in professional society activities.

Comments by former co-workers and supervisors on the role played by a candidate for hire as a source or even as a "pusher" of information provide a good indication of that individual's potential as a contributor of information to others in a group context. A contributory characteristic is, for want of a better term, "niceness." When asked, "With whom would you prefer to work?" respondents in both a non-profit laboratory and a commercial electronics R & D division singled out those to whom they turn for technical information (Shapero et al., 1978).

The interpersonal capabilities of a good communicator are indicated by access to large, extended networks of professionals outside the immediate organization. Typically, a good communicator is in frequent contact with others in various fields and thus brings much more information to an organization than others.

Interpersonal capabilities. The ability to deal with others is recognized as a prized ability in all organizational contexts. When asked by the author, "What is the one thing you wish you had learned in college?" a majority of a one thousand managers and professionals responded, "Dealing with other people," "Interpersonal relationships," "The psychology of dealing with others." Though recognized as desirable, a candidate's interpersonal competence cannot be determined with certainty. A mild correlation between judgements of interview behavior and interpersonal competence has been reported, but the connection is uncertain. Informal references are more useful and accurate indicators.

Disproportionate demands on management time. Anyone who takes a disproportionate amount of management time is a serious drain on an organization. When asked, "What is the worst management experience you have had in the last nine months?" managers frequently answered, "A good worker quit!" Often a competent, desirable employee quits because the manager of the organization has not provided the feedback everyone needs. The good worker is often a person who seldom comes to the manager's office or his attention out of pride in being able to function without constant supervision. Nevertheless, everyone wants to know that management is aware of his or her presence. When there is no feedback, an individual may either create situations that will demand managerial attention or quit. Thus, any individual who takes up a large amount of management time and keeps managers from spending some of that time with others in the organization can be costly in terms of turnover.

KEEPING COMPETENT PERSONNEL

The undesired loss of competent personnel is costly to an organization in both direct and indirect terms. The obvious direct costs are those expended in the hiring and entry processes. Hiring costs include advertising, recruiting travel expenses, time spent by key personnel interviewing, testing and physical examination costs, costs of generating new records, moving expenses, and special inducement expenditures (bonuses, housing allowances, etc.). In addition to direct employment costs there are the entry costs that include orientation and training efforts that can range from formal courses (i.e., orientation sessions, security instructions, etc.) to non-formal orientation efforts such as learning where and how to get internal information, how to get something done within the system, or the location of the nearest sandwich shop.

The estimated costs of hiring a professional for one distributed-data processing company were more than $9,000 for a hypothetical $18,000 a year position, with higher salaried positions entailing higher hiring costs. The same study estimated that training costs were close to $16,000, including direct support to the new employee during the first few months and learning-curve costs. The costs were based on careful surveys of managers and calculations from actual company data (Jindal & Sanderberg, 1978). In another study the total cost of hiring a manager was estimated at $25,000 and $30,000 in 1973 (Hall & Hall, 1976).

The extensive literature on the subject of turnover (Price, 1977) points out that the major factors affecting turnover are organizational and managerial, though there is also considerable evidence relating personal factors to voluntary turnover.

In studies of technicians and engineers (Bassett, 1967), scientists and engineers (Farris, 1971; Shapero et al., 1965), it was found that voluntary turnover is related to age. In general, younger employees are more likely to leave than are older ones. The new college graduate has little information upon which to judge whether a job is a good one, and it is not unusual to hear a young professional say, "I didn't realize until now how good a job I had."

The institutional source of a prospective employee is also somewhat related to turnover. It was found that aerospace scientists and engineers from government stayed with the hiring organization for a longer period of time than those from industry (Shapero et al., 1965). Several other studies show that nongovernment organizations have higher turnover rates than government organizations (Price, 1977).

"Extreme" personality characteristics have been related to a tendency to voluntary turnover. Individuals who manifest such traits to a lesser degree show a higher degree of retention (Meyer & Cuomo, 1962; Farris, 1971).

One study compared retention of high vs. low performers among scientists and engineers (Farris, 1971) and found the personal factors that predicted stayers and leavers were the following:

> High performers stay, low performers leave, when importance is attached to the opinion of colleagues outside the organization and to maintaining contacts outside the organization.
>
> High performers leave, but there is no difference for low performers, when there is high professional orientation.
>
> There is no difference for high performers, but low performers stay, showing independence.
>
> Both stay at the same rate in the case of older employees.

Summarizing the data on personal characteristics related to retention, we see one more argument for hiring the older competent worker, that age is negatively correlated with voluntary terminations. Other important personal characteristics associated with high performers include lots of contacts outside the organization and a high professional orientation.

What is a good turnover rate? Ideas about turnover are often based on the notion there is some utility in maintaining a certain amount of movement in and out of an organization, reflected in the question, "I understand our turnover rate is below 6%, and isn't that bad?" Taking the notion to its practical conclusion, you would fire people to maintain some assumed "correct" failure rate. One Los Angeles electronics firm had an arbitrary policy in the 1950s, of firing 10% of the work force every six months. "Keeps everyone on his toes!" was the president's claim. It was true, all of the best personnel were on their toes and in their track shoes, and the company's turnover rate was on the order of 90% per year. One by-product of firings that reach visible percentages is that the workers you want to keep become uncertain of their place and also leave.

There is no correct turnover rate. For an organization made up of high performers who have a great deal of initiative, who are dynamic in maintaining their technical capabilities, who are good communicators, and who get along well with each other, with clients, and with strangers, a good turnover rate is zero. On the other hand, for an organization full of low performers who are aggressive, constantly demanding managerial attention, uninterested in personal development, and in constant conflict with everyone, a turnover of 100% in six months may be a very sensible rate.

The tenure vs. voluntary termination data raise questions about the value of continuing education being made available for all professional employees. The five-plus year employee is the least likely to leave voluntarily. Should you spend much money on continuing education for employees in their first two years with the organization since they are the most likely to leave or should you spend heavily on continuing education of the five-plus year employees for the highest amount of retained knowledge per dollar expended?

Geography, streams of migration, and turnover. The movements of professional workers to a particular geographic location are strongly correlated with well-trodden general migratory pathways. If a professional is hired in consonance with established migratory patterns (i.e., from within the local area or from "upstream" on an established flow to the area of hire), there is a higher likelihood that the individual will stay with the hiring organization than if he is hired from outside the established patterns. Hiring from "downstream" in the migratory flow patterns results in higher turnover except in the case of individuals who come from the area originally and are returning.

Using the personnel records of thirty-five thousand scientists and engineers, it was found that geographic movements between jobs correlated with the general population migration pattern into each area studied with correlation coefficients on the order of .98 (Shapero et al., 1965; Draheim et al., 1966; Howell et al., 1966). In other words, the geographic origins of the scientists and engineers in a city correlated with those of the general population as shown by the Census data on migration. The professionals studied followed general streams of population migration as old as the country, including one southern and one northern east-to-west flow, a traditional south-to-north movement, with a steady counterflow to Florida from the northeast and midwest. Thus, it was found that a Boston engineer would not move from Boston to a missile company in Denver. A scientist would move from St. Paul to Seattle or to Denver, but would not go to Tucson. In the 1950s a missile company in Orlando, Florida, advertised for technical workers to fill twenty-eight hundred positions and got over sixty thousand applications from the northeast.

A study of new college hires who stayed more than five years in a large Dallas electronics company showed the same patterns. Despite following the prescribed personnel practices, the new hires who remained with the company for five years or more reflected the long-term historical social migration pattern. A personnel manager in Colorado remarked, "It has taken me a long time to learn that we have wasted a lot of money trying to hire engineers from Boston [off stream], and it has taken me another block of time to learn that hiring people from Los Angeles [downstream] is like putting them in a revolving door; they're soon on their way back down there."

Trying to hire someone living "upstream" in a migration flow pattern has a higher probability of being effective, even without great economic incentives, than offering a job to someone living "downstream" with an economic premium attached.

Responsibility

One of the most desired and least understood of the characteristics desired in a professional employee is variously called "initiative taking," "self-starting," "enterprise," and "leadership." What managers seek is the ability and desire to take responsibility, to show spontaneity in doing the work to be done, and to initiate actions rather than to wait to be told what to do next.

One source of data would seem to be the large body of studies on leadership, but apart from goal-setting the leadership literature is primarily concerned with setting tasks for others. A more useful source of information on initiative-taking is found in studies of entrepreneurship that use locus-of-control. Locus-of-control is the perception by an individual of where control over his or her life is located: whether control is within the individual and "internal," or is in outside forces or persons and "external." Thus, the more one perceives control to be within, the more that individual is judged to be "internal"; and the more one perceives oneself as controlled by luck, chance, or other people, the more one is judged to be "external." The relationship of measures of locus-of-control to initiative-taking comes from the suggestion that to take initiative, one must feel able to influence events.

There are several paper and pencil locus-of-control instruments. Two of the most widely used are those of Rotter (1966) and Levenson (1972). The latter measures have been quite widely used, and some of the more interesting and relevant results include the following:

1. Entrepreneurs, managers who are more entrepreneurial than others, and entrepreneurs who survive are far more internal than the general population.
2. Managers who are internal are promoted to a greater extent than those who are not, and attach less importance to salary, job security, and retirement.

3. People who have high internal scores have more information and make better use of information than others.

Creativity: The Most Elusive Virtue

When a manager wants a potential hire to be creative, it implies that he places a high premium on new and different solutions to problems and on uniqueness in outlook. Creativity, thus defined, is the essence of professional work. A manager expects a professional to bring a specialized body of knowledge to unique solutions of unique problems. Creativity is particularly identified with certain professions which consciously seek out more of this quality in their hiring practices. In professional activities associated with the performing or plastic arts, creativity is a leading personnel dimension, as it is in such professions as architecture, research and development, publishing, planning, some aspects of engineering, management, and education. (In advertising, as in other fields, there is the formal title, "creative director.")

A number of theories attempt to explain creativity, and some tests have been developed to gauge an individual's creative ability. However, there is still no valid or reliable method of predicting creative behavior on the job other than evidence of such behavior in the past (see Chapter 6, "Creativity").

Creativity is often sought by a potential employer who, in practice, really does not need it. This is the case in the architectural or engineering-design organization looking for someone to be a detailer. In such cases, the requirement for "creativity" is a cultural trapping of the profession, not a requirement of the job. Asking for a creative person in a situation where creativity will in fact be penalized is bad management, and is costly to the organization.

THE "PURE" CASE: THE NEW GRADUATE

Once a professional has accumulated some work experience records of performance are available. In the case of the new college graduate there is little in the way of a relevant work record: this is the "pure" case. Consideration of the pure case vividly illustrates the gap between what little is known in a systematic way about effective hiring and the actual hiring practices of personnel departments and managers.

Much of what is published about hiring newly minted college graduates is based on the experiences and reports of college recruiters and college placement officials, whose information is severely limited. Typically, two hundred to five hundred companies recruit at any campus, and these are primarily large companies that recruit from several campuses. Considering the fact that there were more than sixteen million companies in the United States in 1983, of which 1% had five hundred or more workers (this does not include nonprofit organizations or government organizations that do college recruiting), this represents a very limited sample of the total number of employers of professionals in the country.

When considering the new college graduate, recruiters are faced with the question how to determine the future work performance of someone without a record of professional work.

Essentially, recruiters and managers turn to the following in judging a new college graduate for hire:

> Grades, in the form of an overall measure such as Grade Point Average (GPA) or in terms of grades in selected courses considered more relevant to the job; seen as indicators of relative technical competence and of motivation and ambition
> Extracurricular activities, particularly sports and leadership positions in organizations
> Appearance (grooming, clothing, demeanor)
> Personality, attitudes, outlook on life
> Personal goals
> Interviewer intuition about the person, which encompasses judgments of future potential, maturity and communications ability

The evidence shows no valid or reliable relationship between any of the above and subsequent performance on the job!

26

Grades

The measure most widely used for evaluating new college graduates is grades. Grades are considered in terms of their absolute number value (e.g., 3.8 out of a possible 4.0), or of the class ranking they indicate (e.g., in the upper 10% of the class). Some recruiters look at grades received in the last two years of college, reasoning that they are more indicative of the mature individual's capacities or that they show a significant trend. Some recruiters consider grades in courses that are specifically relevant to the interests of the hiring organization.

Because of the wide use of grades as a criterion for hiring, there have been many studies of the relationship between university grades and subsequent performance in the working world. The literature is practically unanimous in its conclusion that there is *no* measurable relationship between grades in school and performance on the job. There is even some evidence of a negative relationship between good grades in school and creativity in science and engineering.

Studies of the relationship between grades and subsequent performance have been done with physicians, Navy divers, entrepreneurs, MBAs, managers (male and female), engineers, teachers, nurses, psychiatrists, and ministers. An extensive longitudinal study of MBAs from a prestigious school did find grade point average related mildly with compensation at the five year and ten year points (Williams & Harrel, 1964), *but the GPA used was for grades in the second year of the MBA program, since it was found that the overall GPA was not a good predictor.* The second-year included more optional courses, and it seems that grades in optional courses were far more predictive than overall scores! It is difficult to fathom the significance of optional courses over the rest. Could it mean that required core courses have little relationship to work situations? Some employers agree that grades are not important, though they do consider them. One study found that 53% of the personnel managers agreed that grades did not predict job performance (Drake, 1973).

The subject of grades is emotionally loaded. For a professional, grades have been critical to parental approval, positive teacher feedback, honors, choice of university, scholarships, and acceptance to professional school and/or graduate school for at least sixteen years. Consequently, it is difficult for many to accept data that show little or no relationship between grades and subsequent activities, and this influences the hiring process.

The critical point is that school and the workplace are different environments requiring different behaviors. In school there are fixed problems to be solved, well-known patterns of problem-solving and performance measurement (examinations), relatively mild sanctions, and very benign schedules. A student is seldom "fired" for turning in a late paper or for doing below-average work. Professors are judged by the way their students evaluate them rather than by some external and inflexible criterion such as net profit.

The data on how professionals spend their time, on the other hand, paint a picture of activities marked by meetings and interruptions and a constant demand for improvisation. In the typical work situation few can go one half hour without interruption. The typical professional spends between 35% and 50% of the time in meetings and 15% on the telephone. A major complaint of engineers and architects is professional under-utilization. The information required on the job is never available in neat and ready form. The problems are messy, the deadlines are changeable and abrupt. Several problems must be dealt with simultaneously, and the criteria for evaluation are vague and changing.

School grades measure performance in school-related activities, so college grades correlate with high school grades, and graduate school grades correlate with undergraduate performance. Thus, college grade averages were found to correlate with grades made in basic science courses in medical school, but neither correlated with clinical performance (Hammond & Kern, 1959).

Inflation of grade-based entrance requirements to universities may screen out many who have high potential for distinguished performance. The Dean of Admissions of Harvard College identified fifty graduates of the Class of 1928 who had achieved distinguished careers, and examined their credentials at the time of admission to Harvard. He found that two-thirds of the fifty would have been turned down for admission by the standards used at the time of the study (1958), which were considerably more lax than those applied today (Livingston, 1971).

It must be remembered that every college graduate is a member of a segment of the population already differentiated on the basis of cognitive capabilities. University graduates, particularly the products of professional programs, are highly competent when it comes to cognitive and intellectual capabilities. The classification of school performance (A to F) to differentiate within a population that is already quite capable does not provide significant information. The last person in the class, graduating with a degree in engineering or architecture or medicine, has met rather high standards set by accreditation organizations, and must be considered intellectually capable.

Extracurricular Activities and Leadership

Extracurricular activities, particularly as officer of an organization or as team captain, are sometimes seen by managers to indicate qualities of leadership which are relevant to professional work. The presumptions seem to be that school activity leadership is an indicator of job-related leadership, and that leadership is inborn or the product of a set of traits that will manifest itself in any context. Research shows that effective leadership depends not only on the qualities and attitudes of the individual designated as leader but equally on the work situation, including both the environment and the work to be done. The leader who is appropriate for an automobile assembly line is not likely to be appropriate for an advertising agency project, and the latter is unlikely to be appropriate for an agricultural experiment station. The effectiveness of top executives is found to be limited even between companies in the same industry, as each company has its own particular environment produced by its unique history, organization, and culture and demands a unique combination of leadership skills and approaches (Shetty & Peery, 1976).

Though one study (Williams & Harrel, 1964) showed a correlationship between earnings five years after receiving an MBA and offices held as an undergraduate, the mass of available evidence suggests that extracurricular activities are of little use in predicting effective leadership in a work situation. The same study found no correlation between extracurricular activities in graduate school and earnings.

Appearance, Grooming, Clothing, Demeanor

With the possible exception of an individual who insists on bizzare dress or hair style, there is no measurable link between appearance during a job interview and behavior on the job. Nevertheless, the literature on how to prepare for a job interview stresses appearance and demeanor. The applicant is advised to dress in a particular way, to be sure to give a firm handshake, and to look the interviewer straight in the eyes. When surveyed on the importance of job applicant characteristics, recruiters, students, and faculty all gave appearance a very high ranking. On a scale from one to seven ("very important"), recruiters ranked appearance fifth out of fourteen items with a score of 5.55, students ranked it fourth with a score of 5.79, and faculty ranked it first with a score of 6.19 (Posner, 1981).

Recruiters do place emphasis on appearance, and it behooves the would-be hire to recognize this predilection. However, there is no plausible relationship between appearance and the quality or quantity of professional work. When recruiters are asked why they give weight to appearance during the job interview, typical answers include: "It shows the applicant is serious, and has respect for the company," "A neat appearance indicates an orderly approach to work," "It's more professional." Good, bad and indifferent students all tend to "dress up" and sport fresh haircuts when interviewing, and the incompetent look as barbered as the competent.

Clothing and appearance are primarily functions of the style of the times, and anyone can easily assume acceptable external packaging. The only thing appearance tells the interviewer is the extent to which the interviewee is in tune with current style. Appearance has no relationship to professional performance, except in positions where there is a need to impress selected audiences, as in sales.

Interview Behavior

The interview is the primary vehicle by which a recruiter or a manager makes determinations about the personality, attitudes and outlook on life of the graduate who is a potential hire. The interview also serves as a means for making assessments about appearance and grooming, and about whether or not the interviewee communicates well. During the interview the potential hire is queried about personal goals, ambitions, and motivations, all of which are considered important to the hiring decision. It is during the interview that the interviewer forms opinions about the personality of the potential hire, and makes judgements about how he or she will fit in with the company and what kind of potential he or she has.

Personality, Attitudes, and Outlook on Life

It is the rare sociopath who goes to an employment interview intending to present other than the best front that can be mustered. Few college graduates lack the minimum intelligence required to fathom what is wanted in an interview. The potential professional hire quickly understands how to respond in an interview. Some interviewers take pride in tricking interviewees into revealing themselves in response to trick questions or several drinks, but these methods reveal little.

The question of which personality attributes can be correlated with performance on the professional job has not been answered. Few data show one or another attribute to be required for the successful performance of medicine, architecture, science, engineering, law, or the ministry. Furthermore, it is doubtful that any particular personality attribute can be discerned through the interview process.

Goals, Ambitions, and Motivations

In view of what is known about the dynamics of the interview process, it is surprising that among the questions most frequently asked of the new college graduate are, "What are your five-year goals? Your ten-year goals? Your long-term goals?" The ostensible purpose is to elicit some real notion of the intentions, ambitions and motivations of the potential hire. The interviewee will always contrive some rational answer to the question. After the first interview, the answer to the question is carefully constructed and modified in preparation for subsequent interviews. What would the interviewer (or the reader) come up with if asked to specify five-year or ten-year goals? Few professionals could answer the question. Few find themselves doing later what they expected at time of graduation. What can the inexperienced college graduate imagine of the possibilities "out there?" The future is crowded with a host of interacting unknowns and unknowables, not least of which is a genuine lack of knowledge about situations not yet experienced. TIME Magazine once reported the statement of a forty-year old dentist who complained, "Some damn fool nineteen-year old decided I would be a dentist all my life!"

Fit with Organization; Future Potential

Judgments as to fit and future potential are almost universally made during interviews. In the initial interview, the interviewer exercises intuition based on observations and interviewee responses. When a candidate is interviewed more than once at a firm, the interviewers arrive at a consensus as to whether the candidate is "one of our kind." Once the decision is made, supporting information is sought from references and the school record.

Differences Between Schools

Some organizations place a great deal of emphasis on particular schools, preferring the graduates of some over others, and sometimes offering higher entering salaries to graduates of the preferred schools. They assume that the favored school's graduates will perform significantly better than those of other schools for a number of reasons: the selectivity with which the school admits its students, the presumed excellence of the educational environment (good faculty, fine facilities, and high standards), and the high expectation level of the student body.

There is little evidence of a relationship between the school attended and performance on the job. One study, using salary data on thousands of scientists and engineers in the aerospace and electronic industries (Shapero et al., 1965), found that graduates from prestigious schools (e.g., MIT and Harvard) obtained somewhat higher compensation than graduates from other schools, but that the data were influenced by the fact that many companies offer higher entering salaries to graduates from prestigious schools. Most company wage and salary systems take considerable time to overcome an initial salary advantage, and differences may not be erased for years. Thus, a study relating quality of electrical engineering graduate schools and salary showed an initial advantage for "prestige" schools that disappeared with time. Another study found initial salary advantages associated with grades disappeared with time (Martin & Pachares, 1962). Another study concluded that academic achievement and quality of institution attended were poor predictors of both job retention and salary progression (Schick & Kunnecke, 1981).

EFFECTIVE HIRING

The Hiring Process Itself and Subsequent Performance

The channel through which someone is hired and the way the new hire is put to work are far more predictive of sub-

33

sequent performance than any indicators obtained from interviews, application forms, tests, and assessment center
procedures. The data relating subsequent salary increases (a
very good indicator of an organization's judgment of individual
performance) and retention (a good indicator of individual satisfaction with an organization) to channels of recruitment and
first work experiences within the organization demonstrate this.

Channels of Recruitment and Subsequent Performance

A channel of recruitment is the route by which an individual
comes to an organization. Channels of recruitment include:

Employment agencies
Advertisements (in newspapers and trade and professional
    journals)
Company recruitment (college recruitment, professional
    meeting recruitment)
Self-recruitment (through friends or acquaintances, knowl-
    edge of company's work or reputation, perceived advance-
    ment opportunity)

As can be seen in Table 1–2, the great majority of professionals in organizations are hired through self-recruitment channels. Over two-thirds of the professionals working in three
major missile companies in three widely separated locations
were hired through self-recruitment (Shapero et al., 1965). The
relevance of the data shown in Table 1–2 to other time periods
and industries is shown by other studies such as that of Azevedo
(1974) which explored the utilization and effectiveness of different channels of recruitment in terms of frequency of use by
scientists and engineers and effectiveness in gaining employment in a time of economic downturn in the industry (see
Table 1–3).

Azevedo also found that over two-thirds of the successful
strategies used were methods of self-recruitment. The distribution between use of reference networks and direct applications
differed from what was found in an earlier time period: 31%

TABLE 1–2
Sources of Professional Employees (Channels)

CHANNEL OF RECRUITMENT	CURRENTLY EMPLOYED N = 3045	TERMINATED N = 413
Placement service	5.1	14.3
Advertisements	14.6	25.4
Newspaper	10.6	19.1
Magazine	2.2	4.4
Trade journal	5.1	14.3
Company recruitment	7.6	10.9
College	4.8	10.2
Other	2.8	0.7
Self-recruited	70.9	44.6
Friend or acquaintance	51.1	28.6
Company reputation	17.0	12.1
Advancement opportunity	2.8	3.9
Other	1.9	4.9

SOURCE: Data from Shapero et al. (1965).

TABLE 1–3
Jobs Yielded by Job Search Strategies (Channels)

CHANNEL	HIGH-EMPLOYMENT YEARS	LOW-EMPLOYMENT YEARS
Placement service (State, private, outplacement, college alumni, executive recruitment)	15.7	16.1
Advertisements	14.5	15.5
Newspaper	10.5	8.9
Professional journal	2.0	4.8
Trade journal	2.0	1.3
Employment newsletters	0.0	0.5
Self-recruited	67.4	66.7
Friend, relative, or acquaintance	26.9	32.1
Direct application	40.5	35.6
Other (Includes professional meetings, job shops)	2.4	1.3

SOURCE: Data summarized from Azevedo (1974).

came through friends and acquaintances and 36% through direct application, as compared to almost 52% and almost 20% in the earlier study. The shift in percentages is attributable to differences between "good" and "hard" times in the industry, with "hard" times raising the incidence of direct applications.

Subsequent surveys of a large variety of professional groups by the author show a remarkable persistence in the frequency of use of the different channels of recruitment among architects, librarians, consulting engineers, surveyors, medical research professionals, and computer professionals in state positions covered by Civil Service regulations.

The effectiveness of self-recruitment channels is demonstrated in several ways. The data in Tables 1–2 and 1–3 clearly show the effectiveness of self-recruitment channels, which generate two-thirds of the professionals found on the job and two-thirds of the jobs for professionals seeking work. In terms of who stays (a measure of satisfaction on the part of both employer and employee), a comparison of the data on channels of recruitment with the data on those who terminated shows striking differences. Self-recruitment channels were responsible for 70.9% of those on the job as compared with 44.6% of those who had terminated. The typical personnel recruitment channels such as placement services, advertising, and college recruitment were the sources of the majority of terminated employees: 14.3% came through placement services compared with 5.1% of those on the job; advertisement produced 25.4% of employees terminated as compared with 14.6% of those on the job; and for college recruitment the figures were 10.2% as compared with 4.8%.

Another important measure of the effectiveness of various channels of recruitment is the correlation of average salary increases with channels of recruitment. It was found that those who had come through self-recruitment channels received significantly higher increases than those from other channels (Shapero et al., 1965). Those who applied directly received the highest average annual increase, $92.50 a month, and those who came through a friend or acquaintance, $71.84 a month. The professionals who had come through advertising channels averaged between $54.98 and $64.64 a month, college recruits averaged $58.66, and placement service hires $53.66.

The source of recruitment of research scientists was found to be strongly related to subsequent job performance, absenteeism, and work attitudes. "Individuals recruited through college placement offices and, to a lesser extent . . . via the newspaper were inferior in performance . . . to individuals who made contact based on their own initiative or a professional journal/ convention advertisement" (Breaugh, 1981).

A less frequently used recruitment source worth mentioning is co-operative education. Co-operative education rotates a student between on-the-job training and the university classroom on a systematic basis. An evaluation of recruitment sources for R & D employees at the NASA Langley Research Center at Hampton, Virginia, found that former co-op students significantly outperformed professionals obtained from other sources (Jarrell, 1974). The former co-op students had a lower turnover rate and received more awards for exceptional performance than did others.

Former co-op students are self-recruited since the decision to go to work for an organization is a matter of choice by the former students. In the Langley case, about 30% of the co-op students accepted employment offers from Langley over a seventeen-year period.

Self-Recruitment and the Power of Social-Professional Circles

Why do self-recruitment channels do so much better than channels that dominate formal personnel department practice? The most likely answer is provided by the effects of expectations on behavior. The expectations generated by norms arising from association with a social-professional circle or network, and their activation by the manner of entry into an organization, go far to explain the effectiveness of self-recruitment channels.

A norm is a standard accepted and shared by members of a social group and to which members of the group are expected to conform. A group requires the existence and maintainance of norms if it is to exist for any period of time. Given the norms of a particular group, one can predict with some confidence the behavior of an individual identified with that group.

Norms are enforced by a group in both positive and negative ways, ranging from physical harm and withdrawal of approval to rewarding acceptable behavior. Some norms are maintained by "identification" and "internalization." Identification occurs when an individual defines himself with others and acts in a way that will gain acceptance by those others through meeting their norms. Internalization is the most powerful way in which norms operate, and occurs when an individual defines himself as one who acts by those norms and does so without surveillance by or reference to anyone else.

In our complex society each individual is a member of a bewildering variety of groups: work, social, neighborhood, ethnic, religious, professional, school, and former work groups. Consequently, each individual incorporates and maintains a variety of norms not always similar or even synchronized. One of the ways in which the uniqueness of an individual is achieved is by a particular mix of the norms and values of the many groups with which he identifies.

The groups or social circles, professional and otherwise, with which we identify are crucial to our lives. They are vital to effective job search, crucial to how we get information and even determine to whom we get married. In answer to the question, "How did you meet your spouse?" the same channels of "recruitment" patterns are found: "We met through friends," or "I heard about her and sought her out," or "We met at a church social."

Though few of us are conscious of how dependent we are on our social circles, we consistently turn to them for important personal and work-related information. We are very careful how we act in our social-professional circles. We conform to their norms or are dropped from them and thereby cut off from information essential to professional performance and development. Members of the academic social-professional circles called "invisible colleges" know about research in their field as early as two years before publication. They receive professional recognition, invitations to take important roles in conferences, journals, and societies, and receive desirable job referral through their circles. Those who break with the norms of the circle by such behavior as never contributing information with colleagues who share with them are dropped from the circle. The sanction is not imposed by a formal decision, rather by a kind of withering of one's umbilical connection to the circle (Price, 1977).

An individual hired by an organization through referral by a friend or acquaintance (through a social-professional circle) agrees to an implicit "contract." The new hire feels obligated to live up to the expectations of the person who did the referring, and, thus, is directly controlled or influenced by the standards of that person. The employer reinforces these expectations by attributing to the hire the standards and outlook of the person doing the referring or the circle to which he or she belongs. Consequently, consciously and unconsciously, the new employer makes evident what is expected of the hire.

An individual coming to an organization through an employment agency forms expectations as to what is expected from the agency's interviewer. The individual feels no obligation to the agency since the transaction is commercial and carries with it no strong notions of the standards and expectations of the organization being entered. Just the opposite occurs with self-recruited individuals who come to an organization because of its reputation. They have high expectations and do far better than those coming through other channels.

Entry into the Organization and the First Work Assignments

The first assignments a professional worker receives have a powerful and lasting effect on his or her subsequent outlook and performance. The effect of first assignments is particularly relevant to the newly graduated professional but applies, to some extent, to any professional entering an organization. First assignments establish powerful expectations. Anyone who has worked on a construction crew or in a factory can attest to the short time it takes to learn an expected and acceptable rate of effort. In a matter of hours the new worker learns that to work too fast is to be a "job killer" or "rate buster," and to work too slowly is to "shaft your buddies." Every newly graduated architect learns with amazement on the first job how fast drawings can be produced.

First assignments are critical to the subsequent performance, promotions and pay increases of an employee. Challenging early assignments have been shown to be related to strong early performance, and to the maintenance of performance and competence throughout a professional's career. Early challenge has been found to be effective in professions as diverse as engineering and the Roman Catholic priesthood. When a new worker is expected to perform at a high level he or she does, and, as a consequence, is rewarded and given more challenging work assignments which continue to reinforce the desired performances.

When an experienced professional is hired into an organization, the effects of first assignments are not as clear as with new professionals. Good performance persists, and if one hires an experienced professional who has been competent it is likely competent performance will be obtained. However, the majority of professionals judged as middling in performance can make substantial shifts upward or downward, depending on management actions. In the latter case, the first assignments of the incoming professional can be vital. What the new hire is assigned to do, and who he or she is assigned to work with can effect the subsequent performance of even an experienced worker.

How to Hire: Practical and Operational Implications

The research on hiring professionals leads to two inevitable conclusions: (1) there are obvious ways to systematically improve the hiring of professionals both qualitatively and quantitatively, and (2) the elaborate structure of conventional hiring practices is ineffective for hiring professionals.

Why Conventional Practices Persist

Despite their relative ineffectiveness, classified ads and employment agencies are used as the prime sources of professional hires by 70–80% of 188 large national firms surveyed. What can explain the use of ineffective and costly practices that many experienced personnel professionals readily admit are hit-and-miss?

Several elements interact and reinforce current professional hiring practices. First is the existence of a large establishment with a strong, vested interest in current practices. The establishment is made up of personnel departments, personnel professionals, academics offering personnel courses, consultants, and suppliers of such paraphernalia of personnel work as tests. The present personnel establishment arose in response to the needs of a large, growing industrial manufacturing sector, predominately concerned with routine and predictable work. As a consequence, personnel practices applied to professionals have been drawn from a large, elaborate, and comfortable matrix that was useful for production work.

Another factor in the continuation of current practices is a remarkable lack of systematic evaluation of their effectiveness. There is little evidence of efforts by corporate personnel departments to determine what does or doesn't work when it comes to hiring professionals. With rare exceptions, such as the longitudinal studies conducted by AT&T, companies do not relate data on subsequent performance of professionals to the data used at time of hire.

Conventional practice also can persist because they are bypassed in actual practice. How is it possible that two-thirds of the Civil Service professionals we interviewed had been hired through self-recruited hiring channels despite legal mandates? Typically, an experienced manager asks a colleague to recommend a good engineer. Then the manager calls a long-time associate in the personnel department to ask, "I've got someone really competent I want to hire. How can I do it without going through a month of procedures and three interviews with inappropriate applicants?" The associate replies, "Easy! Hire that engineer as a part-time or temporary worker, and after five and a half months (be sure it is less than six months) we'll process a Change-of-Status Request which will make it legal."

Concentrate on the Hiring Process Rather Than the Traits of Individuals

You can do far better concentrating on elements of the hiring process than on the apparent characteristics of the individuals being considered. To illustrate, if you hire at random from a university graduating class, and concentrate on establishing high expectations in the new hire through a challenging first assignment that entails working with your best professionals, you will get far better long-term performance than by hiring from the top of the class and putting the new hire through a company training program. To put a newly graduated professional into a training program is to delay entry into realistic work situations, and is a continuation of not-yet-ready-to-start expectations far longer than is useful.

Remember, there is no relationship between grades in school and performance on the job. As I have written elsewhere:

> It should be clearly pointed out that people at the top of the class are not less competent than the rest of the class. However, there is little to say they'll do better. There are thus good arguments for hiring from the bottom of the class. Those at the top have been conditioned in a special way by those of us in academe. We encourage them to aspire to join us on Olympus where they can drink nectar with the gods. Their expectations are very high both as to what they will and won't do and as to what they expect in the way of rewards. On the other hand, according to the starting salary data, those at the bottom of the class start out costing a lot less, and as I've pointed out, on average they perform just as well as the class brains. Finally, as Ben Franklin said in talking about a not dissimilar situation, "You'll find they are Oh so grateful." [Shapero, 1977]

Use personal reference networks. Use personal networks to identify good potential hires. Good performers tend to be associated with social circles, professional or otherwise, that maintain high norms of work behavior. The old adage "birds of a feather flock together" could be restated: "birds that flock together be-

42

come of a feather." Watch for the identity of the group through which the individual is referred, since all of us are members of many groups with differing norms and values. Working through your immediate and extended professional social circles, the probability is high you will obtain accurate information about potential hires, and you will get value judgments not available through any formal channels. Information obtained from someone you do not know personally but to whom you are referred by someone you know will still be of high quality.

Concentrate on effective channels of recruitment. Concentrate on "self-recruitment" channels. Hires who come to an organization because of its reputation or through friends and acquaintances are the best performers on the job. Over the long term, it is possible to enhance the flow of high-quality applicants by a program of institutional advertisements (as opposed to employment advertisement) and other public relations activities that convincingly portray the organization as having high professional standards, valuing high-quality work and productivity, and having an appropriate environment. One national research organization ran ads in technical and trade journals with pictures and quotes of great scientists (e.g., Newton, Einstein, Kepler), and in very small print at the bottom of the ad gave a name and number to call for anyone interested in being associated with an organization that valued such people. Similarly, a major aerospace company once took the complete middle spread of several major newspapers to list over four hundred titles of papers written by its technical staff, and to invite those who were interested to request copies and to apply for work in an organization that put such a high premium on technical papers.

Maintaining good public relations pays off over time. A good reputation makes it possible to obtain the quantity and quality of professional manpower desired when needed, which is often hard to do under the immediate pressures of a large project or contract. One caveat should be noted: the institutional advertising and public relations must be realistic rather than fanciful. One company that advertised the glories and pleasures of its professional environment harvested a sharp increase in professional turnover made up of angry employees who contrasted the advertisements with their daily realities. The ads were put up on bulletin boards all over the company with appropriate graffiti.

Enlist friends, acquaintances, relatives, former colleagues, former professors, people met at technical meetings, friends of friends as sources of referrals of potential hires. Using one's own contacts to stir up potential hires is a good way to generate a flow of first-quality potential hires. Most managers will say, "But I do that." Of course they do. That is why such a high fraction of professionals are hired through the channel of "friends and acquaintances," but the process should be systematized. It is a preferred means and should be given precedence in time and resources.

Use professionals already working in the organization to identify and bring in people they know. Many organizations circularize their employees, but few design the effort in terms of what is known about good hiring. It is important to focus on your best performers for candidates. Chances are good that someone referred by a high performer will also be a high performer. Similarly, the professional referred by a low performer has a good probability of having the same standards as the person doing the referring. It is safe to assume the high performer will judge the person he recommends by his own standards. In any case, if you personally ask employees to recommend someone like themselves you have paid a high compliment, which provides positive feedback reinforcement even when it doesn't result in hires.

In times of high demand for professionals, as during the missile buildup of the 1950s, some companies rediscovered an idea invented several times: offering a bonus or fee to employees for every qualified person they referred who was hired. Engineers were in great demand, and the competition was fierce. The situation was exacerbated by the policy of the government to pick up all personnel costs. Large salary increases and promotions were used to attract qualified people. Inter-company pirating was rampant. One missile company sent twenty-three engineers to recruit at an engineering convention and only three returned, all the others having been hired away. In that environment more than one company came up with the idea of paying "bounty" to their own employees for bringing in engineers. Paying bounty did not work well. The practice resulted in poor hiring. By paying the employee for bringing in a candidate the act becomes a commercial transaction rather than a personal responsibility, and the feeling engendered in the employees can be expressed, "If you hire the person I bring in, it's your responsibility. I'll bring in as many people as I can, of all kinds, and leave the evaluation and judgment to the company."

Maintain a program of summer jobs for students, participate in cooperative education programs, and use intern programs for effective, low-risk means for obtaining high performing professionals. The summer employee, co-op student, and intern come to work under conditions in which organization and nascent professional can look each other over without commitment or risk. The managers in the organization can affect the performance of the individuals by the assignments given and the people with whom the individual is assigned to work. Meanwhile, the student becomes familiar with the company and its ways, and can make an informed judgment about the desirability of working there.

Summer jobs, co-op programs, and internships are very popular with students. The best students are anxious to obtain professional experience and seek out such opportunities. One consulting engineering firm in the Pacific Northwest attracts summer students with the promise that they will work directly with the firm's principals—and with no pay! Hands-on programs in architecture, engineering, and business schools are oversubscribed. There is one caveat to be noted. A hands-on program that doesn't put the students to work doing genuine, challenging work will create strong negative reactions. Participants in programs that use them as clerks or that let them study rather than work take home and circulate a poor image of the company. The student employees don't come back, and the organization gets a bad image among other students.

Set high expectations on entry. Locate the new employee, particularly the new college graduate, in a group of individuals with very high standards of performance. The performance

45

of those in the new individual's immediate work environment and their response to his behavior will establish what is expected and strongly influence the individual's behavior. Once set, it takes a long time and a great many different experiences to change the effect of the early expectations experienced by the new employee.

Many organizations undertake the mistaken practice of putting a "young tiger" into a group in need of livening up. Chances are that instead of an enlivened group, the results will be a dead "tiger" or early turnover of the new hire. Group norms are powerful and persistent, and it is extremely difficult to change them. To enliven an organization it is better to build up clusters of high performers, centers of excellence, while allowing low-performing groups to shrink by attrition or to be broken up.

Give the new employee a first or early assignment that is challenging, and make it clear that high performance is expected. It informs the employee of standards and expectations of the organization. A useful way to "save" an employee who has performed well in the past, but who appears to have plateaued, is to put the employee in a lively group and give a demanding assignment that helps evoke earlier standards of performance.

Hire with the flow of streams of migration. To increase the numbers of employment offers accepted and of workers who will stay with the organization, managers should: hire from within the immediate area; hire from upstream; when hiring from downstream, hire people who came from the immediate area (the "return home phenomenon").

To set up a facility in a new geographic area an organization should first draw upon members of the organization that originally came from the area, and should "map" the historic migration patterns affecting the new location as a guide for its hiring efforts. The choice of geographic points of recruitment can make a substantial difference in whether desirable professionals will come to work or stay with the company.

To illustrate the migration path effect, when Huntsville, Alabama, was bustling with space and military work, a large number of contractor and subcontractor organizations set up facilities in the town. Many had large demands for scientists and engineers and expended much on recruitment. One organization needing two hundred professionals placed an advertisement in the local newspaper intending to attract people from other local government and contractor facilities. The advertisement was answered by a large number of applicants from the North, and all the positions were filled. The applications came from Alabamians who had migrated to the North and were ready to return home, a classic pattern. They had obtained the advertisement from relatives who wanted them to return or from their hometown newspaper which they continued to receive.

Similarly, on publication of news of plans to build a plant in Northern Arkansas, a business machine company received over two thousand applications from people who had lived or vacationed in the area, and who wanted to settle there.

Put teeth into the probation period. Hiring is the most important management decision made, and the probation process should be considered a critical element in the hiring process. Firms with more than a handful of employees almost always have a probationary period after hiring. The probation period varies from one month to three months, and is a time when employees can be fired without recourse and even without explanation. Probation is a period in which employees' performance can be assessed before they enter the permanent work force.

Frequently, probation has been a matter of negotiation between union and management to establish a point beyond which an individual is considered a member of the work force with all the protection of the union against layoff. Many organizations have a probation period for all employees, professional and nonprofessional, and it is made clear at the time of hire that such a period must be undergone before the employee is considered a permanent hire.

Despite intentions, few organizations make serious efforts to fully carry out the probation process. In most cases, probation is a perfunctory processing of paper work except in the most flagrant cases of incompetence or behavioral disturbance.

As with the human body, organizations cannot afford to

"ingest" individuals who can seriously affect their ability to achieve high performance. The criterion for probation should be, as with the body, "when in doubt, spit it out." A probation system should establish criteria and operational procedures for evaluating new hires, and for letting people go who do not meet the criteria. Firing is the most painful experience a manager goes through, but there is an important trade off between the short-term difficulty of firing and the long-term costs to everyone of an unsuitable employee.

A useful probation system should include the following:

1. Probationary criteria based on an organization's experience
2. Procedures for making the new hire clearly aware of the probation process, and the criteria used
3. Procedures for probation review applied, where possible, by someone who did not do the hiring, to keep the person who did the hiring from rationalizing the unacceptable performance of the new hire

Organizations suffer from functional amnesia when it comes to their hiring experiences. Few organizations record and review their hiring experience in relationship to subsequent performance. Every organization, even the smallest, should record what was perceived in the new hire in a way that it can be retrieved for comparison against performance. In the absence of the data, subsequent comparisons will be distorted by later impressions.

Low and high performers should be identified and their characteristics and hiring processes (including who recommended them or hired them) compared. Efforts should be made to identify any existing patterns. Efforts should also be made to identify the kinds of organizational events associated with the loss of high performers.

Take Advantage of the Errors in the Conventional Wisdom

Conventional wisdom on hiring is embodied in many personnel practices that have no measurable relationship to the professional performance desired. Consequently, many opportunities are available to enlightened management to gain a competitive advantage in hiring excellent but untapped human resources. The two largest groups of competent and relatively unsought human resources are (1) new college graduates who are not in the upper echelons of the class, and (2) older professionals.

A good opportunity exists for hiring excellent newly graduated professionals, by focusing on the lower two thirds of the class. First, the largest corporations, consulting organizations and government agencies concentrate on graduates with high grade point averages, making it difficult for any single organization to compete successfully for them, bidding up their starting salaries, and giving the candidates an unrealistic notion of what awaits them in the work place. Second, those with the highest grade averages are socialized by their professors to take advanced degrees, to aspire to become academics. The "good student" is asked by the professors, "Have you thought about graduate school? Would you like a recommendation for a fellowship?" The student with lower grade averages is not better (or worse) than the high GPA student on the job, tends to be far more ready to enter fully into the work force, and is happy to be sought out.

The validity of the assertion that there is no relationship between grades in school and performance on the job is easily checked by any organization with more than a handful of professional employees. Any management can rank its employees in terms of performance from highest to lowest, and then check the school records of the employees against their rankings. If the grades scatter, as in all probability they will, it will demonstrate that grades and performance are not correlated.[1]

Older workers are another relatively untapped source of excellent professional manpower. Older workers perform well,

[1] In response to a large number of challenges to a column expressing the point about the lack of relationship between grades and performance on the job, each of the challengers was asked to make the check described here with the assurance that if they disproved the statement the evidence would be published and the statement retracted. No disproof was received.

and bring many other positive attributes to their work. In many cases, the financial situation of the older worker is such as to make them desirable employees. Their children are finished with college, their houses are paid for, their retirement has been partially provided, and they are less likely to make job decisions on the basis of marginal differences in salary. Older workers are not amenable to being underpaid, but are more likely to put a premium on the quality of the work environment, the chance to keep up professionally, and the congeniality of colleagues than on "career opportunities" and promotion.

Some older workers prefer to be hired on a part-time basis or on a part-of-the-year basis so they can take advantage of long vacations to travel or pursue other interests. As a consequence of the predilection for part-time employment, nominally retired professionals are useful in handling the peaks and valleys of project/contract work without the trauma of hiring and firing employees. Some organizations hire "emeritus" professionals on a contract basis so that both parties are freed from a host of procedural and regulatory burdens such as deductions and fringe benefit calculations. Many managements have independently "discovered" the use of older professionals as part-time employees, and are unanimous in praising their capabilities, work performance, and attitudes. Many see the older professionals as good influences in their organizations.

SPECIAL CASES

Special situations in hiring professionals to consider include (1) hiring minority workers and women, and (2) hiring in a seller's market when business is good and professionals are scarce.

Minority Workers and Women

Organizations are concerned with the representation of minority and women professionals in their work force both because of government regulations and a sincere desire for more equity. In spite of persistent and expensive efforts the results have been uneven. There are many reasons for the poor showing to date. Sometimes demographic situations make the task virtually impossible. One nuclear power facility on the Ohio River, ordered by the government to increase the number of black professionals on its staff, found it impossible to convince black engineers to move to an area where less than 2% of the population is black. Another severe limitation can be the absolute numbers of designated professionals available. Though 43.3% of all professional and technical workers in the United States are women, only 2.9% of the engineers, 10.75% of the physicians and osteopaths, and 12.4% of the lawyers and judges are women. The 43.3% figure was achieved by including professions where women predominate: i.e., nursing, 96.8%, teaching, 70.8%.

A more painful dilemma is expressed by the black woman director of minority hiring in a major state agency who said, "We've tried our damndest to hire competent black professionals, but we haven't done well at all. Very few have applied despite the good salaries and conditions offered, and the quality of those who do apply has been poor. What can we do about it?"

As with any professionals, if you want competency, go to competent people for references. If you want good referrals of black, Latin-American, or women professionals, go to competent people and ask them for their recommendations. If you are trying to hire competent black engineers use all of the social-professional circles you have access to and turn to the most competent black professionals of any kind you can contact (physicians, teachers, ministers, social workers) for their recommendations. (The government agency minority recruitment director had to find a way to get referrals into and through the civil service procedures.)

Taking a longer view of the problem, an organization should hire minorities and women for summer work or cooperative-education programs, thus building a long-term flow into the organization. Where a geographic area has very few minority or women professionals in the population, an organization can take advantage of historic migration patterns. By using census data on migration for the past decade, it is possible to identify (1) from where minority professionals in the area have migrated, and (2) the areas to which minority members have been migrating from the local area. Streams of migration all tend to have a two-way flow. The two-way flow was demonstrated in the 1970s by a reverse migration from the North to the South of blacks who had previously migrated to the North, and particularly of those who had achieved professional and technical skills.

No approach to hiring minority or women professionals will have any lasting effect if it is not paralleled by subsequent practices that reinforce the intentions of the organization as expressed in its hiring program. The power of the new hire's expectations is even more important in the case of minorities and women. The organization that hires minority workers in response to governmental pressures, and then proceeds to expect them to perform poorly, generates a self-fulfilling prophecy. Under such conditions, employees will perform as poorly as expected or will leave at a high rate. Those who leave will convey the organization's expectations to the general community, affecting subsequent minority hiring. It would be better to initiate no special minority hiring program if no special attention is paid to initial assignments and locations.

When Business Is Good and Professionals Are Scarce

Professional work tends to be done in terms of projects. The project format typefies research and development, construction, advertising, the performing arts, consulting, and architecture, to name the most obvious. Furthermore, many professional fields have very sharp fluctuations tied to socioeconomic conditions such as booms, slumps, and variations in building, and in the patterns of government expenditure.

As a consequence of the "lumpiness" of project work, many organizations often experience precipitous and simultaneous demands for the same kinds of professionals. Under such "sellers' market" conditions it is important to consider what attracts professionals to one organization over another. Too often, it is assumed that outbidding other organizations is the key to successful hiring. Thus, in the 1950s period of missile buildup, competing companies bidup the salary level of scientists and engineers in the aerospace industry to twice the average for all scientists and engineers in the United States.

Many noneconomic factors influence the employment decisions of professionals. Geographic migration patterns have been discussed. Other clues to the job decisions of professionals come from studies showing that professionals place a high premium on professional challenge, interesting work, reputation of the organization, professional climate, opportunities for professional growth, and recognition.

A final note on hiring in good times: An organization can adopt a long-term stance that assures an adequate flow of good people when they are needed. A long-term stance reflects the view that it is important to maintain at all times the kinds of communications relevant to good hiring, even when the situation is bleak. The best channels of recruitment are those least amenable to being turned on and off with a budget. It is easy to turn on advertising, employment agencies, and recruiting campaigns with a budget, but budgets cannot generate and nurture the social-professional networks and reputations so effective in producing good hires. The latter are maintained by encouraging publication, attendance at professional meetings, and maintaining a host of informal contacts with other professionals in the field on the part of an organization's professional staff, during times when those contacts are not needed.

2

Motivation

A GREAT RE-EXAMINATION of American management practice has been stirred by the success of the Japanese in world markets. Though some cry, "Foul! The Japanese are unfair!," most attribute Japanese success to higher productivity and search for the sources of Japanese advantage. Among the factors credited have been lower wages, more automation, more focused R & D expenditures, and, most of all, better motivation on the part of Japanese employees and managers.

Much effort has gone into explaining Japanese industrial motivation. Credit has been given to Japanese culture (for its homogeneity, devotion to nation, etc.,); guaranteed lifetime employment and its subsequent benefits in terms of long-term vs. short-term decisions (i.e., R & D expenditures, lower wages, acceptance of innovation capital investment, long-term cost-benefit analyses); and Japanese management styles (e.g., consensus decision-making, and worker participation as exemplified by quality circles).

Most of the attributions are without much substance or are relevant only to a limited segment of Japanese industry.

Guaranteed lifetime employment applies to less than twenty-five major corporations and not to the 75% of the Japanese work force found in small companies. There is little long-range planning, in the U. S. industrial sense, in Japanese companies. There is a great deal of competitiveness in Japanese society and industry. Many, of the admired worker-participation methods, such as quality circles, have American roots, and were introduced to the Japanese by American efforts through the occupation authorities and U. S.-sponsored productivity centers. Quality circles, an admired feature of Japanese management, derive from work simplification programs and quality control methods that were the hallmark of much of U. S. industrial practice four decades ago. The most useful clue to the Japanese success is found in motivation.

Motivation is certainly one of the most frequently mentioned concerns of U. S. managers. One often hears them complain, "If we could only motivate our people . . ." or "Workers are not motivated the way they used to be." Yet, as with quality control, it is the United States that has always dominated the subject. American scholarship and thinking pioneered and still leads the field of motivation research.

Historically, managers have been concerned with the morals and morale of the workers since the feudal relationship between the lord of the manor and his serfs. However, serious interest in understanding what influences the behavior of workers and how to use that knowledge did not begin to develop until the early 1920s. In the 1930s the field took off with a tremendous increase in the space devoted by management texts to behavioral concerns, and textbooks of the period bristled with such terms as "adjustment," "status," and "social environment." In the 1950s the terminology showed a preoccupation with "informal groups," "roles," "job satisfaction," "work performance," and "work motivation." Through the mid-1970s the term "motivation" was second in frequency only to "leadership" in management texts: in twenty-eight textbooks it was mentioned 611 times, compared with 860 times for "leadership" (Aronoff, 1975).

It must be pointed out that when managers complain that "the workers are not motivated" they are dead wrong. There is no such thing as a sentient human being who is not motivated. It is impossible not to be motivated. Even to lie in bed and refuse to move is a motivated inaction. When a manager says that someone is not motivated, what she or he is saying is that the individual is not motivated to do what the manager wants that person to do at the time and in the manner that the manager deems appropriate. What the noncooperating individual is showing is not lack of motivation. He or she might actually feel a strong motivation to do something to frustrate the manager or to accomplish something counterproductive to the needs of the employing organization.

The complaint of the manager about motivation should be reinterpreted to read, "How can I get these others to do what is in the interests of the organization rather than what they might do if left to their own devices?" The problem is one of work motivation, and the manager must find ways to effectively influence the behavior of those managed. Work motivation is central to what managers do since most management work consists of influencing human behavior, and in professional activities the proportion of management work devoted to influencing human behavior is much higher than for other kinds of work.

Except for rather infrequent events—such as when a contract is bid for and accepted, a project is launched or terminated, a campaign is undertaken or completed—the management of professional activities is primarily concerned with influencing the behavior of the professionals doing the work of the organization. Managers spend the bulk of their time listening, evaluating, encouraging, defending, criticizing, coaching, and advising—in other words, responding to the needs of or influencing the behavior of subordinates. The more the work of an organization is human-centered, the more the manager must be an influencer of human behavior. In organizations primarily engaged in professional activities, the work is almost entirely human-centered, and thus the manager is primarily a work motivator whether consciously or not.

In a sense, every chapter in this book is concerned with influencing human behavior or motivation, whether we are discussing this directly or are considering incentives, evaluation, creativity, technical obsolescense, burnout, information-communication, or hiring.

Incentives are institutionalized influencers of behavior. Incentives (such as compensation, for example) are used to elicit kinds of behavior other than might have been chosen in the absence of incentives (Gellerman, 1968).

Evaluation is another way of influencing future behavior. In evaluation the manager provides verbal feedback of judgments together with instructions, advice, and suggestions.

Creativity, technical obsolescence, and "burnout" are human processes, relevant to professional work, that can be influenced to some extent by the actions of managers.

Information-communication behavior is a vital work-related activity that can be influenced significantly by managerial actions.

Organization structures and processes are concerned with configuring, channeling and affecting the ways people in the organization relate to each other in carrying out their work. A good deal of what managers do with organizations has to do with the effects of their actions and of the organizational structure on the work of their employees.

Hiring, too, engages us in a discussion of motivation and the influencing of human behavior. As was underlined in the chapter on hiring, the most effective means of hiring positively influences the behavior of those hired (i.e., the use of networks, the importance of first assignments and locations, etc.).

Thus, the subject of motivation is the logical place to begin consideration of how managers can go about achieving influence over worker behavior through incentives, evaluation, organization, and so forth. A manager needs enough information to feel comfortable in dealing with the subject from a rational, data-based perspective rather than from hearsay and gut feeling. An understanding of motivation, of the dynamics of influencing behavior, provides the manager with the knowledge from which specific means of influencing employee behavior can be developed.

Drawing upon the growing pool of research data on motivation, and particularly on work motivation, the process of work motivation is mapped below to help managers find a useful path through the maze of factors identified as influencing work place behavior. The "map" is eclectic in that it draws upon various theories and upon empirical studies, and is designed to identify for the manager what can be influenced in the work situation, and what important factors are outside that situation, and outside the reach of the manager. The map also helps identify which factors are more important than others in influencing the work behavior of professionals, and identifies available motivational tools.

MOTIVATION IN GENERAL AND MOTIVATION IN THE WORKPLACE

The word "motivation" is used to describe goal-directed behavior, as differentiated from reflexive behavior such as the blinking of an eye or the knee-jerk reaction to a knock on the knee which are unconsciously activated. According to one definition, motivation is concerned with:

> how behavior gets started, is energized, is sustained, is directed, is stopped, and what kind of subjective reaction is present in the organism while all this is going on. [Jones, 1955]

In the work situation, motivation is narrowed to questions of work performance: the starting, energizing, sustaining, directing, and stopping of behaviors relevant to the work situation.

When researchers in the field of work motivation, such as organizational behavior specialists and industrial psychologists, write about motivation, they are concerned with the "whys" of an individual's motivation to work. Behaviorial scientists raise questions like: why does an individual choose to work for one employer rather than another, or prefer one task to another? why does an individual choose to initiate a particular piece of work? why does an individual put as much effort into a task as he does? why does an individual complete an effort or even come to work every day?

When managers refer to motivation, they are concerned

with the "hows" related to an individual's motivation to work: how to get an individual to work for his organization rather than another, or to prefer an assigned task to another? how to get an individual to initiate pieces of work chosen or preferred by the manager rather than others? how to get an individual to put a desired level of effort into a task? how to get an individual to complete an assigned effort and complete it on time. How to get an individual to come to work at the appropriate times?

AN ECLECTIC MODEL OF WORK MOTIVATION

A number of theories have been developed to explain work motivation. Each of the theories offers a plausible framework which a manager can use to derive operational clues, but to limit one's perspective to any given theory deprives one of what can be gained from other theories and from the many available empirical studies. To make more of the available information available in a form that can guide managerial efforts to understand and affect motivation, a simple model has been developed (see Figure 2–1) to depict the factors that affect an individual's motivation in the work place. The model is "eclectic" in that it draws upon both a range of available theories and empirical studies. In addition to the eclectic model, the major work motivation theories are discussed from the viewpoint of the manager of professionals.

How an individual's work motivation is affected is described below in terms of an Expectations-Motivation-Performance-Experiences-Comparisons -Expectations cycle embedded in three overlapping fields: the work motivation field of the individual, the work situation, and the larger environment. The primary or central field is that of the individual, and within it is embedded the motivation cycle. At work, the individual's field is surrounded by the work situation which includes the organization, the physical facilities, and all of the conditions of work such as tools, materials, assignments, resources, rules and procedures. The larger environment encompasses all of the world outside

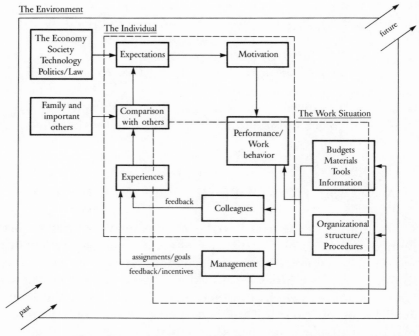

FIGURE 2–1. Work Motivation of the Individual

work that is significant to the individual and includes family, friends, other significant people, political and economic factors, technology, and law.

The Work Motivation Cycle and the Individual

Work behavior begins with *expectations*. What we expect to happen affects what we are motivated to do. The individual starts with a set of expectations about what will occur as a result of various work-related and social actions. It is the individual's expectations that are transformed into those predilections that we usually refer to as *motivation:* the propensity to move, the tendency to act in a particular manner or to work at a certain rate, to volunteer or withold suggestions, to express or hide enthusiasm, to act creatively or "play it by the book," to put in extra hours or not.

Motivation leads to *performance:* performance of the work to be done, as well as social and other behavior in the work place. Once the individual has done something in the workplace, several kinds of feedback—both external and internal—are received: the responses of managers, colleagues and clients, personal feelings of pleasure or displeasure at the outcomes, and other formal and informal signals of all kinds. The sum of all these kinds of feedback is the work *experiences* of the individual, which determine whether one feels that one has done a good job, is appreciated, or had a bad day.

Work experiences, however, do not occur in a vacuum. The individual is part of a work group, an organization, a profession, and a social group. Consequently, to be able to evaluate one's experiences, to decide whether they are good or bad, getting better or worse, the individual compares them with those of others. By making *comparisons* of one's experiences with those of others, an individual determines whether the treatment received is "fair," or should be protested. Most important, by evaluating what has been experienced as a result of the way one has performed, and by comparing it with what happens to others, expectations are re-examined, and, where it appears required, modified.

It is a dynamic cycle, constantly in action, constantly being modified. A change in the work situation, including what happens to others, leads to a change in the results of comparisons, changed expectations, and changed motivation.

From the viewpoint of the manager, it becomes apparent that exhortations to "change your motivation," or "change your attitude," are superficial and likely to be ineffective. The actual way motivation is changed is far less direct. Motivation is affected by what happens daily on the job, what happens to others, by rules and organization, and by the availability of all those other elements that go into doing the work, among which are the reactions of colleagues and what the manager says and does directly.

An examination of the cycle suggests where the manager can and cannot act directly on work motivation. The cycle begins with expectations which immediately suggests that the manager might help establish initial expectations and continue to affect them through a variety of actions. Realizing that the individual's experiences are partly a product of reactions from others and that those of the manager are the most influential suggests the importance and power of a frequent flow of managerial feedback to the individual. The alert manager can gear salaries and conditions to those of comparable individuals and organizations and can make sure the comparative data are freely available.

The Work Situation

The work situation is the domain of management, and it is the field in which the manager has most control. Managers determine the form of organization, the facilities to be used, the work rules and procedures, and the formal system of rewards. Managers make the work assignments, allocate resources, assign the schedules, and determine who works with whom. It is through manipulation of the work situation that managers have their greatest impact on the motivation and subsequent work behavior of the professionals that work for an organization.

The performance of an individual can be described in the form of an equation:

$$P = M \times A \times N$$
where P = performance
M = motivation
A = ability
N = necessaries (resources, information, budgets, organizational structure and procedures)

The job performance of the individual is the result of an interacting mix of the individual's motivation and ability, and of the availability and quality of the items necessary for performance of the work to be done. All of the elements are relevant, and all can be affected—one way or another—by management.

Availability of the necessary situation elements is almost

completely in the hands of management. Ability and motivation cannot overcome a lack of instruments and technicians. An organization's structure and procedures can make it difficult to get the timely decisions, resources, or information that can be crucial to whether work is performed well or not. Examples abound of the negative effects of various kinds of organizational structures or bureaucratic procedures on a firm's ability to carry out effective research and development or to deliver construction projects on time.

Further, the highest motivation cannot overcome an individual's technical incompetence. The inherent and acquired abilities of a professional combine with motivation to affect work performance. Management can affect technical competence and abilities by providing for technical updating, and by enabling the individual to continue developing personal professional skills and knowledge through a variety of means (see Chapter 5, "Technical Obsolescence, Burnout, and Staying Alive").

The manager, by all counts, has the most influence, directly and indirectly, in determining the nature and quality of an employee's work experiences. As has been pointed out above, the manager determines the employee's resources, information, organizational constraints, assignments made, goals set, as well as providing feedback in terms of approval, criticism, rewards, incentives, and recognition.

The manager affects work motivation indirectly by locating the professional employee physically and socially (organizationally) in a particular environment. Where and with whom one works closely has a distinct influence on one's work motivation. Assigning a new employee to an established group means the employee will be given all kinds of direct and indirect signals by members of the group as to what they consider good work behavior. Thus, assigning a new employee to a group with a low output rate is likely to set the new person's expectations to a low level of performance. Research has shown that a new employee's values tend to converge over time with the values of those already in the organization at time of entry (see box, "The Power of Expectations").

THE POWER OF EXPECTATIONS

The psychologist R. Rosenthal created a furor in research circles in the early 1960s when he found that the attitudes of individuals carrying out an experiment affected the way rats performed in running mazes. Using rats drawn from the same strain, he presented one group of experimenters with some of the rats with the explanation that they were specially bred for brightness. He assigned them the task of teaching the rats to run a maze. With a second group of experimenters, and rats from the same strain, he explained that the rats had been bred to be poor at running mazes, and he also assiged this second group the task of teaching the rats to run a maze.

Right off, the rats believed to be smarter did well, and the rats thought to be dull did very badly, sometimes refusing even to leave the starting position. Students who thought they had brighter rats found their subjects to be more pleasant and more likeable than those who thought they had dullards.

Rosenthal's results raised a lot of laughter as well as furor. Why did the rats act as they did? What did this mean to all the data based on rat experimentation? One could picture laboratory rats asking each other, "Hey, what's the hypothesis?" and knocking themselves out to prove it. Could it be the experimenter projected expectations that affected the performance of the subjects? What might the same kinds of expectations mean in human situations?

The Environment

The larger environment encompasses all the institutions, persons, and events significant to the individual and the work situation. The larger environment includes family, peers, and other significant people; the economic and political situation; and what is going on in technology and the profession. The way family and peers perceive and react to the work an individual is doing, to his or her position and pay, and to the employing organization has an influence on the individual's expectations and subsequent performance. Working for an organization held

64

In 1968 Rosenthal and Jacobson created similar kinds of expectation conditions in an elmentary school in South San Francisco. They told the teachers they needed further validation for a new kind of test to predict academic blooming or intellectual gain in children. They used what was then a new standard intelligence test unfamiliar to the teachers. Before school opened the following fall, using random numbers, 20% of the students were arbitrarily designated as potential "spurters"; about five to each classroom. The names of the so-called spurters were transmitted to the teachers casually at the end of the first staff meeting in September, and the students were subsequently tested and retested three times throughout the year.

The children whom the teachers were led to expect to show the greatest gains did show the greatest gains: the designated spurters showed the greatest increase in total IQ, in verbal IQ, and in reasoning IQ. At the end of the first year the greatest gains were made by those in the first and second grades. At the end of the second year the greatest gains were among the fifth grade spurters.

Those designated as spurters were judged by the teachers as having a better chance for success in later life, as being happier, more curious, more interesting, more appealing, better adjusted, more affectionate, and less in need of social approval than other children. Among the undesignated children who gained in IQ during the year, the more they gained, the less favorably they were perceived.

in high or low regard by the general public does have an influence on work performance. There is a long-term value for an organization in projecting a positive "image." It attracts desirable applicants, offsets their decisions to accept other positions, their decisions to come to work or be absent, and their on-the-job performance.

The general economic and political environment has an impact on the expectations of the individual professional. Most obviously, in hard times expectations shift in the direction of concern for security. In hard times it is important to keep professional employees attuned to the condition of the company with regard to the economy. In times when professional employees are in demand, there is a different weighting of incentives than when work is scarce. In recent years the legal environment has become more influential in the work situation with increasing exposure to professional liability and requirements for hiring minority and women workers. Professionals are acutely aware of what is happening in the legal environment and it influences their expectations. It is vital that management convey to its employees how the organization will respond to new legal requirements, in terms of hiring, promotion, rewards, and treatment.

Perceptions of what is going on in the world, economically and politically, and of what is going on with others in the same profession in other companies influences an individual's expectations and are a major cause of comparisons of work experiences. When times are bad economically and unemployment is high, an individual's perceptions of the relative value of work experiences will be influenced by that fact, and professionals may lower their expectations. When times are better and it is easy to find other positions, the standards will change. One is constantly comparing one's work experiences with what is happening to others in the same organization, as well as with what is happening to peers in other organizations. An individual may be happy with his or her work experiences until they are compared with those of professionals in other organizations. The results of such a comparison may produce greater job satisfaction or disgruntlement.

A manager cannot significantly affect the larger environment that operates on the employee but can take the existence and influence of that environment into account. Since individuals are constantly comparing their experiences with those of others, it is important the manager be aware what comparisons are being made. The most obvious comparisons are concerned with salaries. This is recognized by managers, and enlightened organizations survey the general salary climate to see how they stack up. Comparisons are also made of promotion policies, special bonus arrangements, the experiences of colleagues who have gone into business for themselves, technical content of work, and degree of autonomy.

Managements usually recognize the importance of the environment in deciding where to build facilities. The nature of the locale in which an organization is situated affects the employment decisions of professionals, and their subsequent decisions to remain with an organization. Thus, the availability of educational, cultural, and recreational offerings in a community should be of interest to managers. When there is a shortage of professionals in a given field, some organizations will deliberately locate facilities with an eye to gaining a competitive advantage in hiring or to retaining desired professionals. During the defense system buildup of the 1950s, major facilities were located or relocated to the "sunbelt" states (i.e., Florida, Arizona, Colorado, California) to keep and attract scientists and engineers. One major company, Contral Data Corporation, built a facility in a rural community in Minnesota because of the predilections of its key computer designer.

The Past and Initial Conditions

Each individual comes to the work situation with a set of purposes, drives, needs, and attributes—the product of whatever moves humans in general and of the individual's particular biological and historical past. The individual's past manifests itself in the work situation as a collection of talents, skills, and knowledge called "ability," and as a collection of expectations as to how the organization and the work to be done relate to the individual's purposes, drives, and needs. An individual prefers one organization to another because of some perception of what future experiences can be expected in that organization in terms of rewards, personal growth, interaction with others, image, etc. When hiring, the manager is really trying to match the products of the past, as expressed in the apparent abilities and attitudes (expectations) of a candidate, with his own perceived need in the workplace.

The individual professional comes to the hiring process with expectations formed by what has been learned about the organization from relatives, friends, or publications. Initial expectations motivate the individual to go through the hiring process, and, during that process, to act in ways that are a product of those initial expectations. An individual's experiences with the hiring process, and the explicit or implicit employment contract that results, are the first test of initial expectations. Far more powerful is the first operational test of expectations in first assignments and first interactions with managers and colleagues.

First experiences on the job in an organization have an influence on later performance that is very difficult to change. An individual's entry into an organization and its impact on subsequent performance suggests a number of important implications for managers.

Feedback from the Manager, Evaluations, and Incentives

No matter how we try to create organizations that are flat in terms of hierarchy and informal in terms of authority, the hierarchical model is so deeply ingrained that a manager has to work very hard to play other than an authority role. There have been many attempts to create "dual ladders" in organizations that give equal status and pay to individuals going up either the managerial or professional track, but research has shown that no one believes the two are really equal after a few months in the organization. Managers, in the end, control the real sources of power, the budgets, and the organizational structure. Managerial power is exemplified by the fact that managers have the power to decide whether to end the dual ladder system and how to fund it.

What the manager says and conveys through actions has an influence often far greater than intended. An inadvertent remark by a manager can lead to interpretations by others of organizational policies diametrically opposed to what was intended by management. How a manager reacts to the work or comments of an employee is interpreted as the way the organization views what has been done or expressed, and helps form the expectations of the employee.

The daily feedback received by the professional employee is a constantly reinforcing set of experiences with much more influence than a once-a-year or once-every-six-months formal evaluation. The daily feedback from a manager can generate a movement in the work motivation cycle that will determine what happens at the time of a formal evaluation. Frequent positive feedback and coaching establish and maintain expectations that motivate the professional to perform in a way and at a level that evokes more positive feedback, thus exercising the work motivation cycle over and over again in the direction of desired performance. Managers who do not actively exercise the cycle over and over again, and who remain remote from the day-in, day-out work situation, can hardly expect to seriously influence work performance with evaluations only every six months or a year.

Humans are so in need of feedback from the environment they will generate it even if they have to do something quite counterproductive to get it. An example we instinctively understand is the apparently atrocious behavior of a child to which we typically respond with, "He's only looking for attention!" In the work situation, where frequent feedback is not supplied by the manager a worker will give more credance and weight to feedback from colleagues, from gossip, from the smallest signs to be found in memoranda, or from the actions or inactions of managers.

WHAT CAN A MANAGER AFFECT?

The work motivation model highlights ways managers can systematically and effectively influence the work motivation and resulting performance of the professional employee.

The New Employee

The lasting effect on subsequent performance of the way the individual enters an organization suggests a number of important guidelines for managers:

1. Establish realistic expectations as to the work to be performed, the conditions of employment, and the reward system. (A chance to provide a clear understanding of

what is expected on the job without great risk is one reason summer hire programs are so successful in producing good hires.)

2. Treat the first assignment given a professional as the important event it is (this is almost never done). Make sure the first assignment is a demanding one, and that the first people the newcomer works with are your best workers. The professional's first assignment and colleagues provide important experiences that have a long-term effect on a newcomer's expectations.

3. Be chary about establishing or using long-term training programs for new, entering professionals. Unless done extremely well, a formal training program is a good way to establish the wrong set of expectations in new hires. A training program puts a new hire right back into a school situation, in a student role, and delays the appropriate work experiences. Seen in its proper light, a tough first assignment with high demands on quality, quantity, and delivery time constitutes a very effective training program more in consonance with the model of work motivation than a training program.

4. It is important that initial conditions and experiences are not out of line with what happens to others. Perceptions of equity are very important to each of us. We are always comparing our experiences with what we think others are experiencing. It is amazing to find how many managers believe the salaries and work arrangements negotiated with individuals can be kept confidential. All workers find ways to learn what others are getting, and professional workers tend to be more ingenious than most at doing so. It is not necessary to publicize every individual arrangement, but don't operate on the assumption that they can be kept secret.

Give Motivation a Fighting Chance

Professionals start out with a higher level of positive work motivation than most other workers. Their work has high status in society, and by its nature professionals have more opportunity than most to do things that are interesting and varied. It is the responsibility of the managers of professionals to provide the conditions and where withal that will let the naturally motivating force of the work itself operate.

Motivation cannot overcome the lack of the "necessaries" to do the work. Management is responsible for providing the budget, equipment, materials, time, information, and organizational arrangements to accomplish the work assigned. Making it impossible to achieve good work performance by denying the means for success results in both internal and external negative feedback and lowers expectations. It also generates resentment and feelings of inequity.

Provision of the wherewithal to do the job is obviously required of the manager. Not quite as obvious are the many actions the manager can take with regard to the provision of "necessaries" that significantly enhance work performance and, eventually, motivation. This can be illustrated in the area of information. There is much that managers can do to obtain large improvements in the flow of information (discussed in depth in Chapter 4, "Managing Information"). Designing organizational structures, procedures, and physical arrangements to encourage and increase communications—particularly informal communications—among an organization's staff, and between the staff and professionals outside the organization, will result in improved performance. The manager can hire people who are good communicators, design physical facilities and organizational procedures to promote information exchange, provide liberal budgets for telecommunications, travel, and publications, and encourage coffee-klatsching and reading, all of which not only encourage the exchange of information but also result in the kinds of experiences that lead to high expectations and high motivation.

By encouraging and even requiring the professionals in an organization continually to upgrade their professional abilities, and by providing them with the means for professional development, management can upgrade work performance. Even more effective in the development of the professional abilities of the staff is a conscious effort to broaden and deepen their professional experiences through the progression of work assigned them.

Feedback

The vital part played by managerial feedback in motivating and shaping the performance of the professional cannot be over-emphasized. The manager is the most important source of the feedback that reinforces or modifies expectations, subsequent motivations, and performance.

Management should recognize the role played by feedback, in affecting motivation and that the part played by the manager in providing that feedback is the critical first step to consciously influencing the motivation of the professional worker. This should force a certain amount of unwelcome but necessary self-consciousness on the manager in dealing with those who report to him.

The importance of feedback is recognized in all organizations by a number of formal mechanisms, and the manager is the primary channel for formal feedback. The forms of feedback include the universal, patterned, performance evaluations scheduled on an annual or biannual basis (discussed in Chapter 3, "Performance Evaluation"). Another form of feedback is the salary review, which is often coupled with the performance review. The whole spectrum of nonsalary incentives are other forms of feedback to the professional, many of which are governed by procedures and written instructions.

Formal means of feedback are important, but the informal feedback received by the professional can be far more effective in shaping, directing, and motivating work performance. Formal feedback occurs too infrequently, and, because of its very formality, becomes ritualized and generalized. Professionals want management to be interested in what they are doing, and to comment on it regularly. They don't like to be told how to do the job but want and expect reaction to what they are doing.

The colleagues one works with are also major sources of

feedback on work performance. The individual's new peers will be giving feedback day-in, day-out. Assigning a new, lively person to a low-performing group probably won't raise the standards of the group; the reverse usually results because of the power of the feedback from the group on the individual. It is usually better to break up the low-performing group and reassign its people to higher performing groups.

Management should consider the value of their five-year plus employees. On the order of 85% of all the professionals that voluntarily leave an organization have had a tenure of less than five years. Those that remain more than five years are most likely to stay much longer and, in the main, determine the operative value system of the organization. Whatever new management policy is adopted, if it is in conflict with the prevailing value system of the majority of the professionals in the work force, it will have a hard time succeeding. Managers should measure the prevailing value system to gain an understanding of what predominates in order to do better hiring, make better assignments—and also to ensure that the values are in consonance with the values of management.

The values of the existing work force exert a powerful influence on what happens to professionals who join the organization. Newcomers to an organization go through a process of socialization if they are to become effective members of the group, and, if they don't, they are isolated or pushed out by social pressure. As Brim defined it (1966), socialization is "a process by which individuals acquire the knowledge, skills, and dispositions that enable them to participate as more or less effective members of groups and society." Socialization is a lifelong process. An individual is socialized to his or her profession, and, within the work situation, an individual is socialized to the organization. In a study of the socialization process in a research and development organization, Dewhirst (1970) found the values of the majority of professionals who were new to the organization converged with those in the organization by the fifth year.

The manager's own work performance and behavior become a model that gives the people reporting to him a number of signals as to what is expected. The manager who comes in early will find that most of his people begin to come in early. The manager who reads at work will encourage others to read at work. The way a manager spends money on a trip sets a standard that is noted by all under him.

Taking Comparisons into Account

Individuals compare the feedback and rewards they receive with their efforts. Further, they make comparisons of their rewards, treatment, and situation to those of others within and outside the organizations for which they work. They compare salaries, promotions, perquisites, and general treatment. If inequities are perceived, the individual will act to reduce the inequities by asking for different treatment or by a change in performance.

Alert managements frequently survey salary and other work-related conditions for professionals in other organizations and modify their own practices to either minimize differences or skew them in favor of their own organizations.

The feeling of equity is important within an organization. It is impossible to keep salaries secret for any length of time. Professionals in organizations eventually learn the relative salaries of others, and will make personal comparisons. Managers should have a rational, defensible system for distributing rewards, and be prepared to use it to explain differences.

Affecting the Greater Environment

The manager can have little direct effect on the larger environment of the professional. It is possible, however, to influence how the organization is perceived by the world outside and thus indirectly affect the expectations of candidates for hire, employees, and important people outside the organization. Development of an organization's positive public image has a number of benefits, including an effect on the motivation of its employees. An organization perceived by the general public, or the professional public, as being a good place to work, a place where a professional can develop, an organization that has high professional standards, a company that emphasizes advanced technology (and/or quality, integrity, etc.), attracts and keeps the best professionals. A good public reputation increases self-recruitment and assures a flow of good professionals when general demand rises.

Develop a policy for active public relations. An appropriate program should encompass policies on attendance and exhibits at professional meetings, advertising in professional media, contacts with universities, and community relations. A well-designed public relations program is a concrete way to help develop the kind of high expectations that result in high initial motivation in new hires. Institutional advertising in professional and trade journals that feature desired values are particularly effective.

A steady flow of high-quality publications, public appearances, and press releases about the professional accomplishments of an organization can have a variety of positive side effects, ranging from increased sales to ease in obtaining resources when they are needed. There are many examples of the potential effects of good public relations. In one case, a newly hired controller of a West Coast electronics firm initiated a policy of issuing press releases whenever anything of positive technical value occurred in the firm. Every time one of the staff gave a paper at a professional organization a press release was sent out. The technical staff was thus given very positive feedback as to the way the organization valued their technical activities, and there was an increase in the number of good applicants for positions in the company. Furthermore, appearance of the positive company news created a public awareness of the company, and the price of the company's stock doubled on the stock market! (It should be noted that an effective public relations program cannot be built on "hype." Advertising that portrays a false image can backfire in very direct ways.)

Diversity

Diversity enhances productivity of professional workers: diversity of projects, of functions performed, of people communicated with. Using as a measure of productivity "overall-usefulness"—in a development context (rather than the more science-oriented measures, "scientific contribution," "papers," and "unpublished reports" used by Pelz and Andrews)—it was found that higher productivity was associated with the following (Pelz & Andrews, 1976):

Spending half or less than half of one's time in technical work increased productivity; productivity dropped precipitously as the percentage went up.

Those with no areas of specialization were very productive, surpassed only by those with three; those with one area of specialization were least productive.

Performance was highest for those engaged in five different R & D functions, and lowest for those engaged in only one.

Deliberate steps should be taken to encourage and assign diverse tasks, including a number of projects, a mix of administrative and professional work, and a mix of functions. Encouragement should be given to the development of a number of specialties. The manager who frowns on diversity in the interests of short-term efficiency generates signals that tell the professionals to narrow their perspectives. The consequences will be loss of those very productive people who naturally seek diversity and a long-term drop in productivity among those who remain. Of course, there are times when all attention must be concentrated on a crash program, but they are rare and should not set the style. At the least, the manager should smile upon efforts to achieve diversity, and at best should deliberately take steps to generate it: (1) don't always give an assignment to the person who has done that kind of thing before; (2) deliberately assign some nonprofessional work to technical people; (3) give professionals some administrative assignments; (4) occasionally make assignments that put an individual into another group, temporarily or permanently; (5) don't let the inertia and comfort of group managers or the professionals themselves keep you from enhancing diversity.

Diversity also enhances creativity, which may also influence productivity. One definition of creativity is the ability to make associations between widely separated items, and the more widely separated the items are that you can associate, the more creative you are. An increase in the diversity of input made available by participation in different kinds of activities and functions can significantly raise the probability of making creative sense out of that input.

A question that may be raised by the data is whether or not it is the "nature" of people to seek diversity or whether they will be more responsive to diversity if management deliberately provides it. Whatever the answer, stimulation of diversity is good for any capable professional. Professional work is not linear and repetitive in the manner of production-line assembly. When a professional is plateaued or stymied on a given project, a switch to another project or function or task is refreshing and energizing, and often permits the first project to work itself out below the level of consciousness.

Merit Salary Increases and Promotion

Merit salary increases and promotion to higher rank are the most often used and most expected forms of incentive. Both managers and professionals rank merit increases and promotion first and second in terms of their value. A major reason for this is that they are almost the only formal, explicit incentives used by organizations and, therefore, they make up the perceived spectrum of incentives. There is abundant evidence that professionals are moved by many incentives other than pay and promotion, yet there is little evidence of efforts to broaden the repertoire of formal incentives offered.

Merit pay rewards are unequivocally more motivating than non-merit pay rewards—e.g., piece rates as opposed to hourly pay, merit reward rather than seniority—and all organizations claim to use merit reward policies of one kind or another. There are, however, significant differences between organizations in the effects of their pay systems, and what companies claim is often different from what is perceived by their employees. When employees see themselves as above-average in comparison with their peers, and yet do not get above-average pay increases in one period (since not every individual will be judged above-average every time), the overall effects can be negative. And negative effects of merit pay rewards have a more lasting effect than positive ones.

As a consequence of all their difficulties, no matter what management's intentions pay practices tend to become routinized, to follow a "least trouble" pattern. When performance declines, an employee's salary is almost never reduced, and though subsequent increases are kept to a minimum, the differences between the lowest increase and the highest is often not very large. When performance is really high, it is seldom rewarded adequately. There is a strong tendency to keep the whole salary structure moving together without letting anyone's salary get "too far out of line." This is easier on the manager and on the personnel department. It takes a great deal of continuing effort and an ability to accept large variations in pay structure to keep a merit pay system in line with performance, and, thus, actually working as an incentive.

The more a merit pay reward can be linked to specific performance, and the shorter the time interval between performance and reward, the stronger the effect of the reward. Bonuses given to reflect specific accomplishments are far more effective than merit salary increases given at fixed intervals to reflect overall past performance. Unfortunately, it is often difficult to find explicit events that occur frequently enough to fit into a bonus scheme for professionals. It is easier to reward a salesperson whose sales can be measured monthly. However, where and when bonsuses can be used, they are very effective. One company that designs and installs automation systems rewards its project managers and key project personnel with substantial, on-the-spot, money bonuses for delivering a successful system on or ahead of time. An Air Force missile project office made a point of issuing nonmonetary awards to groups and

individuals working for the company being monitored whenever something outstanding had been done. The awards were
carefully given, were treasured by the recipients, and were effective as incentives.

Promotion into management is used as an incentive because
(1) professionals aspire to management even though they often
don't respect it or like to practice it, and (2) management is
hard put to think of other meaningful ways to reward its best
professionals. Too often, the result is the proverbial "We lose
an excellent professional to gain an incompetent manager."
All of the signals in the environment, both within the organization and in the larger world outside, indicate that it is desirable
to be a manager. Management is associated with power, pay,
and perquisites. (This is more true in the United States than
in Europe or Asia where Engineer or Architect are honorific
titles preferred by managers.) As mentioned above, the "dual
ladder" system has been tried, without much success, to keep
professionals from aspiring to management positions. The results so far indicate that the method is ineffective.

Inventing Incentives for Professionals

We need to invent more incentives because our available
set is surprisingly limited and insufficient. Relevant data are
available on what professionals respond to and what motivates
them—the data should be intelligently acted upon. In addition
to aiming for high quality and quantity in professional performance, the new repertoire of incentives should have among
its major goals reinforcement of the professional's desire to
do professional work rather than to go into management, and
encouragement of the individual's efforts at personal professional growth. The author has experimented successfully with
an incentive as simple as a budget for books, journals, and technical meetings that increased over time and according to performance, and that was completely within the discretion of the
individual. This technical materials incentive works and is easy
to administer and justify.

Another longer-term incentive that meets all the relevant

criteria is the accrual of time and money for each month the professional does satisfactory work on organizational projects until some given time period has been accumulated—say, three or four years. Then the accrued time and money can be used for any project the professional proposes as long as it is approved by a committee of peers (not managers) using a very broad, but accountable definition of organization interest (i.e., meets accounting criteria for legitimate business expense such as "internal research and development"). The catch is that if the professional goes into management he or she doesn't qualify for the incentive—it is not available to managers.

Incentive Programming

The ideal incentives are those tailored for the specific individual and are flexible over time. It would, of course, be impossible to conduct a completely individualized incentive system for an organization of more than a few people. It is still possible, however, to come much nearer the ideal than is commonly done.

Within a given suborganization or group, the manager can go a long way toward individualizing incentives other than pay and promotion. This will depend on observation of the individual professionals to see what it is that moves each one—a matter of daily and but thoughtful interaction, and of a conscious effort to learn about the individual. The kinds of incentives that can be applied include assignments made (to provide diversity), recognition, chances for personal growth, and chances to do something different and even risky without penalty.

The younger professional is more moved by money than is the older professional; with time, other incentives become more powerful. These priorities can be taken into account by an organization's formal incentive system. For example, if a large group of professionals is asked to choose between incentives such as a large salary increase or a chance to go to school for an additional degree with only regular salary increases, there will be a split in the responses. If that same group is given a choice between work that will lead to promotion and work that will accrue money and time for a project, there will again be a division among the choosers. Similarly, if a group of professionals is asked to choose between a pay increase and a chance to work for the company in Europe for two years, their responses will be different. Basic differences in outlook, as represented by the examples, inform an organization as to the pattern of incentives that would motivate each group of choosers. Each choice reveals something about the kinds of incentives that an individual responds to. It is feasible to develop an individualized incentive program that takes the effects of time and at least two kinds of individual outlook into account, and that isn't hopelessly complicated.

3

Performance Evaluation

Hiring is the most important decision made by the manager of professional activities, firing and disciplining are the most painful, but performance evaluation may be the most difficult. Performance evaluation exemplifies one of the persistent characteristics of the management of professionals: it has to be done, and there is no neat, objective way to go about it.

For a great many managers of professionals, the task of performance evaluation and salary review is distasteful and dreaded. Once or twice a year, managers are required to conduct performance evaluations of each of the individuals working for them, and to determine how to divide up the budget allocated for salary increases. Despite the counsel of theoreticians that performance evaluation and salary reviews should not be linked, there is no serious separation of the two.

When it is time for formal performance evaluations, the manager is faced with a stack of forms to be filled out and a limited pot of money to be divided up among the professionals in his or her organizational group. In making these evaluations, most managers are caught between conflicting pulls. The individual professionals want to be evaluated—they want to know how they are doing. Higher management wants a rational distribution of rewards that will assure a high level of performance, and that can be justified to organizational insiders and such significant outsiders as stockholders, bankers, and clients. Personnel departments and employee organizations prefer evaluations that result in a minimum of complaint and provide a rational basis for personnel decisions such as promotions, development programs, and transfers.

Complicating the task of performance evaluation for the manager of professionals is a feeling that both manager and subordinates are professional peers. There are also distasteful questions. What might the manager have done to improve the performance of individual professionals in the period under review? To what extent were the matters being evaluated in the control of the manager rather than of the individual professional? To what extent was the individual's performance a matter of unavoidable circumstances?

Performance evaluation is inherently a difficult task, particularly when it comes to professional activities. How do you evaluate one-of-a-kind activities? What can you compare them with? Typically, more than one discipline is represented in the professional organization, no two of the professionals are doing exactly the same kind of work, and all are working on projects that have never been done before. It is also not unusual in professional work that different professionals in an organization are working for different internal or external clients with varying objectives and standards.

While most routine activities are directly measurable in terms of output such as product or activity counts, most of what professional do is not measurable in neat, direct terms. While routine activities can be standardized in terms of time requirements, it is impossible to establish a rigorous time standard for professional work. How does one predict and estimate the time to produce a movie the like of which has never been produced? How does one predict and judge a rare surgical procedure on an individual patient with a unique physical system and a unique personal history?

Take the example of a group of medical doctors. How would

you compare their individual performances? Would you judge them on the basis of cures per head? Opinions of patients? Opinions of other doctors? Attitudes and personality? Some other criterion? When the author presented the preceding choices to a broad audience, 29% opted for record of cures, 29% for the opinions of other doctors, 21% for the opinions of other patients, 7% for attitudes and personality, and 14% for other criteria. Despite the foregoing responses most people judge their doctors on the basis of attitude and personality. There is little possibility of obtaining a record of cures or other doctors' opinions.

One could choose any of the criteria for picking a doctor, but none would leave one truly satisfied. How can you compare a doctor whose specialty is oncology with a pediatrician? The possibilities of cures for cancer cannot be compared with those for children's diseases. On what basis are the opinions of other doctors formed, and how do we obtain them? What can be said about the objective value of opinions of patients? No one has established a significant relationship between the personality of doctors and their medical competence.

The same dilemmas are found in any professional field. Despite a host of efforts to find an objective way to measure as widespread and historic an activity as teaching, there are still no satisfactory tools. The efforts of teachers and professors are judged on the basis of highly questionable student evaluations, peer opinions, or supervisor judgments. The same dilemmas are found in research and development, advertising, engineering, architecture, and the performing and plastic arts. In some professional fields the marketplace and history eventually judge whose work is acceptable or great, but this does not help the manager who must make judgments long before the marketplace or history render their final determination.

DILEMMAS IN EVALUATING PROFESSIONAL WORK

There are many dilemmas in evaluating performance in professional activities. Some difficulties are due to the non-comparability of work among professionals. There is the problem of dealing with highly uncertain subject matter in which the approach taken and the level of effort are unquestionably good, but the undertaking results in failure. Even the definition of "good" performance is not an open and shut case.

Noncomparability

The work of two professionals is hard to evaluate because the problems they work with and the way they go about dealing with those problems are not strictly comparable. No two professionals deal with exactly the same problem despite the fact that the problems dealt with fit into some definable category. Whether it is pulling a wisdom tooth, designing a tract home, or doing a parametric analysis for a weapons system design, no two problems are ever quite the same. Though pulling most wisdom teeth is rather routine, each person's body is somewhat different, and for some the difference is significant. Patients certainly want the dentist to recognize and treat them as if they were unique. Though the basic design of a tract home may be something less than a design breakthrough, no two sites are exactly the same, and the architect is required to take variations into consideration. A particular analytical technique may be the stock in trade of an operations researcher doing a parametric analysis, but each situation requires different assumptions, weightings, and data preparation.

No two professionals attack the same problem in exactly the same way. Though both professionals will come up with satisfactory or acceptable results, their approaches will vary, often radically. Style is important in professional work, and each individual develops a particular style and way of doing things.

The Effort and Approach Were Good, But the Project Failed

There are many reasons why a professional undertaking can fail despite superb efforts and impeccable approaches. The project or case being undertaken may simply be intractable, or the timing may be off. Research and development and medicine are replete with examples of problems undertaken in good faith by responsible, intelligent people, that were inherently intractable. Leonardo da Vinci, unquestionably one of the great geniuses of all times, left notebooks full of feasible inventions that could not be realized in his time because of the state of technology. Chemistry was given a great boost by the many alchemists who were consumed with the problem of transforming grosser metals into gold—something that is finally possible (but not economical) through the use of atom smashing equipment. Cancer, schizophrenia, and the common cold have been subjects of very large research efforts but have not as yet been defeated. Would we have denied Leonardo a merit salary increase or give a negative performance evaluation to the dedicated and competent medical research workers working on cancer?

By its very nature, professional work is beset with high uncertainty. There are unknowns and unknowables. The unknowns are amenable to research, and with time, money and effort can be diminished. Then there are the unknowables for which there are no parallels or precedents. Take the case of the drug Thalidomide. It was developed as a tranquilizer, and was demonstrated to be very effective. Years after it had been on the market an insightful medical practitioner saw a relationship between the use of Thalidomide by pregnant women and the subsequent birth of children with crippling deformities. Now it is widely understood that pregnant women should take no drugs at all (at least not in their third month). There was no way to know about the effects of Thalidomide on pregnancy before the damage had been done. There is no way to know the combined effects over time of much of what we ingest and daub ourselves with until time has passed and someone is astute enough to perceive the relationship. When dealing with unknowables, we have the choice of doing nothing new or going ahead. How should the scientists who developed Thalidomide be evaluated with regard to performance?

Another virtual unknowable is what someone else is doing in the same area of work. In many cases, one worker doesn't know that someone else is doing something that will impact on what he or she is doing, while the second person may very well know about the work of the first. In science there is a rich history of simultaneous discoveries, but what credit is given to the individual or group that publishes second? A fascinating case study of a scientific race in which one side was aware of what others were doing but didn't take their work into account is the discovery of DNA, which resulted in Nobel laureates for Crick and Watson, who published first. Would you give two-time Nobel Prize winner Linus Pauling a bad performance evaluation because they beat him? At one time, Stanford Research Institute had an outstanding radio tube research group which lost all purpose with the advent of semiconductors. What do you do with fifty tube research and development experts in a semiconductor world—and how do you evaluate their performance?

In the case of the development of new products or services for the marketplace, the company that enters the marketplace first often gains great advantage over later entries. The development of new products and services is usually shrouded in secrecy, and in many cases there is no knowledge in one organization of what other organizations are doing in the same field. How should the professionals who developed and brought the product or service to the marketplace second be evaluated? Their efforts were crowned with success in terms of development of the product, but they were a failure in the marketplace for which the product was developed.

Short-term Failures But Long-term Successes

The "success" of creative efforts in many professional fields depends on the opinions, tastes, or acceptance by others. A case can be made that the more an innovation differs from what already exists in form, fit, or function, the more likely it will have a hard time getting adopted. Hence, many of the innovations and works of art now recognized as among the world's greatest did not gain acceptance for decades. There is a rich history of scientists, writers, composers, artists, and inventors whose works were not appreciated during their life-times and of others who received broad recognition in their own times but are forgotten today. In many instances an excellent product comes onto the marketplace too early for its acceptance, a good example of which is the Cord automobile. Cord stopped production in the mid-1930s because of a lack of market acceptance. Later the Cord was hailed as an example of outstanding design, and limited production was resumed in the mid-1970s.

A significant fraction of the professional work force is engaged in industrial activities aimed at generating new products and services. Extensive efforts are made to identify and measure the potential for such new products or services to determine whether they should be developed and what their chances are for success once developed. Nevertheless, a substantial number of these products are failures in the marketplace, some of them despite their technical excellence and the talent and dedication of their developers. Hundreds of millions of dollars were invested in computer developments during the 1950s and 1960s that had to be written off because the market was not ready for the products. In the 1980s the market is burgeoning. The Edsel automobile is a well-known example of a product that failed in the marketplace. Yet it was technically sound and is a collector's item today. How shall we evaluate the performance of the technical professionals who developed the computers of earlier decades and the Edsel?

What Is Good Performance in Professional Work?

Finally, the greatest dilemma in evaluating professional work is to agree upon what is considered good performance. Nearly half the Nobel laureates believe they were awarded the prize for work that was not their best work. Whose judgment of performance is more valid, that of the committee that awards the prizes or that of the creative professional?

In production work, emphasis is on delivery of a product or service that is minutely specified. In professional work, however, a professional who delivers something other than what was specified may be rated highly and even honored. Fleming, credited with the discovery of penicillin, was engaged in research that had nothing to do with the discovery of an antibiotic. The accidental observation of the effects of mold on bacteria in some laboratory preparations was the beginning of the penicillin story. In many laboratories the appearance of mold might have been considered indicative of sloppy work, and someone would have been reprimanded. Fleming was knighted. Fleming was evaluated and rewarded for something he wasn't working on. How would his work have been evaluated before his great discovery?

The British story of the discovery of radar is another instance of great results that were not sought and that had nothing to do with the task assigned. In the 1930s a group of technical professionals was given the task of testing the popular notion of a "death ray" that could knock down aircraft. The group beamed electrical energy at test aircraft, and found that they were getting an echo on their instruments. Someone perceived the possibilities of using such echos to identify and locate aircraft for purposes of defense. The project goals were shifted, and the radar was developed that is given much credit for the survival of Great Britain when it was bombed by the Germans in World War II. Though he didn't achieve what he was charged with doing in the first place, Robert Watson-Watt, too, was knighted for his efforts. In professional work, achieving something other than what was intended can subsequently be judged as superb performance.

The Final Dilemma

Evaluation of the performance of professionals is something that has to be done, but there is no nice, objective, systematic way to do it.

WHY EVALUATE

If there is no objective way to evaluate the performance of professionals, then why do it? The most immediate reason for conducting formal performance evaluations is that implicit and explicit evaluations are made whether formalized or not. Where formal evaluations are not conducted, implicit evaluations will be assumed, and what managers say and do, even casually, will be interpreted and weighted as organizational evaluations. Formal performance evaluations serve both the individual professional and the organization in several additional ways.

From the Viewpoint of the Individual

All individuals want to know how they are doing from the viewpoint of the organization, which means from the viewpoint of management. When people are not informed how they are doing, they will find ways to push the system to get some response. Some will push the system for a response to the point of quitting. It is not exceptional to have a key professional give notice of taking another job. The manager, caught by surprise, asks, "Why? You're one of our best people. Can I get you a raise?" only to get the explicit or implicit response, "You never told me! It's too late now." In the absence of explicit, formal evaluations, an individual will assume an evaluation and it is likely to be negative.

Formal evaluations are needed by every worker and are markedly important for professionals. Since professional work is nonroutine and inherently uncertain, professional workers have no ready, objective measures they can use to inform themselves how well they are doing. As a result, the professional has a need to receive some judgment or evaluation from respected others. The most individualistic of artists and authors needs formal feedback from other artists, authors, gallery owners, critics, publishers—from *someone*. They need to determine if the direction of their work is acceptable, even if only to get a negative response with which to disagree and reaffirm their current direction and efforts.

Interaction with people in management is essential to high performance for most professionals in organizations. Where managers show an interest in a project and take part in decisions about the project with the professional, peformance is high. Pelz and Andrews (1976) found that, with a few exceptions, performance was highest where project decisions were shared by the professional and his or her chief. Next in ranked performance were situations where decisions were made mainly by the chief or by the chief and other executives, rather than by the professional. Interestingly, performance improved if the decisions were made by higher executives rather than the professional's immediate supervisor. The exceptions were the scientists and engineers who had a strong interest in breadth of research rather than in depth and detail (those generalists again). The latter did better making project decisions by themselves. A study of 223 medical sociology projects (Gordon & Marquis, 1963) came to similar conclusions. The study of medical sociology projects found that twice as many projects were judged highly innovative when the project director had an administrative superior who took some responsibility for the project and influenced the project funds and design, as compared with projects with no administrative superior or in which the superior dominated the project.

The picture that emerges from the research shows the professional responding to managerial interest and decisions concerning the work being done. The data also indicate that the input that works is concerned with the direction and design of the project, but not with the internal conduct of the project. Though autonomy is appreciated, there is an advantage to and a need for the expressed interest of management in the work that is being done. Performance evaluations ensure that management formally reviews and responds to what the individual has been doing.

From the Viewpoint of the Organization

There are several organizational reasons for conducting formal performance evaluations, and the need for formalizing performance evaluations increases with the size of the organization.

In small organizations the continuous interaction between manager and professional worker may be sufficient. Management is not an impersonal entity in the very small organization. The professional worker gets constant and immediate feedback and has a clear idea, daily, of what management thinks about the work. In larger organizations, there is far less contact with management. Uncertainty as to how management feels about things requires means to make sure that the individual professional gets a formal indication of those feelings. Organizational reasons for performance evaluation include the following:

Feedback on performance
Compensation administration
Promotion decisions
Identification of development needs
Human resources planning
Validation of hiring and selection procedures

Feedback on Performance

From the viewpoint of management, performance evaluation provides an opportunity for coaching, encouraging strong performance, and strengthening weak performance. In terms of the expectations–motivation–performance–experience–comparison–expectations model of motivation, formal evaluation provides management with a powerful platform for feedback to the workers. The formal evaluation is also an important input for comparisons by the individual to judge his or her position vis-à-vis others in the organization. In large organizations, formal performance evaluation is also used to assure that the individual does get feedback periodically, something often avoided by managers.

Compensation Administration

Performance evaluation is used as the basis for merit increases in salary. It provides an equitable and justifiable basis for compensation bonuses, raises, and perquisites. For managers and personnel departments it is important that the reward system be justifiable and orderly for purposes of organizational governance. A formal performance evaluation system allows the manager to draw upon or point to "the system" as a reference point in compensation judgments. The increase in recent years of laws concerned with compensation and hiring practices has underlined this role of formal evaluation systems. Much recent job-related litigation has been concerned with questions of equity with regard to sex, minority status, and age, and a clearly enunciated and practiced evaluation system is a basic legal defense for an organization.

A cautionary note should be inserted here about the limits and dangers of formal personnel systems. Orderliness can be carried too far. Management's drive for uniformity and consistency also leads to rigidity and a tendency to forget what the work is all about in an effort to maintain the internal management systems. Some organizations would rather lose their most productive people than disturb the established "wage and salary system." A case in point is the company that lost its top salesman because it wouldn't let him earn any more bonuses—after he had earned the permitted amount by the second month of the year—because it would disturb the established system. Another example is the company that lost the head of its most profitable acquisition by insisting on making the head change from his hard-won, familiar, debugged computer system to one used by the rest of the company. It never occurred to higher management that it could "translate" his reports into the predominant format—neatness became more important than performance.

Promotion Decisions

Performance evaluation provides a systematic basis for key personnel actions such as promotion, transfer, firing, and layoff in times of cutback. The formal performance evaluation system contributes a modicum of objectivity to many personnel actions. By establishing criteria for promotion and incorporating those

93

criteria in the formal performance evaluation system some rationality can be introduced into the promotion process. It can incorporate what an organization has learned about who makes a good supervisor, and it informs the individuals about its priorities and where they fit with regard to chances for promotion. Formal evaluations can be a useful means for determining an employee's potential to be a supervisor or to undertake a new and different kind of responsibility.

Transfers, firing, and layoffs can also be rationalized, justified, and explained, offering a greater sense of equity to all in the organization. Formalization of performance evaluations contributes a little to offsetting unconscious systematic biases concerning race, color, religion, appearance, school tie, and the like. (Nothing short of sanctions can overcome conscious biases that will find a way to deliberately color the evaluations given.) Again, the results of formal evaluations are vital on those occasions when an organization is accused or sued on questions of bias or prejudice in personnel matters. Of course, a formal evaluation system also provides managers with an out when they have to perform distasteful personnel actions such as firing. The manager can take refuge in the rules of the system, implying that the system is responsible.

Identification of Personnel Development Needs

Performance evaluations are a useful means for identifying the development needs of the individuals evaluated and of the organization as a whole. A well-designed performance evaluation process should supply systematic grounds for determining what kinds of courses and experiences might help the evaluated individual. The aggregate of evaluations can help determine the developmental needs of the organization as a whole. The results of evaluations can be used as the basis for education policies and program development. For example, if ineffectiveness in a particular technical area shows up in several evaluations, it may indicate a need for training in the area of deficiency. If the performance evaluations show that many of

the professionals are having problems in dealing with people—
a common problem in some professions—then a special program may be called for.

Intelligent use of the evaluations provides valuable information on the manager's developmental needs. Systematic discrepancies in the evaluations of given individuals made by different
managers can indicate a need for a program to bring managers
to some common consensus on criteria for evaluation. Systematic evaluation errors tending to rate everyone high or low
can also be identified and called to the attention of the manager.
Existing and incipient organizational problems can be identified
by a perceptive reading of the aggregate of evaluations. If many
evaluations in a group are significantly lower than previous
ratings, it may be indicative of a serious problem in the group
similar to a sharp increase in turnover rates that should be
looked into. It could indicate a problem with the manager, a
work situation problem, a salary system discrepancy, or some
environmentsl problem needing attention.

Human Resource Planning

Performance evaluations help identify personnel gaps in
the organization. If the evaluations show that many of the professionals in an organization are lacking in some particular specialty, such as computer aided design, it might indicate a need
for a training program and/or the need to hire someone who
is proficient in the area of deficiency. Evaluations are also helpful in determining what should be done with regard to the
loading and distribution of human resources in an organization.
They can indicate where personnel are overloaded, and where
there is slack.

Validation of Hiring and Selection Procedures

Though not done by most organizations, performance evaluations are an excellent means for validating and improving hir-

ing and selection in an organization. Performance evaluations help determine whether an organization's hiring criteria make sense. For example, with regard to the use of grade point averages as a significant criterion for hiring the new college graduate, if subsequent performance evaluations show there is or isn't a significant relationship between subsequent performance and grades, the results should be used to inform the hiring process. Similarly, the worth of different channels of recruitment can be determined. An organization can measure the relative value of "porthole" hiring (hiring right out of college), hiring at conventions of professional societies, advertising (including personnel ads vs. institutional ads), and hiring through reference networks. In the same way, evaluations of managers can provide useful information on the value of the promotion policies of an organization.

EVALUATING

Formal evaluation or appraisal systems are widespread in industry. Surveys of R & D organizations made in the 1960s found that between 79% and 87% of all of the organizations surveyed used formal systems. A survey of manager appraisal systems made in 1977 found that 74% of the organizations used formal systems to evaluate their managers. The need for performance evaluation is clear and widely recognized. Doing such evaluations is another matter. It is a highly problematic undertaking for several reasons.

First, because evaluating means placing a value on something. A value is a concept of the desirable, and when evaluations are made someone or something is being judged or appraised from the viewpoint of what the organization considers desirable. Performance evaluation is the act of judging the desirability of someone's actions, behavior, or characteristics from the viewpoint of the organization. Many organizations and managers have never thought through what it is they consider desirable, what importance to give the various values they hold. There is a tendency to adopt a system that is in general use and operate it without considering whether the values incorporated in the system represent those of the organization.

Second, few managers think about whether they want to use the performance evaluation as a way to elicit future behavior, as a way to judge past behavior, or as a combination of both. The tendency is to just evaluate, but judgments of past behavior should be used as a starting point for the improvement of future behavior. The problem can be stated in terms of something as familiar as school grades. If someone started as a high A performer, but by the time of evaluation is performing barely above a B level on some arbitrary scale, should the grade be an A, or a B with some advice on improving performance?

All present methods of performance evaluation are limited in their application because of common, systematic sources of error. Nevertheless, since some method of evaluation will have to be used and will probably be a variation of generally used methods, it is important to understand both the nature of these methods and the common sources of error.

Errors in Evaluation

To be useful, a method of performance evaluation must be both reliable and valid (Szilyagyi & Wallace, 1980). By reliability is meant that the method must be consistent and stable. Consistency is achieved when two different people make an evaluation—or two different methods are used—and the results are the same. When a method is stable we mean that the same performance evaluation instrument or evaluator gives the same results over time.

Reliability. Many factors can affect the reliability of a performance evaluation method. Some factors are situational.

The time of day can affect an evaluation, but even more important from the viewpoint of professional activities is the phase of the project being worked on. Many professional activities have a long time constant, and it is hard to judge performance en route to the completion of the work. A cancer is considered cured if after five years there has been no recurrence of the disease. Aircraft development takes ten years. How can we reliably judge performance on a cancer research project or an aircraft development project every six months or year during the life of the projects? Another problem with long-term projects is that their objectives may shift due to changing circumstances or to discoveries made during the course of the work. The original justification for the British effort on the Concorde SST aircraft was that it would bring together distant parts of the Commonwealth, such as Australia and England. By the time the project was completed, far different goals and criteria applied. The British discovery of radar illustrates a change of objectives due to what had been discovered en route.

The evaluator's mood, physical health, or general mental health at a given time can affect the content of an evaluation. There are times when we are more tired, more impatient, or more inclined to be generous and lenient. Mood can be a function of personal circumstances that have nothing to do with the evaluations being made, the time of day, or the day of the week.

A given evaluation may also be affected by the previous evaluation of someone else. If the previous evaluation was of someone with very superior or inferior performance, the contrast can affect a subsequent evaluation.

Evaluators vary and are subject to systematic errors based on their tendencies. The three major categories of evaluator error (Landy & Trumbo, 1980) are leniency errors, halo errors, and central tendency errors. Some evaluators are systematically lenient or harsh in their ratings. Given the same group of individuals to evaluate, the lenient evaluator will consistently give better than average ratings and the harsh evaluator will give lower than average ratings. Halo errors occur because of a generally good or bad impression the evaluator has of the individual being evaluated. The good or bad "halo" persists despite the actual performance record of the individual. For example, if the evaluator has a good general impression of an individual who has not performed well in the period under review, the performance will be explained away as "due to circumstances beyond his or her control." Central tendency errors result from a propensity to avoid extremes at either end of the performance spectrum. A particular case of a directional tendency in evaluations occurs in the military, where ratings tend to drift to a narrow band at the top of the rating spectrum.

Inadequate definitions of what is meant by good or bad performance can cause disagreement between different evaluators. The problem is easily demonstrated by asking a group of managers to check off which of the following describes someone who is prompt:

1. One is always early or exactly on time.
2. One is always within five minutes of the required time.
3. One is always within 15 minutes of the required time.
4. One is always within a half hour of the required time.

It is surprising to see how much variance there is between managers within the same organization. This variance can lead to serious disagreements. The person who chooses the first description is assured by someone who chooses the third that a particular worker is very prompt. After some experience with the individual who is consistently ten minutes late, the first manager feels the second manager has misled him. If the first manager says something about being misled, there may be sincere indignation and conflict.

Another source of unreliability is disagreement between methods. It has been found, for example, that interview ratings usually differ from formal, written ratings. Which method is more accurate?

Validity. By validity it is meant that a method is well grounded and actually represents what it is supposed to represent. To be valid a method of performance evaluation must accurately represent the nature of the work and the behavior that pertains, and should not include irrelevant considerations. Validity becomes more of a problem as we go up the occupational scale from simple motor tasks to professional work. With routine, repeatable, simple tasks, it is relatively easy to depict the dimensions of the work and to determine the relevant behaviors. A line assembly job can almost always be described completely and each part of the process delineated. The quantities and qualities of output expected and the requisite skills and behavior can be described and measured. In the routine case, performance is standardized and quantifiable. As we move up the occupational scale to the work of, say, a maintenance trouble-shooter, validity becomes somewhat harder to establish, and when we come to the work of a professional it is very difficult, if not impossible.

Lack of validity is perhaps the greatest inadequacy in methods for evaluating the performance of professionals. Since professional work is concerned with one-of-a-kind outputs, for the purposes of performance evaluation the work dimensions and the appropriate behavior have to be depicted at a level of abstraction that can encompass many different projects through time. How can we depict the work of an editor, a medical research professional, an architect, or a lawyer in a way that accurately reflects the job's key dimensions and requisite behavior, and that applies to other professionals in the same organization? The research question, project, or legal case worked on during the period under review is different from the one worked on the year before and different from those being worked on by others. The higher the level of abstraction used in describing the work and the behavior required, the more difficult it is to deal in anything but very broad generalities.

All professional work faces the same problems of validity. How much easier it would be to measure professional performance in such terms as "copies sold per book per month," or "number of valid findings per page per publication per year," or "sold square feet of buildings designed per month," or "number of dollars per days in the slammer per client per year." Instead, all of the problems delineated above apply and, since performance evaluation has to be done, managers often retreat into any method that measures some apparently appropriate traits, process behaviors, or mutually developed general objectives whether they are valid or not.

Some Widely Used Methods

The three basic methods of performance evaluation are (1) those based on objective performance data, (2) those based on personnel data, and (3) those based on judgment.

Evaluation methods based on performance data are not usefully applied to professional activities. All of the problems with evaluation of professional work already described militate against the development of objective performance data: noncomparability, good methods but failed output, short-term failure but long-term success, and the question of what is good performance.

Methods based on personnel data are used only with hourly, lower-level workers and concentrate on such variables as attendance and length of time with organization. Methods based on personnel data are clearly of little use in evaluating professional performance.

All the methods used to evaluate the performance of professionals are based on subjective judgment. Despite great variety of methods and the many kinds of efforts to increase the "objectivity" of the methods used, they all essentially and eventually depend on judgment.

Methods of Evaluation Based on Judgment

Rating scales. The majority of rating scales are basically graphic scales in that they present the evaluator with either a set of traits or of job dimensions and a set of graduated valuations to be checked off against each trait or job dimension. Typically, a trait-based rating scale might include such traits as job knowledge, judgment, attitude, quantity of work, quality of work, communication ability, and an overall evaluation. A rating scale based on job dimensions for a professor might include key job dimensions such as research, public service, and teaching; for a professional in a contract research laboratory it might include proposal preparation, field research, laboratory research, report preparation, dealing with clients, presentation, and the helping of colleagues. For each trait the evaluator might be asked to pick a valuation from a graduated list that best corresponds to the person being evaluated, such as "excellent," "good," "satisfactory," "fair," or "poor." Some rating scales attempt to spell out briefly what is meant by poor, fair, satisfactory, good, and excellent. For example, in the case of the contract research activity, the ratings for the work dimension item, "proposal preparation" might be spelled out as follows:

Poor = Does not do any proposal preparation

Fair = Helps in proposal preparation but needs heavy editing

Satisfactory = Helps in proposal preparation and input is useful

Good = Prepares good proposals that have moderate success

Excellent = Takes initiative to prepare good proposals that have a high rate of success

Many organizations combine evaluation of both job dimensions and traits in their performance evaluation systems. To illustrate, one large organization's rating form for scientific and engineering personnel had an array of four levels of job dimension performance and twenty traits to be considered in answering general questions concerning the individual (Krantz, 1964). Each of the job dimension performance levels clustered several statements concerning performance. Level one, the highest performance level, had the following kinds of statements:

The employee and/or his unit have made some extremely valuable contributions . . . results achieved far exceed those normally expected of the great majority of engineers or scientists of comparable education or experience . . . exhibits a high degree of creativity or ingenuity in producing useful, practical, often unique solutions to problems . . . gets things done well with established deadlines and at minimum cost . . . consistently productive . . . uses time effectively . . . good teamwork and enhances work of other groups . . . all have high regard for ability . . . personal shortcomings are minor and have virtually no effect on ability to achieve results.

Level four, the lowest performance level, had the following kinds of statements:

The accomplishments of the employee and/or his unit have been limited . . . work accomplishment tends to be erratic or inconsistent . . . frequently too much time, effort, and money devoted to projects . . . unimaginative and routine . . . often goes off onto unproductive tangents which could be avoided by better analysis . . . work often has to be rejected or redone . . . others have some doubts about competence . . . unless performance improves serious questions concerning continued employment.

The traits included for consideration were the following:

Job knowledge
Accuracy
Safety
Attitude
Initiative
Industry or drive
Decisiveness
Judgment
Analysis
Ability in meeting associates and public
Effectiveness in relating assignments to other activities
Profit and cost consciousness
Effectiveness in presenting facts or ideas
Flexibility
Creativeness and resourcefulness
Handling of confidential information
Effectiveness in relating assignments to other activities
Maintaining high morale
Effectiveness in training and developing subordinates
Effectiveness in delegating

There are two main criticisms of rating scales. The first is concerned with selection and definition of the traits for a particular job. There is little evidence of a significant relationship between particular traits and performance of a given professional job. Many so-called traits are really a function of the job situation rather than something inherent in the individual. Consider the traits "flexibility," "decisiveness," "attitude," and "industry or drive" from the above listing. The traits sound desirable enough, but what do they mean exactly, and how, exactly, do they apply to doing (for example) architecture? Are those traits inherent in the individual or are they a product of the job situation? What kind of initiative might be expected in an organization where the management gives little leeway for it?

The second major criticism of rating scales is that they are subject to lenience (and strictness), halo, and central tendency errors. To overcome the tendencies of the evaluators some organizations use the method of "forced distribution" of ratings. In the forced distribution method, the regular rating techniques are applied, but the evaluator is required to distribute the ratings according to some fixed rule. A common example of forced distribution is used in education when a class is "graded on the curve." When forced distribution is used in performance evaluation, the evaluator is required to place some fixed percentage of those evaluated into each of three or four categories (e.g., one fourth in the lowest category, etc).

Though forced distribution helps overcome evaluator error tendencies, it creates a special problem of its own. It requires the evaluator to rate people in each category without regard to how intrinsically competent they may be. Forced sorting can destroy the morale and performance of a high-quality performance team, lower the expectations and consequent performance of good workers, may result in the loss of competent people. The U.S. Air Force introduced forced distribution ratings for officers, which resulted in the loss of very competent, expensively trained pilots who were put in the lower evaluation categories regardless of their absolute capabilities and performance.

Behaviorally anchored scales. Behaviorally anchored scales (BARS) are a relatively recent development in performance evaluation. BARS is a rating method that attempts to overcome some of the problems inherent in conventional rating systems. The scales used in BARS have anchor points directly relevant to the jobs being evaluated. The BARS method combines job analysis and the critical incident technique in generating its scales.

To develop a BARS requires that the dimensions of the job are determined by groups of supervisors and experts in the area of work being considered. Relevant dimensions might include such things as job knowledge, relations with others, motivation, and supervision required. Once the dimensions have been agreed on, a large number of critical incidents are generated by supervisors and experts. Critical incidents are specific descriptions of effective, average, and ineffective work behavior relevant to the job. Another group of supervisors and experts is then asked to individually sort the critical incidents and assign them to the job dimensions. Only those incident assignments that receive a high consensus (e.g., 60–90%) are retained. The panels are then given the remaining incidents with instructions to locate them on a scale of one to nine, ranging from very good to very poor. Finally, the results are edited and checked for agreement.

BARS is considered by psychologists to be the best of the current appraisal instruments. The scales are behavioral and cast in terms of reference used by supervisors and employees. Actual descriptive incidents are used to describe when someone is considered a one or a nine. A lot of the uncertainty and vagueness encountered in the use of such terms as "very good" or "very poor" are done away with. There is some evidence that the scales need not be as job-specific as first assumed; some of the scales are common to a number of jobs. BARS have been used to evaluate some kinds of managers, professors, and, to a limited extent, engineers. The rating process lends itself to providing feedback to the employee. However, developing BARS is expensive and tedious. Studies comparing BARS with other carefully developed rating scales or checklist methods have been inconclusive, and suggest that the large amount of time and expense required to develop BARS may not be warranted.

Checklists. The checklist method presents the evaluator with a set of statements about work behavior. The evaluator is required to check those items on the list that best (or least) describe the performance of the person being evaluated. Depending on the particular kind of checklist method used, the items checked by the evaluator are compared to reference profiles or are summed up using a weighted key to give the individual a final ranking. The values of the profile or the weightings are not available to the evaluator and are scored by the personnel office of the organization.

The checklist is made up of very specific characteristics of job behavior such as:

Can be counted on to help colleagues

Never volunteers to assist others

Needs very little explanation or support once assigned a piece of work

Needs repeated explanations of assignment from management

Checklists are useful in making the evaluator think in very specific terms about what the professional actually did at work, thus overcoming much of the fixed tendency problem. The major obstacles to using checklists, however, are that they are quite costly to develop, and, in professional activities, they can seldom be kept current with what the professionals actually do. To develop a good checklist requires the expenditure of much time and effort on the part of management and professional staff.

A valid and reliable checklist requires the development of a long list of statements describing both effective and ineffective work behavior. The statements have to be scaled by a number of independent judges who must reach a relatively high consensus. To develop a relevant profile or set of item weights demands the extensive calibration of statements with the performance of the kinds of workers to be evaluated. Separate checklists have to be developed for each job or job family.

Though expensive to develop, checklists can be very useful as long as the work being performed does not change substantially. In the case of professional work, change is inherent, and it is difficult to develop a checklist that will be appropriate for a length of time that makes it worth the expense of development. Another criticism of checklists is that they do not lend themselves to providing feedback to the person being evaluated, particularly when the manager doesn't know how items are scored or weighted.

As with rating scales, checklists are prone to evaluator bias, and forced choice methods for checklists have been developed to overcome that bias. In a forced choice checklist, statements (usually four) about work behavior are clustered, and ten to twenty are developed to describe each job or job family. Each cluster contains both favorable and unfavorable statements. When doing a performance evaluation the evaluator is required to choose that statement from each cluster that is most (or sometimes least) descriptive of the behavior of the person being evaluated. Only one of the positive statements and one of the negative statements actually discriminates between favorable and unfavorable performance. Both the manager and employee do not know which statements are significant, and so neither the manager or employee know whether the evaluation is favorable or unfavorable until it has been scored by the personnel people. It has been reported that despite its complexity and apparent statistical nicety, the results of forced choice checklists are no more valid than those of graphic scales. Because of its disadvantages, the forced choice checklist method is not widely used.

Employee comparisons. Employee comparison methods, which have been in use since World War I, compare employees with each other on one overall measure or on a number of specific dimensions. The primary methods of performance evaluation through employee comparisons are ranking, paired comparisons, and forced distributions.

Ranking requires the evaluator to array those being evaluated from best to worst along either one overall or several individual dimensions. Sometimes, to make it simpler for the manager with several employees to evaluate, alternation ranking is used. In alternation ranking the manager is instructed to pick the best and worst employees and set them aside, and then to repeat the process with those remaining until all employees have been so paired.

Paired comparisons require that each person is compared, one at a time, with every other employee. The evaluator is required to choose the better of the two in each comparison. Final ranking is done in terms of the number of favorable pair rankings each individual obtained. In addition to all of the weaknesses of straightforward ranking, paired comparisons take an inordinate amount of time with a group of any size. The number of comparisons that have to be made can be calculated by the equation,

$$N = \frac{n(n-1)}{2}$$

where N = number of comparisons

n = number of people to be evaluated

As can be quickly calculated, the number soon becomes prohibitive. With a group of five, the number of comparisons is only ten. With a group of ten, the number of comparisons is forty-five, and with a group of fifteen, it becomes one hundred five.

Forced distribution requires the evaluator to assign each employee to a scale category in each dimension being appraised. Forced distribution methods have already been discussed in connection with rating scales. Ranking introduces a variation in that each individual is ranked within the category to which he or she is assigned.

Employee comparisons have the apparent advantages of being relatively easy to do, of forcing the evaluator to differentiate between the individuals being evaluated, and of helping overcome the leniency and central tendency biases of the evaluator. Comparison methods have several weaknesses. Ranking does not give any indication of the distance between the ranks. The two top-ranked people may be very close in performance while the next person is far below them, yet they would simply be ranked one, two, and three. Where one overall dimension is used, comparisons do not give any information on components of the individual's performance, and, thus, are not helpful for improving performance. Comparison methods are not comparable across groups or locations and so are useless for promotion or overall development purposes. Where more than one dimension is used, comparison methods tend to suffer from halo tendencies. With comparisons it is quite likely that an individual can improve performance significantly without getting a change in ranking if everyone moves up, at a consequent loss in incentive.

Essay. In an essay evaluation the evaluator is required to write an essay describing the performance, traits, and behavior of the employee including his or her strengths and weaknesses. In some organizations the essay can be written any way the evaluator wants to write it. In other organizations the evaluator is provided with guidelines that require comments to be made under specific headings, such as job performance, technical effectiveness, leadership ability, quantity and quality of work, potential for promotion, and development needs. One survey of how major corporations evaluate the performance of managers found that 37% of them used an essay method (Conference Board, 1977).

One value of the essay method is that it provides a three-dimensional view of the individual being evaluated, even when it follows a set of guidelines, permitting the evaluator to add observations not easily included in a standardized format. The three-dimensional quality of the essay makes it an excellent vehicle for giving feedback and coaching to the person being evaluated. Another value of the essay method is that it forces the evaluator to spend more time consciously observing the people to be evaluated.

A difficulty with the method is also one of its virtues. It requires the evaluator to spend a great deal of time composing the essay, and few managers are likely to want to spend the necessary time. Other weaknesses of the essay evaluation method are that it is very subjective, it does not permit easy comparisons of employees for other personnel purposes, and it subjects the person evaluated to the writing ability of the evaluator. The evaluator who writes poorly can do harm to a career.

Critical incident technique. The critical incident technique is not so much a performance evaluation technique as it is a method for collecting good data to provide the basis for an accurate essay evaluation. The critical incident technique requires the evaluator periodically (e.g., once a week or once a month) to record incidents of an employee's work behavior that represent the individual's best performance and the performance most needing help. The method requires explicit rather than general records. Examples of best performance incidents might be, "stayed late to help out on a rush proposal without anyone asking him to do it," or "helped new engineer get settled in and oriented her on the project." Examples of incidents of ineffectiveness or needing help might be, "missed schedule on delivery of drawings—needs help in getting organized for timely delivery," or "Criticized secretary severely in front of several other people—needs to learn how to deal with nonprofessional staff." Not acceptable would be unspecific comments such as "was uncooperative" or "was cooperative."

The incidents are collected in a notebook, and at the time of review they provide material for an essay or become the basis for ratings using one of the rating techniques. In some organizations notebooks are issued for the purpose and categories for classifying incidents and recording them are provided. The categories might include productivity, interpersonal relations, etc. The collected incidents also provide a basis for explicit periodic feedback to the employee.

One of the benefits of the critical incident technique is that it makes the manager really observe the people who will be evaluated. It is very easy for a manager to become caught up in the daily flurry of improvisations, meetings, telephone calls, and interruptions, and suddenly to realize at evaluation time that the employee was seen every day but not observed. The critical incident technique forces the manager to stop and observe those for whom he or she is responsible—the beginning of really doing the management job. Where there are a large number of employees reporting to a manager, the technique makes sure that everyone comes to the attention of that manager. Another benefit of the technique is that it provides a sound basis for the more frequent, informal feedback that is essential to coaching and shaping work performance long before formal performance evaluation is called for. A manager can sit down for a cup of coffee with an employee and say, "I want to thank you for pitching in and picking up some of the load on that rush presentation last month, it really got us out of a bind." This has much more effect than saying every twelve months, "Your work has been between 'good' and 'very good' this year." It also makes it easier subsequently to make less positive comments, such as, "And, by the way, you've been having trouble getting reports in on time. Is there something we can do to help you?"

The problem with the critical incident technique is that it requires a serious shift in how managers observe their employees. In some cases it can become a matter of "breathing down the necks of the employees." If handled badly, the notebook can become the classic "little black book" in which all missteps are recorded, which is not the purpose of the technique at all. Some companies that have used the technique gave it up because it required too much record-keeping on the part of the manager.

Even where it is not part of the formal system, the critical incident technique is useful for informal feedback purposes. In fact, the technique is widely applicable to other purposes than performance evaluation. It is an excellent method for identifying and measuring many kinds of phenomena. The technique was developed in World War II to determine and measure problems with aircraft instrument panels. Several hundred pilots were asked to identify the worst problem experienced with an instrument while flying. The great majority identified the altimeter as their worst instrument problem. A subsequent experiment found that 14% of the pilots tested made errors of one thousand feet or more when reading the instrument, and corrective steps were taken. In the same way a management can identify critical areas that need correction in an organization.

Try a critical incident technique experiment with your family. Start each dinner with a round of, "What is the best thing that happened to you today?" and see how it changes the tenor of the evening.

Management by objectives. Management by objectives (MBO) is not strictly classifiable as a method of performance evaluation, though it is used widely as such. In fact over 50% of major corporations surveyed in one study cited MBO as the method used to evaluate the performance of their managers (Conference Board, 1977). MBO is a management system sometimes referred to as management by results, performance planning and evaluation, work planning and review, charter of account-ability, individual goal-setting, group goal-setting, and participatory goal-setting (Szilyagyi & Wallace, 1980). In each of these systems of management there is (1) participation of both management and employees in setting performance goals at every level throughout the organization, (2) agreement on the criteria to be used to measure and evaluate subsequent performance, and (3) a requirement for periodic reviews of progress towards the goals, at which time performance is appraised, goals are modified, and coaching is supplied. The emphasis on periodic reviews links MBO to performance evaluation.

MBO is attributed to Drucker (1954) and Odiorne (1965), both of whom emphasized an orientation toward results and participation of employees in the setting of goals. The idea was that participation would lead to responsibility for achieving the desired results on the part of those who participated. The goal-setting approach received theoretical support from Locke (1968), who postulated that an employee's conscious goals regulate his or her work behavior. Locke's laboratory studies and subsequent field studies give strong support to his theory. The implications of Locke's theory (Wexley & Yukl, 1977) fit nicely into the MBO approach. They are as follows:

1. Specific performance goals help maintain individual motivation and guide individual behavior.
2. Goals can be assigned or set jointly, but joint setting is recommended.
3. Goals should be set at levels that are perceived by the employee as challenging and possible to accomplish.
4. Feedback is required to determine progress and to modify goals where needed.

MBO achieves many different useful purposes. First, it makes managers plan, with all the attendant benefits of planning. By planning and setting objectives it helps focus management efforts on achieving those objectives and on helping employees reach their personal objectives. Setting objectives helps managers rationally set priorities and avoid stimulus-response behavior. MBO aids in focussing performance evaluations since there are operational goals and criteria against which individual performance can be compared, and there is a focus on what manager and employee need and can do to reach the objectives. MBO is attractive for evaluation of the performance of professionals since it is individualized and, thus, concentrates on the specifics of what each professional is working on rather than on vague generalities.

Some of the general problems with MBO include a short-term orientation at the expense of important long-term considerations and a concentration on output measures such as production, costs, and profits, thereby ignoring important process measures such as employee development, turnover, and morale. MBO requires constant monitoring to make sure that objectives are not deliberately set low for easy achievement and that it doesn't encourage activities that artificially or destructively inflate output reports.

As a performance evaluation method, MBO has certain difficulties and disadvantages. Developing meaningful and reasonable objectives for each level of the organization and each individual is very difficult and requires considerable training, effort, and time. It is extremely difficult to integrate all the individual sets of objectives into a sensible whole. It is very easy to slide into a mode of generating very general objectives or objectives that don't quite meet the criteria of being challenging and attainable. The system is sensitive to being arbitrarily dictated from above, thus diminishing the degree of participation. MBO is so individualized in terms of standards that it is difficult to use the system for allocating salary increases or for promotion.

Studies of MBO effectiveness have raised serious questions about its value. A review of 185 studies of the effects of MBO on employee productivity and/or job satisfaction (Kondrasuk, 1981) came up with mixed results. The review found that the more sophisticated the design of the study of MBO effectiveness the less support there was for it. Since studies of goal-setting strongly support its effectiveness, the mixed results on MBO may be a comment on the difficulties encountered in establishing and maintaining a comprehensive goal-setting system. A review of ongoing industrial MBO programs found that the successful programs were those where MBO had become the way the company conducted all aspects of its business. Where companies used MBO only for performance evaluation, compensation purposes, or management development there was less satisfaction with the approach (Wikstrom, 1968). Many of the studies of MBO effectiveness make the point that it requires strong commitment and continuous monitoring on the part of top management. Some point out that MBO works well while top management is strongly interested, and goes downhill sharply when top management's interest shifts (Ivancevich, 1974). Similar results have been shown for the effectiveness of organization development (OD), which leads to the conclusion that almost any method works as long as top management focusses on it, and that any method will decline when top management loses interest.

Group methods. Group evaluation methods represent a variation in who does the evaluation rather than in the technique of evaluation. Group evaluations of the performance of an individual shift the evaluation process from the individual's supervisor to others. The groups of evaluators that have been used in such evaluations include the organizational peers of the individual to be evaluated, the subordinates of the individual, and persons outside the individual's immediate work organization. None of the group evaluation methods are widely used, despite some positively reported efforts for peer assessments in military and industrial settings.

Peer assessments include peer-ranking, peer-rating, and peer-nomination. Peer-ranking requires all members of a group to rank all other members of the group from best to worst. A variant of peer-ranking asks each member of the group to partially rank one person by naming one person in the group who is better and one who is worse than the individual being evaluated. Peer-ranking, peer-rating, and self-ranking have been used by research-oriented organizations where the individual works quite autonomously and the supervisor is not familiar enough with the individual's work to appraise it. Organizations such as Bell Laboratories, the Battelle Research Institute, the Rand Corporation, and the Brookings Institute have used peer- and self-evaluation (Szilyagyi & Wallace, 1980).

Peer-ranking suffers from all of the disadvantages of ranking methods already pointed out. In addition, peer-ranking puts each individual doing the ranking under conflicting pressures. If the evaluation is too critical, is a colleague being harmed? If the evaluation is too lenient, will it elicit a negative judgment from management? If the evaluation is too laudatory, does it affect the relative ranking of the evaluator? There has been little research on peer-ranking, but interviews with professionals who have participated in peer-ranking strongly suggest that it is resented by those who have to do it because of the dilemmas the evaluator faces. As one of those interviewed put it, "It's just a way management gets off the hook. They can blame whatever evaluation they make on us. Management is paid to do evaluation. Let them do it!" Peer-rating is subject to all the criticisms of rating schemes, and, in addition, puts pressures on those who do the ranking.

Peer-nomination is a method of evaluating individuals for promotion. In the peer-nomination method, the evaluators are asked to nominate members of their group who are outstanding in general or who are outstanding in terms of some performance characteristic or personal trait. Studies of the peer-nomination method have concluded that it is fairly reliable and accurate in separating the best workers from the worst in a group, but that it has little utility in terms of feedback (Kane & Lawler, 1978). Another criticism of the method is that it does not help discriminate between those defined as outstanding or best.

Evaluation by subordinates can give managers some important feedback not usually available to them. It provides a manager with some information on how subordinates perceive him or her and can be useful in suggesting ways the manager can improve performance. However, as a method for the manager or the personnel department to use for purposes of promotion, transfer, or compensation, it is fraught with political overtones. Managers feel threatened by formal subordinate evaluations that are used by others, and there is little evidence that the method will be used widely. One form of subordinate evaluation is student evaluations of professors. There is much argument as to their reliability and effectiveness, but in any case, unlike the industrial situation, the professor does not have to continue to live and work with the students who do the evaluating.

Evaluation by people outside the immediate work organization includes evaluations by the personnel department, outside consultants, and assessment centers. There is some evidence that outside evaluations might be useful for promotion purposes because the outsiders can be more objective in identifying and evaluating the characteristics, skills, and experiences of a firm's employees. The argument is that the judgment of others in the same work unit may be clouded by personal relationships with the individual evaluated and by feelings of personal comparison.

The Evaluation Interview

The evaluation interview is difficult for both the evaluator and the evaluated individual. When a large sample of managers was asked by the author (using the critical incident technique) to specify their worst managment experience in the previous six months, evaluating their subordinates ranked high among their answers. Where it is not required, managers will tend to avoid giving postevaluation interviews. In fact some students of the subject claim that managers will not give such interviews unless there are strong control procedures to make them do so. There is a strong emotional buildup in both the evaluator and the individual employee. The employee enters the interview on the defensive since he or she is being personally judged, while the manager enters the interview rather uncomfortably, especially if the evaluation includes criticisms or questions concerning the work of the individual. The situation has elements of confrontation where one individual is in a subordinate and, therefore constrained, position.

A consensus holds that performance evaluation is nevertheless useful, since every individual should learn where he or she stands with the boss and the organization, and therefore the manager ought formally to deliver the results of the evaluation. The consensus holds that the evaluation interview provides an opportunity for constructive criticism and coaching. The evidence, however, suggests that the evaluation interview can have lasting negative effects, and that the manager/evaluator should be conscious of the relationship between the way the interview is conducted and the subsequent feelings and performance of the person evaluated. A study of GE's comprehensive performance appraisal process (Meyer et al., 1965) found that:

1. Critical comments during the interview, rather than resulting in improvement, create defensiveness and have a negative effect on subsequent performance.
2. Praise has little effect on performance one way or the other.
3. The great majority of employees (82%) see their manager's evaluation as being less favorable than their self-estimates.
4. There is a nonlinear relationship between the number of negative comments made during the interview and defensiveness on the part of the person being evaluated—defensiveness goes up faster than the number of negative comments.

Some of the implications of the GE study are that comprehensive, formal, annual performance evaluations are of questionable value, they are a threat to an employee's self-esteem, and they can harm relationships between manager and subordinate. A further implication is that negative comments should be fed back to an employee in limited doses throughout the year and not all at once at the time of the formal evaluation interview.

The results of the GE study also suggest that, since you have to follow the rite of the annual review, it should be handled carefully, and that criticisms should be saved for informal daily and weekly feedback sessions when the emotional charge is far lower. The way the performance evaluation and feedback are handled is important. One study has shown that satisfaction with the company and with the supervisor are tied closely to satisfaction with the performance evaluation and feedback system (Landy et al., 1978). It can be seen that one of the attractions of MBO is that it provides explicit, measurable goals and criteria available to both manager and employee, and minimizes the vague threats to self-esteem that are inherent in some of the other evaluation methods.

From the Viewpoint of the Manager of Professionals

Once again, the major point to be made about performance evaluation for professionals is that it has to be done, but there is no objective, reliable, and valid way to do it. Performance evaluation is demanded by each individual and serves many organizational functions so that there is no escaping the task. However, the difficulties and discomforts of the task can be substantially ameliorated in a number of ways.

1. Develop a performance evaluation system that finds a comfortable fit in your organization. Since there is no correct method, the field is wide open for pragmatic, eclectic approaches. Many of the formal systems have elements that can be usefully combined. Some organizations have combined BARS and MBO to take advantage of the useful features of both systems. Don't "buy" an evaluation system off the shelf, and, if you do, take the time and make the effort to modify and redesign it until it fits. Be very conscious of the inherent problems in all performance evaluation methods, and design around them. In general, not enough organizations take an experimental, trial and error approach to their own system.

2. Treat the formal evaluation system as only one part of a comprehensive feedback system in which frequent, informal feedback sessions bear the brunt of the coaching and criticism effort. Let the formal review come as no surprise. Do not let the formal review become the draining emotional experience it is in the majority of instances.

3. Use some form of goal-setting, whether an approach as comprehensive as MBO and its variations or something far less formal and hierarchical. People perform better against goals than in the absence of goals. Shapero's fourth law is, Organiza-

tions and individuals that plan do better than those that don't, *but* they never follow their plan. Goal-setting and planning make everyone more outward and forward-looking and broaden their horizons and awareness.

4. As an individual manager, use the critical incident technique whether it is part of the formal system of the organization or not. The technique makes you observe the people who work for you in a constructive and thoughtful way, and it can help improve one's general management capabilities.

4

Managing Information

PEOPLE AND INFORMATION are the essential resources in professional activities, and it is the task of management to bring those resources together in a way that will raise the probability of relevant and good results. All managers are clear on their responsibilities for obtaining the best people they can, motivating them, and organizing them to do the work of the organization. Managers are far less conscious of their responsibilities regarding the information resources used in their work. Even where they know that information is important, they are unaware of the available data on how people get and use information and of what can be done about managing the information-communication processes in their organizations.

Successful management of the information resources in professional activities begins with a clear realization of the following general rules at both the organizational and individual level:

> Anything that improves the quality and quantity of information available to a professional organization, and/or

improves its ability to receive, process, apply, and transmit information, will improve that organization's productivity.

Anything that improves the quality and quantity of information available to a professional and/or improves the professional's ability to receive, process, apply, and transmit information, will improve that professional's productivity.

Once responsibility for management of information is consciously accepted, a manager can find sufficient data on the information-communication behavior of professionals to translate the general rules into systematic management applications. The available data suggest management actions with regard to the individual professional, the organization, physical facilities, and the transmission of information.

INFORMATION-COMMUNICATION ABILITIES ARE CENTRAL TO PROFESSIONAL WORK

With few exceptions, professional work consists of transforming information from one state to another. The few exceptions include the surgeon, sculptor, and dentist who not only need skills with information, but also require motor skills to translate what they perceive and interpret into physical results in the form of operations, objects of art, and dental operations.

To illustrate the information-communication character of professional work, consider the medical doctor's activities. A patient calls her doctor and reports that she has a fever, a headache, and an upset stomach (information input). The doctor replies, "There's a lot of that going around" (the result of information inputs previously received from others). The doctor asks, "Are you allergic to antibiotics?" and the patient answers, "No" (another information input). The doctor asks for the telephone number of the patient's pharmacy (another information input), and, drawing upon what she has heard from other medical practitioners and drug detailers, what she has read recently, learned in medical school, and personally experienced (previous information input stored in her head), the doctor diagnoses (integrates the information) and prescribes (a transformation of information received and integrated into an information output). If the patient gets better or dies it is the end of the transaction, but if the patient calls again and says she is still suffering the doctor will tell her to come in. What ensues is another round of information activities. The patient is weighed, her temperature and pulse are taken, and she is observed. The patient's records are reviewed. Then the doctor prescribes again or sends the patient with her records to a specialist who iterates the information-communication process in its general form.

Similarly, the engineer translates design objectives and specifications into plans and reports using varied input from handbooks, catalogs, and reports. The lawyer translates the client's stated problems into briefs and trial statements drawing upon the extensive records of previous litigations as well as information specific to the case at hand. One can readily see the parallels for accountants, design professionals of all kinds, teachers, advertisers, and other professionals.

The importance of information-communication behavior to professional work can be demonstrated in a number of ways. The Pelz and Andrews (1976) studies of productivity of scientists and engineers show a strong correlationship between productivity and the number and variety of work-related conversations an individual has with colleagues within and outside the organization. The Pelz and Andrews data paint a picture of professional productivity being enhanced by frequent exchanges with other professionals. It is a picture that is directly in contradiction with that of the traditional "bull of the woods" production management view that "If they're talking, they ain't producing."

Using one of the Pelz and Andrews measures of productivity—"overall usefulness," as applied to Ph.D.'s in development labs—it was found that productivity rose sharply when the average contact with colleagues went from weekly to semi-weekly and remained far above the fiftieth percentile when

TABLE 4–1
Time Distribution of
Professionals and Managers

Activity	Time Spent (%)[a]
Meetings	35%
Speaking on the telephone	14
Reading	16
Dictating, writing	14
Other secretarial interface	5
Observation	7
Personal breaks	3
Thinking, planning	7
	101%

Source: Data collected by author, previously unpublished.
[a] Self-estimates.

the average contact increased to daily. Similarly, productivity rose with the number of close colleagues in one's group (the number of people to interact with), being highest when the number was fifteen to twenty. In terms of the number of colleagues outside one's group but within the organization with whom a professional exchanged information, productivity went up until the number reached ten to nineteen and thereafter declined.

Another very direct measure of the importance of information-communication behavior in professional work is the amount of work time spent in such behavior. As can be seen by the data on the use of time by two thousand managers and professionals, they spend well over 80% of their time in information-communication activities. The data in Table 4–1 are estimates made by managers and professionals studied. An actual time-study made of a group of managers and professionals, using a self–time-study instrument, found systematic discrepancies between their self-estimates and the actual time spent in various activities (Vorwerk, 1979). Those studied spent more time in information-communication activities than they thought. It was found that they consistently underestimated time spent in meetings (closer to 50%), and overestimated the time spent in reading and thinking.

In contrast, Allen (1977) reported that engineers on twelve development projects allocated 77.3% of their time to analysis and experimentation, 16.4% to all communication (including literature use, 7.9%) and 6.3% to other activity. However, no breakdown was made as to how the analysis and experimentation time was spent in terms of communication with others through informal and formal meetings with one or more people.

A strong case can be made that anything that improves the quality and quantity of information available to a professional and/or improves the professional's ability to receive, process, apply, and transmit information will improve that professional's productivity. This is not to denigrate the importance of creativity or other professional capabilities. In fact, creativity illustrates the relationship of information to other professional capacities. Creativity is widely defined as the ability to relate remote bits of information—the more widely separated the items that one can relate, the more creative one is. Koestler (1964) describes the creative act as taking the contents of two drawers in one's mind and dumping them together on the floor. The capacity to impose or recognize a relationship is central to the creative act, but without the presence of information from different sources the act cannot take place.

Information-communication abilities and acts are relevant to a wide range of managerial activities in a professional organization and affect all of the following:

Hiring
Individual performance
Individual growth
Team capabilities and growth
Dealing with subordinates
Dealing with other parts of an organization
Dealing with vendors
Dealing with clients
Dealing with banks, insurance companies, other professionals
Dealing with the government

Learning from What People Actually Do

The ability to handle and communicate information has been an important—probably the most important—survival mechanism of the human race. As a consequence, nearly all humans are superb information handlers. The ability to make it through any given day is a testimony to human information-communication competence. Witness the morning rush hour on the freeways of any major city. Thousands of half-asleep humans pilot tons of steel at breakneck speeds through unpredictable, intricate patterns with a minimum of accidents. Each of the drivers is receiving and processing a very large number of signals, making sense of them, and responding in meaningful ways.

Observing and measuring how humans actually get, respond to, and use information can provide us with data relevant to the management of professionals. Information-communication behavior is pervasive to all human activities, and data about such behavior is to be found in a wide range of fields. The data most directly related to the management of professionals comes from a large number of "user" studies concerned with how scientists, engineers, medical, and other professionals get and use work-related information. Other relevant data are found in studies of the diffusion of innovations, studies of advertising and propaganda, studies of attitude change, and in the history of science and technology.

Studies of diffusion of innovation are concerned with how innovations are adopted by their potential users. The diffusion studies are particularly relevant to questions of how new ideas, processes and materials are recognized and accepted, and are important to the maintainance of professional capabilities, and to the marketing of the products of professional work. Advertising, propaganda, and attitude change studies are relevant to an understanding of how information is perceived and how it influences those who receive it. The historical record provides data on the relationship of information to the creative process and can lead to an understanding of how information-communication processes affect the fate of professional activities and their products.

From the viewpoint of management, information-communication behavior is usefully described in terms of the following:

1. Sources and channels of information
2. Contexts
   a. Nature of work
   b. Physical location
   c. Attitudes of management
   d. Logistic or nutrient needs
3. Individual differences
4. Two-person communications
   a. Effects of sources
   b. Two-person bonds
5. Social-professional circles and networks

Whenever two or more individuals or organizations are engaged in an endeavor, the quality of communications has an important effect on the outcome. The quality of communication is least important when the endeavor is routine and concerned with highly specifiable items. When someone has need of a standard item, communications can often be effectively carried out using a teletype machine. All that is needed is a sentence that includes a catalog number. Where the endeavor is unique, complex, shot through with the uncertainties and anomalies that characterize professional work, then the quality of communications becomes critical. In professional work it is often difficult to convey important ideas or observations that deal with abstractions, new concepts, or complex, new shapes from one person or organization to another.

Sources and Channels of Information

Think of your own experiences. How did you come to the company you work for? What were the channels through which you heard about it? Did you come to the job through an employment advertisement, an employment agency, college recruitment, through the information or recommendation given you by a friend or relative? Where did you get the most important bit of work-related information received in the last three months? Did you find it by accident or did you get the information from a book, memo, report, trade-press publication, or journal? Did you get it from a salesperson, from a colleague over the telephone or over a cup of coffee, or did you get it at a meeting, in a class session, or by overhearing it?

Sources of information include people (interpersonal), documents (including publications, film, computer displays or printouts), personal files, memory and observations. Channels are divided into formal and informal channels. Formal channels and sources are those formally committed to the transmission of information, including books, journals, reports, data systems, classes, meetings, conventions, and exhibitions. Informal channels are those involving person-to-person interactions such as informal conversations (e.g., over a cup of coffee, over the phone, in the halls outside a convention meeting) and correspondence, and they require drawing upon oneself (memory, files) and on information found by chance (e.g., the book next to the book I was looking at while browsing through some apparently irrelevant materials).

Without question, the most important source of work-related information for the professional (and probably for everyone else) is other people, and the most important channels are informal ones. Reviewing several studies of channel utilization by scientists and engineers, Bodensteiner (1970) found that informal communication channels were used far more than formal ones: an average of 55% of the time vs. 45%. It was also found that informal communication channels were used 65% of the time for the transmission of information. Further, studies that explored how respondents happened to use the formal sources and channels they reported, found that much of the time they had been recommended by someone using an informal channel. Among the informal sources and channels, "found by accident" is reported 18% of the time—that is, the information was found when the respondent was not specifically looking for it. "Found by chance" is reported so consistently that Menzel (1958) speculated that the "accident is no accident."

Use of informal channels is not an example of resistance of humans to innovations in the field of data retrieval but is something more fundamental. A number of studies found that the use of informal communications is associated with professional productivity (Pelz & Andrews, 1976; Parker et al., 1968). Informal transmission of information by colleagues, and by colleagues of colleagues, is characterized by other elements not available or only partly available in formal channel modes of information transmission; i.e., participation in stating the question, value judgments, and richness of communications (discussed below in the sections on the two-person information system and the social-professional circles.)

Informal channels and interpersonal sources are preferred by high performers in professional work, and when they use formal sources they tend to be what librarians call "ephemera," e.g., proceedings of meetings and technical reports. A survey of the information behavior of technical professionals working for the RCA corporation (Jenny & Underwood, 1978) measured differences between high and low performers (those in the upper and lower thirds of the three thousand engineers included in the study). The survey found that high performers drew upon far more sources of information, and valued informal sources and channels of information far more, than the low performers. Neither group placed highest value on technical journals or libraries: the low performers made no mention of them at all, while the high performers placed them in fourth and seventh place respectively. The low performers assigned highest value to standards, handbooks, and catalogs. The high performers assigned highest value to conference proceedings, papers, and conventions and meetings.

In a study of winners of the *Industrial Research* magazine award given to the one hundred most significant technical products of the year (IR 100) for the years 1970–1974, Goldhar (1971) obtained data on three hundred cases and found that informal and interpersonal sources and channels dominated as having produced the "greatest stimulus" and "greatest value." Informal sources accounted for three-quarters of those reported and informal channels for 73% of the channels.

Studies of how professionals divide their time between the formal and informal literature in their field (Allen, 1977) emphasize again the relative importance of the informal over the formal. Engineers spent about three times as much time on informal literature (unpublished reports) as on the formal literature (books, journals, and periodicals). Even the methods used for obtaining the formal literature were dominated by informal methods, which were used 73% of the time by the engineers and 63% of the time by the scientists studied. The formal methods included personal library search, search by a library assistant, and technical abstract search. The informal methods for obtaining the formal literature included "on desk" or "in personal file," "borrowed from a colleague," or "other." The only formal method used by the scientists was personal library search. Interestingly, Allen reports that an analysis of technical solution quality vs. the kind of information used showed the higher-rated solutions were based on written sources far less than were lower-rated solutions: 4% vs. 16%.

The data on channels of recruitment (discussed in Chapter 1, "Hiring: The Most Important Management Decision") provide another measure of the importance of informal sources and interpersonal channels of information. The recruitment channel that provided the greatest number of professionals was referral by a friend or acquaintance. With the exception of those who were self-recruited (which often meant they heard about the job from someone they knew), those who were referred by a friend or acquaintance received the highest raises and stayed the longest.

Channel use plays an important role in the effectiveness of communications between two organizations or between client and contractor. The channel used is of particular concern when there is trouble associated with the matters being communicated. One study of the way communication channels were used in communications between clients, contractors, and subcontractors in R & D projects related the use of different channels to various events (Bodensteiner, 1970). The research found:

1. A significant increase in telephone and face-to-face communications was recorded every time there was any kind of technical or contractual uncertainty, which diminished as the uncertainty or problem was resolved.

2. There was no similar increase in written communications. There was an apparent trade-off between face-to-face and telephone communications. The data further suggested there were fewer periods of uncertainty or trouble and they were of shorter duration where there were more frequent face-to-face exchanges. No one seemed to write to communicate, only for the record.

Bodensteiner's findings (1970) and the previously described data on the superiority of informal communications channels can be explained in terms of "richness" of communications. Written communications are far less rich than voice-only (telephone) communications, which, in turn, are far less rich than face-to-face communications. The more complex, abstract, or sensitive the message, the greater resort to richer forms of communications. It is no accident that we get most of our important information from informal (i.e., face-to-face and telephone) communications, or that when there is a problem on a project we switch to the next richer channel. Richness also pays off in terms of effective problem-solving. Experiments comparing effectiveness of problem-solving using ten different modes of communication found the time required decreased with an increase in the richness of the mode of communication. Face-to-face was faster than voice alone, though the two were quite close, and both were far faster than written or typewritten modes.

Richness of a particular mode or channel of communication results from the number of symbols each provides for use. In the written English language there are twenty-nine significant symbols that can be manipulated with twenty-six letters and three significant punctuation symbols. In spoken language there are an estimated thirty-two symbols (phonemes) to be manipulated with accent, pitch, pauses, and intonation. Face-to-face communication has all the symbols of spoken communication plus a large number of nonverbal signals in the form of gestures, body language, and eye position.

There is a tradeoff between telephone and face-to-face in communications between organizations and within organizations. When people are located on the same floor, face-to-face communications make up 80% of their exchanges. When two different floors are involved, face-to-face exchanges drop to one-third of all communications and telephone communications make up the difference. Bodensteiner (1970) also noticed the tradeoff and suggested that it was influenced by the difficulty of travel between organizations (i.e., weather, distance, accessibility).

The tradeoff is not surprising, since telephone communications are about as efficient as face-to-face communications in terms of exchanging information. The substitution of the telephone for face-to-face contact is affected by whether those communicating have previously met face-to-face. "The use of video for conferences is helpful to people who have never met. The act of seeing one another's expressions contributes to communications. Once the first meeting has occurred, however, video is no longer necessary, and phone conversations become just as revealing" (Goldmark, 1973). Once having met people we talk to them on the telephone as if we can see their faces.

Written communications are the smallest fraction of all communications within an organization—something under 5%—while face-to-face and telephone exchanges are used on the order of 75% and 20+% of the time respectively. Even when organizations are separated geographically, written communications make up less than 15% of all the communications between them (Bodensteiner, 1970).

Written communications are used when a large amount of information is to be transmitted, when a large number of recipients are going to receive the same message (e.g., notice of a meeting), and when accuracy of detail is important (e.g., when a lot of numbers are involved and when a record is desired). A telephone discussion may be followed by "I'll send you a note to confirm what I've just said." One of the signs of trouble within an organization is a sharp increase in written correspondence, particularly memoranda written "for the record." A large number of internal written communications signifies that people are writing for all to know what they told you, to cover themselves rather than to communicate.

Spoken and written language are different forms of communication with different ways of handling the same information.

Written language requires "good English"—good spelling, punctuation, and grammar and good sentence and paragraph structure. It is hard to write correctly and harder to write well. Spoken language, even when grammatically correct, is completely different from written language. In spoken exchanges, sentences are not finished. Thoughts are not completed. More than one subject is discussed in the same exchange. Half sentences, affirming grunts, different subjects all make sense in spoken language. Nothing can make one squirm more than to read from a transcript: though it all made sense when presented, it reads atrociously. Words spoken take on a different meaning than when written. Hesitation, intonation, and inflection all enter into the spoken message, and cannot be captured by the written language, thus obfuscating the meaning of the transaction recorded.

Contexts

The type of information used and the sources and channels employed vary with the context in which the work is conducted. Contexts include the nature of the work being done, environmental elements such as physical location and physical barriers, the attitudes of management, the size of the work group, and the nature of the information needed. From the viewpoint of management, an understanding of the relationship between context and information-communication behavior provides a guide to decisions affecting budgets for publications and physical facilities, and the role the manager has in eliciting desirable information-communication behavior.

Nature of work. There are variations among information-communication behavior patterns by profession and by the kinds of functions for which the information is to be used. Information-communication behavior varies between research and applications work, basic and applied research, academic and nonacademic work, and corporate and professional practice, thus the management of information must vary accordingly.

As would be expected, professionals engaged in research and/or academic work make more use of professional journals than those engaged in applications and nonacademic work. Practioners tend to get more of their work-related information from colleagues, reports, salespeople (vendors, medical detailers, etc.), and the trade press.

Written communications are more likely to be used by technical professionals working on basic research projects than by those working on applied research projects. Basic researchers are more likely to need information from professional colleagues working in different locations, even different countries, and are seldom under the time pressures faced by applied researchers.

The problem of the logarithmic growth of the formal journal literature has been overstated and is based on an idealized rather than an actual view of the role of the formal journal literature in professional life. The majority of professionals work in the world of applications and make little use of the journal literature. Journal publications are used primarily by research professionals and academics. The flood of journal publications is a response to a market demand that has nothing to do with potential users of new knowledge. The writer of a journal article is the primary market for the publication. The journal article is the means by which the author establishes "property rights" to the findings presented. Publishing second earns no Nobel prizes. Journal publication earns the academic author promotions and tenure since it is truly "publish or perish" in academic life.

Physical location and physical barriers. Who communicates with whom and the frequency of their communications is affected strongly by an organization's physical arrangements. The distance between the work locations of two individuals, which is determined by management, has a considerable effect on the frequency of their work-related communications. The probability that two persons will communicate on professional matters drops sharply with the distance between them. The probability of two persons communicating at least once a week drops sharply from just about 0.98 at a separation distance of six feet to half that at fifteen feet, and keeps dropping with distance, practically disappearing at fifty feet. (Allen, 1977) Any physical barrier that impedes easy access on a given floor will have a similar effect. Individuals will sooner walk one hundred feet to communicate with someone on the same floor than walk up twelve stairs to talk to someone on the next floor, even when the stairwell is adjacent to their desks.

Within organizations there are frequent moves of groups and individuals organizationally and physically. When professional personnel are moved to new locations, the pattern of interpersonal communications changes accordingly. Within as short a period as four months after a move, the patterns of communication on work-related matters shift as much as 46%, with people turning to those physically nearest to them even though they had not turned to them before (Shapero et al., 1978).

It is a familiar professional experience to have a good, informal, communicative relationship with another professional who works in the same office. The relationship is both professional and social and results in having lunch together frequently, playing chess together, and the like. Then comes an organizational move which separates the two colleagues physically and organizationally. Within a very short time the relationship attenuates to the point where they wave at each other when they meet accidentally, and promise to "get together pretty soon," but they seldom do. People tend to fall into very fixed patterns of movements in their work life, walking the same path to coffee, going to the same places for lunch, and talking with those nearest to them physically.

Attitudes of managers. Motivation is important in any consideration of information-communication behavior. If the individual professional is motivated to want information, to value information, and to want to share information with others it will make a difference to his behaviors and consequent productivity. In the same way, the professional who has learned that active participation in information-enhancing activities will be penalized is hardly likely to seek out and exchange information in such a way as to enhance productivity.

The attitude of managers toward such information-communication behaviors as reading in general, reading on the job, informal exchanges, coffee breaks, and attendance at conferences and professional meetings is an environmental element that affects the behavior of professionals. If management gives negative feedback with regard to them, the activities will not occur or will be seriously diminished. On the other hand, the manager who reads on the job, calls attention to interesting material, participates in informal exchanges and coffee breaks, and encourages attendance at professional meetings will elicit more productive communications. A general management policy that recognizes and rewards the desired communication behavior can have a positive effect. Managers shouldn't make the mistake of their German colleague who was described by one of his employees as "believing so much in the importance of the coffee break that he had the coffee delivered to everyone's desk so they wouldn't be interrupted by all those people."

The information need being satisfied. The kind of information needs to be satisfied can be divided into what may be termed "logistic needs" and "nutrient needs." Logistic needs occur when the kind of information wanted is known, but its content isn't known. Examples include the following:

> We want the name and telephone number of the vice president for marketing of the United Astrology Corporation.
> We want to know the magnetic properties of a particular alloy.
> We want to know what is available in the way of certain kinds of components with characteristics that fall within given limits, their costs, the companies that make them, and whom to call to order them.
> We want a list of everything available in the literature on the disease, multiple myeloma, and then abstracts.
> We want material on the design of stairways.
> We want to know what information retrieval systems contain information on agricultural economics.

All of the above are logistic needs, and are the kinds of needs satisfied by a library search, and by the use of handbooks, catalogs, and well-organized filing systems. Logistic needs are ideally suited for fulfillment by a mechanical retrieval system.

Nutrient needs for information are satisfied by information where it is not known when it will be used. The expression "nutrient needs" (for want of a better term) is used to denote the flow of information needed by the human animal to maintain and develop itself. Nutrient information is required by professionals to maintain themselves and to grow professionally. Every event experienced by an individual, and every significant input of information is registered somewhere in that individual's memory. All of us have had *dejà vu* experiences, recognizing some place we have never been before because it evokes some memory from our large storehouse. No two individuals have the same store of information, not even identical twins, and it is our unique stores of information that distinguish each of us from every other individual.

When faced with a problem, a nonroutine question, or a creative opportunity, we consciously and unconsciously draw upon our unique store of information. A design professional faced with a design problem might draw upon something seen in a trade magazine a year ago, a previous design experience, something learned in a course, a paper heard at a convention, a personal experience with equipment while working on a summer job, and something seen as a child while fishing with an uncle. All of these stored memories come together in some complex, and as yet unexplained, way to form a new design concept.

The notion of information as a nutrient generates a number of inferences. Given equal capabilities, the larger and more varied the store of information in an individual, the greater probability of a creative solution. The more one's store of information is exercised, the easier it will be to avail oneself of all parts of that store. The notion of stored information from previous significant experiences suggests that more importance should be given to feelings than is often assigned them. Our feelings are evoked by experiences with past events. Though we cannot always assign labels or rational explanations to those feelings, they represent uncatalogued information in our store. Though we should not take precipitous actions on the basis of our feelings, we should also not ignore them. Our feelings are a basis for intuition, and are important to inductive thinking and pattern recognition.

Individual Differences

There are, of course, individual differences in information-handling capacities. There are differences due to age, experience, and training. Various cognitive capabilities, such as short-term memory, change with age. In general, however, the information-handling capabilities of almost all humans are so good that, from the view point of the manager of professionals, most individual differences are insignificant.

There is one exception, an individual who has been labeled variously in the literature but who all agree plays a central role in the information-communication process. That central figure, who will be referred to here as "the high communicator," has also been variously referred to as "the technological gatekeeper" (Allen, 1966); "the scientific troubador" (Menzel, 1964); "the information specialist"; (Bernal, 1958; Hodge and Nelson, 1965); and "the special communicator" (Holland, 1970).

Whatever the label, all are agreed on the existence of individuals who play a special part in facilitating and increasing information flows into, within and from an organization. The high communicator is primarily identified by the relatively high frequency with which he or she is cited by others as the person they go to for information. These high communicators raise the total information capabilities and content of an organization. The majority of studies about high communicators have been concerned with scientists and engineers, but the findings about technical professionals are pertinent to other professionals. Among the characteristics of the special facilitators of information are the following (Shapero et al., 1978): High communicators:

> Read considerably more than their colleagues
> Read more sophisticated technical journals than their colleagues

Participate more frequently in professional meetings and conferences than their colleagues

Play a pivotal role in professional social circles

Have and use more personal contacts outside the organization than their colleagues

Have more intraorganizational contact than their colleagues

Use more technical specialists within an organization than their colleagues

Maintain close communication with other high communicators in their organizations

Are high technical performers

Present significantly more papers at professional conferences than their colleagues

There is more than one kind of high communicator. No one is a high communicator for every kind of information in the workplace. In research and development, high communicators have been differentiated with regard to three categories of information: project-task information, state-of-the-art-information, and research-laboratory technique information (Holland, 1970; Shapero et al., 1978; Myers & Huffman, 1982). It is not surprising that the high communicator for project-task information tends to be a first-line supervisor and more likely to be a person who communicates a lot with others outside the organization. The high communicator for state-of-the-art information is more likely to be a producer of both published and unpublished papers and to read more technical journals. The high communicator for research-laboratory technique information is more hardware-oriented and has more patents.

Differences among high communicators are associated with the institutional contexts in which they work: differences in technology, institutional purpose, organizational structure, and organizational history. For example, the high communicator in a twenty-year-old, nonprofit, contract-research physical sciences laboratory will have a different profile than one in a profit-making, hardware-development electronics company that is fifteen years old (Shapero et al., 1978).

As might be expected, in the hardware-oriented electronics

organization, the high communicator is likely to have more patent applications, more communication with outsiders, will read more unpublished papers, have more years of technical experience, go to more meetings and receive more awards. High communicators differ from other professionals in the extent and intensity of their information-communication activities, but there are logical differences among them depending on the kind of work they do and the kinds of organizations for which they work. We would expect patents to play a larger role in a hardware organization and to make more sense in the laboratory-research technique than in the state-of-the-art function. We can easily understand the greater importance of writing reports in a research organization.

Two-Person Communications

The two-person exchange is the basic unit in communications. Communication implies a sender, a receiver, and a message. Even when we speak of mass communication, a large number of two-person exchanges with one source and many receivers is implied. In addition to the factors already discussed, two-person exchanges are affected by the receiver's perceptions of the source of the message and by experiences with previous exchanges between sender and receiver.

Effects of sources. Communication is concerned with the transmission and *reception* of information. Effective delivery, which means effective reception, is the main goal of communication. The management of professionals wants to be sure that messages transmitted will affect the recipient's behavior in the direction intended. Whether the intention is to affect work-related behavior, or to be assured that employees (including the managers themselves) are updated professionally, or to raise the likelihood that clients and prospective clients will be affected by its messages, management has to be concerned with effective reception.

A major influence on whether a message will be accepted and acted upon is the receiver's perception of the characteristics of the source of the message. Research has identified three source characteristics associated with the transmission of messages which are effective in terms of persuasion, attitude change, and diffusion of innovation: source credibility, source attractiveness, and power (McGuire, 1969 and 1973).

Source credibility. The same message sent by two persons, one perceived as credible and one as not credible, will be received and remembered equally by a recipient, but the effect of that message (i.e., attitude or opinion change) will be far greater when sent by the credible source.

The credibility or believability of a source depends on his or her perceived expertise and objectivity. The more the source of a message has professional or social authority, the more the recipient is likely to accept and use the transmitted information. Most professionals quickly check a source's degrees, rank, place of work, publisher, and/or school attended before deciding whether and how to listen to or read the information presented. A lecture on the history of architecture by someone identified as a very intelligent butcher will not be taken seriously no matter how good the content of the material.

Advertisers have long understood the effect of credibility on target audiences. Hence the advertisements with a man in a white laboratory coat with a stethoscope dangling around his neck urging the use of a particular headache remedy. When medical associations protested the ads, the stethoscope and white laboratory coat were removed and a microscope substituted.

The status or prestige of the source of information affects the believability of the information, particularly if the status of the source is seen to be higher than that of the recipient of the message. Status and prestige are associated with expertise, among other things. Another element in the perception of the credibility of a source is perceived objectivity. Sources are believed to be more objective when they are seen as having nothing to gain as a result of convincing the recipient.

Something can be learned from the data on source credibility and the use advertisers have made of them. When transmitting important information to clients, prospective clients, higher management, and other branches of an organization thought should be given to who is transmitting the information. This is intuitively sensed by many, but it should be considered more systematically. Thought should be given to the credibility of the messenger in the eyes of the recipient—the best messenger may not be the person most readily available or the one with the highest rank.

If a management is serious about bringing new professional information into the organization, it should consider sending its most respected (credible) people to professional meetings. They are the ones most likely to be listened to when they return, raising the likelihood their information will be used. Proposals for projects provide a good example of where credibility is achieved in terms of the biographies of the proposed staff that accompany them. When an organization making a proposal for work feels it needs more credibility, it can often obtain it by engaging consultants with the requisite credibility—a way of "renting" credibility.

Source attractiveness. Attractiveness here means being likable, admired, and/or similar to the recipient. People tend to agree with those they like, and on learning that someone they like feels negatively towards an idea or object, people will tend to share that dislike. One will adopt a position taken or urged by a liked or admired source to enhance one's own self-esteem by identifying with the source. The use of popular and admired figures from sports and entertainment is a staple of consumer advertising. Naming lines of clothing after popular figures has resulted in significant increases in sales.

Factors that influence likableness in the work situation are suggested by the literature on interpersonal attraction (Berscheid & Walster, 1969) and social exchange (Chadwick-Jones, 1976). The factors include the following:

Propinquity: the closer two individuals are located to each other physically and socially, the more likely they will be attracted to each other and the more likely they will select each other as information sources.

Reciprocity: we like those who cooperate with us in attaining rewards for ourselves, those who like us, and those who give us something. A benefactor is liked better when the recipient has a chance to reciprocate and disliked when there is no chance to reciprocate (Gross & Latane, 1974).

Similarity. Similarity is associated with liking. In addition to being more likely to accept and be influenced by someone who is perceived as likable, an individual is more likely to seek out such a source for information. Conversely, individuals will go out of their way to avoid going for information to someone who is unlikable or who makes them pay an unacceptable psychological price (Shapero et al., 1978).

Substantial evidence suggests that individuals are influenced by messages from sources similar to themselves. The more the recipient perceives the source of the message as being like him/or herself, the more he/or she will be influenced by the message. The more someone perceives another to be like him/or herself the more it is assumed they share common tastes, standards, and goals.

For example, making use of the data on similarity, advertising on television is becoming more and more regional. The same advertisement, shown in different regions uses people with local accents and appearances. Television advertising increasingly uses "ordinary-looking" people who are similar to a larger audience (like you and me). Ads for computers and laboratory equipment show someone who is a business person or a scientist, give the individual's name, title and company, and statements about satisfaction with the advertised equipment: an example of using similarity for effective message transmission.

As with credibility, management can make use of the data on source attractiveness in many situations. For one thing, it is possible to enhance and shape the flow of information in a laboratory by use of what is known about the effects of propinquity in making office assignments. Putting a development group next to the people responsible for marketing will result in more marketable developments. Putting an R & D group next to a university will result in more publications. Putting an electronics group next to a materials group will result in more exchange and understanding between the two groups. Sending research people to spend some time with salesmen in the field can change the research man into an "attractive" source of information for the field people and vice versa, enhancing the useful flow between the two functions.

A thoughtful matching of the characteristics of whoever is selected to transmit information with those of the intended receivers will raise the chances of the transmission being successful. An ideal choice is someone who is both credible and similar to the intended receivers. For example, if one is mounting an effort to increase the number of minority applicants for a summer intern program, it would be ideal to send someone from the organization who is both a respected professional (for credibility) and who is from the same minority group (similarity). The intelligent manager in charge of the marketing of professional services studies the background and characteristics of those being contracted and sends someone who might have the best chance of being listened to.

The two-person bond. Two-person communications are affected by the history of past communications between the individuals, and their experiences with past exchanges affects the impact of subsequent exchanges. A relationship established over a series of exchanges creates a two-person bond which has a particular strength and which carries with it a set of norms and expectations that do much to determine the attention paid and the value placed on a message sent between the two persons. Knowledge of how two-person bonds operate with regard to information can be employed in many useful ways to enhance the flow of work-relevant information in professional activities. This knowledge is useful in maintaining and increasing the general flow of professional information into an organization or to an individual while simultaneously developing positive relationships with outside organizations and individuals.

A two-person bond begins when "liking" or "attraction" is established by some initial exchange between two persons. Two persons communicating for the first time generate a relationship that has a potential for becoming a continuing bond between them. The initial level of liking is in large part a function of similarity between the two individuals. The more the two persons share in the way of values and characteristics the more likely they will like each other if the context and the situation provides the opportunity.

Subsequent strengthening of the bond occurs as a result of propinquity, reciprocity, and shared experiences, and in their absence the bond weakens and disappears. If there is no physical propinquity, the bond depends on the number, variety and value of the subsequent exchanges (reciprocity). A continuing and growing relationship comes from a series of exchanges of information interlaced with social and professional exchanges of many kinds. The professional exchanges include invitations to lecture or give a paper, recommendations for jobs, recommendations of potential hires, and consulting. Social exchanges include anything from a Christmas card or a drink to invitations to be a house guest.

The length of time between exchanges affects the strength of the bond (and the liking). The strength of the bond weakens with the length of time between bonds, unless there have been so many exchanges that the bond takes on a permanent high level of strength, the kind that occurs with childhood friends. When two "old" friends meet again, it is often as if they are picking up a conversation again in the middle.

There is a norm of reciprocity in exchanges: exchanges must be reciprocal, and they cannot become too unbalanced. When exchanges between two persons become too unbalanced the bond cannot be maintained. Reciprocity does not imply a *quid pro quo*. *Quid pro quo* exchanges are commercial transactions, and each has a one-transaction life. Each of the parties is quit of the other once the exchange has been made, and another "deal" may be negotiated when needed. Bond-strengthening exchanges just happen naturally in context.

Two simple experiments that anyone can try will demonstrate the dynamics of two-person bonds for the readers, and, incidentally, strengthen some of their own social-professional bonds.

In the first experiment, mail some interesting professional material to a selection of people you have met professionally more than a year ago. Draw the names from your address list or collection of cards. Attach your card or a very brief scribbled note to the material. Keep a record of the returns in the following weeks. I sent a copy of a paper I had written to forty people drawn rather randomly from my files. Within ten days I received a number of letters conveying thanks for the materials, stating that they were glad to hear from me, and some filled me in about themselves and what they were doing. Within a month a number of articles, papers, and a report, accompanied by cards and notes, were received from the target group. Within three months a call was received from one of the addressees asking me if I could be included in a proposal for a major piece of research work.

Try a second simple experiment that strengthens bonds. From your address list draw three names of people you have not talked to in over a year. Call each of them, and tell them nothing more important than that you have been thinking of them or that you were wondering what they were doing. During the subsequent conversation note how much useful information is exchanged. This is a form of networking (it is also a very pleasant experience that can brighten a gray day). The last time I made three such calls I unexpectedly ended up helping someone hire a good professional, I was informed of some new technical material, and I committed myself to writing a chapter in a book.

The experiments just described also suggest useful management actions. By regularizing and encouraging professional-to-professional exchanges between people in the organization and others, a reciprocal flow of information will be generated, bringing valuable information into the organization, possibly including recruitment and business opportunities. Professionals should be encouraged to keep a mailing and telephone list of professionals they have met, and to keep them active through calls, mailing of working papers, articles, and correspondence. Institutional mailing will have far less effect than person-to-person mailings. Managers of professionals might also promote the establishment and maintenance of regular information means, such as working-paper series, newsletters, reprint series, and the sponsorship of talks to other groups.

The Social-Professional Circle or Network

The professional social circle or network is built upon an aggregation of two-person bonds. A multiperson information communications system is usually referred to as a network, but the term "network" evokes an electro-mechanical model of communications that does not adequately describe the social nature of human communications. It is more useful to refer to the expression "social-professional circle," but since "network" is used so widely the terms "social-professional circle" and "social network" will be used interchangeably.

The social-professional circle is more amenable to organic/ biological or social terms of reference, which can include relevant concepts of age, attraction, norms of behavior, transactions, and the like. As was discussed in Chapter 1 ("Hiring"), social-professional circles are crucial to our lives. Our social circles determine our norms and standards, provide us with trusted and useful work-related information, and often bring us jobs or suitable employees.

Data on how information flows in social-professional networks are found in studies of the so called "invisible colleges," in the international science community, and in the literature on social networks, social change and interpersonal attraction. The literature describes a social network as based on social contacts, kinships, friendships, professional ties, and on physical propinquity (Lin, 1973).

The individual professional can be a member of many social-professional circles, for example as a member of an international professional circle linked to a group studying the phenomena in a limited field of science, or as a member of the advertising department of a corporation.

"Invisible colleges" are the social-professional circles of scientists working in a given field of basic research and found

146

in a variety of institutions in many different locations and countries. The scientists in an invisible college maintain their social networks through correspondence, visits, small invitational meetings, and informal exchanges at larger meetings. Their exchanges are marked by a high overlap between the professional and the social. The formal meetings are marked by informality while their social meetings are filled with discussion of their work (the napkins and tablecloths at dinner might be covered with diagrams and equations). Personal bonds are formed in face-to-face meetings and strengthened by exchanges of notes and drafts of articles long before they reach formal publication. In the science community, members of so-called invisible colleges know about new findings one to two years before they are published, obtain their leads to formal sources, and receive feedback and recognition before having gone through the formal process of publication (Price, 1963; Crane, 1972; Compton, 1973).

Membership in professional social networks is obtained through sponsorship or, in the case of science, publication followed by an invitation to a meeting or a visit. To maintain membership an individual must follow the norms and standards of the network, most fundamental of which is reciprocal exchange. Those who only take from the network and do not reciprocate are dropped. An individual may be dropped from the network for not behaving according to its accepted norms: e.g., not giving due credit to the work of others, using material without attribution, taking part in the political repression of colleagues.

Extended social-professional circles are found in all professional fields, though they may not play quite as central a role as in advanced fields of science. Extended social-professional circles are particularly important to professionals who work alone or in small groups in widely scattered locales. Artists need the company and exchange of other artists. Architects who aspire to doing new and advanced work need to exchange ideas with other architects. Medical practioners, particularly specialists, need to talk to others in their specialty.

Many social-professional circles are spatially anchored in

a given city, and in professions where this occurs it is almost necessary to locate in that city or to make regular pilgrimages there to keep abreast of what is happening professionally. Examples of the latter are publishing, advertising, *haute couture* design, film making, theater, and financial analysis. In cases where a particular kind of professional activity concentrates in a region, as in electronics, social-professional circles will be made up of some of the professionals that work for the many organizations in the region.

The extended social-professional circle takes on different forms in larger organizational contexts. In such activities as engineering and industrial R & D, the extended network (beyond the organization) does not play as great a direct role in the conduct of work-in-progress as in science. Much of the information used in industrial activities comes from within the organization. What comes from outside is usually obtained and transmitted by high communicators who play the part of boundary spanners, or from sales people.

Organizational social-professional circles form within an organizational work situation. Links form between individuals for some purpose or because of some consciously recognized interest on the part of one or both of the people interacting. The links are characterized by a daily intermingling of formal and informal exchanges that include job assistance, social conversation, and personal service. The benefits obtained from daily exchanges are both intrinsic and extrinsic. Among the intrinsic benefits are information transmission and verification, friendship, and play. The extrinsic benefits include recognition and influence. In the work situation, intrinsic and extrinsic are intertwined. Joking is easily combined with recognition. Information relay and verification are easily combined with influence.

The small world of social networks. There is a great deal of interconnection between social networks. The interconnections occur because individuals within the networks have multiple memberships. All individuals, with few exceptions, are members of a large number of different kinds of social networks based on church, school, neighborhood, military service, sport, social interests, hobbies, and profession. An engineer within a given organizational social network also belongs to a church group with someone who is a scientist at a university, and is also on a committee at her child's school with someone who is an investment banker. If asked a science-related question at work, she may freely call her acquaintance for information. If the question is one of a financial nature, she can contact her fellow school committee member. Her contacts may need to reach into their professional social circles to obtain information for the requestor. The very fact of the request creates the first act in a reciprocal relationship that may strengthen with more exchanges.

Because there is so much interconnection between social networks in the United States it is usually possible to identify and locate the source of needed professional information in three to five telephone calls. In addition, starting with a fairly unstructured question, the question will become more accurate, the terminology more precise, and value judgments about the various sources of information available will be proffered and refined in the course of the calls. To illustrate, if you wanted to obtain information on what is known about the costs and benefits of alternate methods of psychotherapy, where would you start? If you went to a library to use its mechanical information retrieval system and queried it for everything on costs and benefits you would get hundreds of references. If you requested everything on psychotherapy, it would produce a similar outpouring. However, if you cross both terms to get everything that combines costs and benefits and psychotherapy you would get nothing.

Take the same question to your network of acquaintances. Where to start? You might call a psychologist friend or someone who would know a psychologist. You make your call to the psychologist, apologizing for your ignorance. Your friend might tell you "It's a dumb question" but will consider it seriously anyway and say, "Call Professor Black at State University. If anyone might have a clue about the subject, he will." You call Professor Black, telling him that your friend suggested that you get in touch with him, and admitting that it might be "a dumb question." Professor Black is sociable and asks about your friend. He tells you, "It is an odd question, but it seems to me that White, at the University of California, spoke about something on those lines."

You now call White, telling him that Black had referred you, ask your question, and apologize again for your ignorance. White is immediately responsive. He tells you your question is improperly framed. "The terms are all wrong! We don't use those economic terms in our field, and you'll never find anything under those terms. We use cures per time of treatment per person." White tells you of the work of Brown and Green, stating, "Green is an idiot! Her work is misdirected and dated. Brown is first class! Brown's done the only useful work on the subject." He goes on to say, "Brown did a lot of his work at Cambridge, but he's now at Sussex." Now, you are on target, and are able to go to the library and ask for everything by Brown of Sussex.

Analyze the process in the example. You started in almost complete ignorance. You used a personal bond in your social network to start. You followed a trail of personal bonds through personal references which meant that you would be given thoughtful responses no matter how far-fetched your question. You have had your question and terminology reframed to fit the field. Because you have come through social networks, you have been given value judgments that no retrieval system would contain.

This would be relatively fast and efficient, and in the process you might learn much more about the subject and about attitudes in the field. You might even form an acquaintanceship with someone in your chain of questions who shares other interests or who wants to know what you learn. If you reciprocate, you have created the beginnings of a two-person bond.

The question was raised some years ago, how many personal social links it would take to link up two individuals picked at random from the two hundred twenty million people in the United States. A preliminary answer was provided by Milgram (1967) in an elegant study called "The Small World Study." Packets were mailed to individual names picked at random in the Midwest. Each packet contained the name and description of an individual in the Boston area, giving the person's home and work addresses. The recipients were asked to send the packet to the target person if they knew him by first name, and, if not, to send it to someone they knew by first name who might be more likely to know him. Each of the chain of recipients were asked to return an attached postal card describing their relationship to the person to whom they sent the packet.

Of the completed chains of referral, the average number of links was five. The study was a demonstration of the effective way in which two-person bonds imbedded in social networks link up a very large population. Typically, someone in Nebraska sent the packet to a fellow engineer raised in Massachusetts who, in turn, sent it to a former high school teacher in a small Massachusetts town. The former teacher sent the packet to a haberdasher in the town where the target person lived, who then completed the chain. Other packets reached the target person at his or her place of work in Boston, most of them coming through work colleagues. Two of his or her colleagues at work and a shopkeeper in his or her living area were the principal conduits, and they could be high communicators or boundary spanners.

Managing Information–Communication Behavior at the Individual Level

Management can affect information-communication behavior by who and how they hire, the resources they make available to the individual professional, education, and motivation.

Hire high communicators. Make extra efforts to hire high communicators. Hiring the high communicator is probably the most direct way to improve the information content of an entire organization. The high communicator brings an organization (1) access to an extended body of information imbedded in links with many sources of information, (2) an active information-seeking mode, and (3) an active information-communication–transmission style that creatively connects people and information within the organization (i.e., the individual who thrusts information on you, saying, "Remember you were asking about . . ."). Hiring the high communicator is not just a matter of accessing the information in the individual's head, but of accessing the information made available to the organization through that individual's information-communication behavior.

To identify a high communicator when hiring, look for a record of continuing information-dependent output (a number of recently published and unpublished papers, patents, etc.), evidence of continuing professional networking (professional meetings frequently and recently attended, honors and awards, professional directory listings), and evidence of continuing active information-seeking behavior (number of journals read). Of course, these characteristics should be looked for in addition to what is sought in any professional—a good work record and reputation and likableness (both of which are commonly found in high-communicators).

Hire "nice" people. To maximize the information available within your organization, hire people whom others will readily go to for information and to whom they'll readily give information. The most impressive formal education without the ability to make that information readily available can result in a net loss to an organization. The measure to be applied is "net available information."

Facilitate your high communicators. If you are fortunate enough to have one or more high communicators in your organization, make it easier for them to play the part. Give them unlimited budgets for books and journals—they will get the information to more people than most libraries. Locate them where they are easily accessed by others. Encourage them to travel to see what is going on in their fields. Do not make the mistake of designating them as "information specialists" and removing them from the normal working processes and tasks. High communicators function best in context, where they are part of the regular flow of work and social exchange.

Provide liberal budgets for formal information. Information serves to enhance and save professional labor, and is cheap relative to the cost of that labor. The price of a book or an annual subscription to a technical journal may be roughly equivalent to one fully costed hour of professional labor. If a book or journal saves one hour of labor, it has already earned its way, and if it has improved the output of a professional its payout may be very large. Unlike the professional hour, the book or journal remains available after being used. In light of their potential worth and economy, it is startling to find organizations surrounding the acquisition of books, journals, and reports with an amazing amount of bureaucratic procedure that lowers or prevents the use of the formal sources of information. Typically, the purchase of information is treated as the purchase of materials and equipment, and is justified and inventoried accordingly.

Remember that information serves a "nutritive" purpose as well as a logistic one. The preferred rule is to have a larger quantity and diversity of books, journals, and reports around than is needed for any given project rather than to require justification on the basis of identified, and often painful, immediate and explicit need. If you make the book budget unlimited, probably only one or two people will make heavy demands on it. The individual who does "abuse the privilege" will likely be the high communicator who will subsequently distribute the information within the organization. It may be a good way to identify your high communicators.

Education. Education is one means of achieving improved information-communication behavior. Informing professionals how they can get and use information can make some difference in their behavior. When formal materials are combined with exercises in improved methods for obtaining information and are reinforced through practice and reminder, new behavior patterns can be established and maintained. Seminars have been successfully held in which, for example, the participants are asked to compare several modes of obtaining information such as "three to five phone calls," library search, and mechanical retrieval systems.

Motivation. Perhaps the most effective actions are those that motivate the individual to shape his or her information-communication behavior to be more effective. Eliciting the desire to read, to exchange information with other professionals within and outside the organization, and actively to improve transmission of information are tasks for the manager. Professionals can be motivated to increase and improve their information-communication behavior through positive feedback and through incentives. Among other things the manager can do are the following:

Make information-communication contributions part of the review process

Make a deliberate point of encouraging professionals to read: by managerial example, by making approving comments, and by encouraging discussion of what the professionals read (e.g., the formation of a weekly, informal "brown bag" journal club in which participants including the manager report on articles they have read)

Encourage use of the telephone to contact outside professional colleagues for information

Encourage participation in both formal and informal exchanges of information outside the immediate organizational group (e.g., seminars, classes)

Reinforce information-related activities with relevant rewards (e.g., trips to review state-of-the-art technology, subscriptions and books, time to review the literature)

Networking. Managers should encourage professionals to develop and maintain their memberships in social-professional circles that cross organizational lines. The social networks are important sources of good information for technical matters, hiring, and business-related information. Effective access to outside networks provides an organization with an extended family of information, and access to useful social-professional networks is only freely available to individuals who are "members" of them. Management should encourage and support participation in the social-professional networks to which their professionals belong for its value to the organization and its educational value to the individual professional.

Many organizations support or encourage their professionals to take part in local professional societies, and some organizations consider membership in such societies an obligation for
some of their senior technical people. Membership in professional societies can lead to the kinds of personal relationships
that enter a professional into a social-professional network, but
this is only one form of networking. Far more effective are
those things that bring the professional as a participant to
smaller, less formal groups, such as seminars, small invited conferences of experts, or task forces. The preparation of articles
and papers has a beneficial effect on networking just as much
as it does on the individual's and organization's reputation.

At the Organizational Level

Management can affect information-communication behavior by the use of formal and informal organizational mechanisms, including rules and procedures, and by the allocation
of resources.

Encourage informal workplace communications. The manager
has a large effect on informal workplace communications. The
manager who understands and accepts the importance of the
informal, even playful, kinds of exchange that take place on
the job is at ease in such an environment. With the manager
at ease, the information exchange is rich. The manager who
is still firmly fixed in the "production line" ethic, and who
feels that "if they're just talking, they aren't working," sends
out a host of signals that suppress exchange.

In addition to passive encouragement, the manager can formally help to develop an environment for productive informal
information exchange by use of a number of informal mechanisms. The manager can encourage the daily coffee gathering,
sponsor and take part in an informal weekly lunch with different mixes of professionals in the organization, provide architectural aids including a good lunchroom that becomes a gathering
place. At one time, the Ramo-Wooldridge Corporation had coffee alcoves in their California plant to encourage just such infor-

mal exchanges. Scratch pads on cafeteria tables may encourage the exchange of information during lunch hour.

Rules, procedures, and resources. Rules, procedures, and resources channel or block desired information-communication activities. Rules regarding the buying of books and journals can make it easy or difficult to get some material when needed and, eventually, can determine whether a professional will even make the effort. The availability of resources acts in the same way and conveys a message as to what is considered to be in the organization's interests and what isn't (e.g., a rule that requires special clearance from a high level of management to use a company car tells one quickly that the management does not see company cars as just another tool.).

Uses of travel. Face-to-face communications with people in other organizations is a valuable activity that is also expensive in terms of time and money. The cost of travel makes it more difficult to be as liberal with it as with other sources of information. However, travel should be encouraged for the following reasons:

Early-on face-to-face meetings between key professionals in your organization and others with an important role in or concern with a new project: i.e., clients, subcontractors, suppliers, public interest groups and their professionals

Regular, periodic face-to-face meetings between your professionals and other parties with an important role or concern with an ongoing project

Exchange of needed information on highly abstract or uncertain subjects which require very rich communications, e.g., certain kinds of professional subjects or incompletely stated problems

The first face-to-face meetings between people who will be working together on a project but are going to be separated by organizational and spatial distance provides the necessary means for each person to "calibrate" the others, to know what to expect from them. Face-to-face exchanges are vital to the establishment of trust, and make it possible subsequently to carry on reliable and useful communications over the telephone. Subsequent, periodic meetings are needed to maintain trust, to prevent misunderstanding from developing, and to defuse difficult situations. The more the work that engages two parties is of a nonroutine nature, the more the need for face-to-face exchange. In any field concerned with highly abstract material, visually dependent material, or where the questions are incompletely formed, face-to-face exchanges are essential. For example, it is difficult to conceive of an architectural project carried out completely by correspondence and telephone. It would be difficult to convey a complicated medical procedure by telephone (though this is now being tried by television hookup).

Travel should be liberally supported for the development and maintenance of linkages between professionals in an organization and professionals elsewhere. Budgets for travel to professional meetings are widespread, but travel should also be encouraged for visits and exchanges with others in the profession at universities and other institutions. The Japanese have been exemplary at understanding the value of having professionals meet other professionals to hear and to see what they are doing. Japanese recognition of what others are doing, and the Japanese custom of gift-exchange, generate the reciprocity that assures them of more information over time.

Travel by professionals from whom others in the organization will accept information should especially be encouraged. High communicators should be encouraged to travel as a way of obtaining more information.

Physical facilities. Through the design and arrangement of facilities, management can facilitate informal exchange within a group and between groups, as well as stimulating organizational changes.

Facilitate informal exchange within a group. The informal exchange of information within a group can be enhanced by locating the members fairly close together, by removing physical barriers between them, and by designing the facilities to increase "eddying" patterns (i.e., patterns that encourage encounter and interaction in the normal, daily flow of movements). Information-communication–oriented facilities design would do some or all of the following:

Locate a group in a contiguous space where possible

Place the "coffee pot" so it is easy for more than one person to share coffee and talk, and encourage group rather than individual coffee facilities

Arrange the physical layout of the group to increase the probability that all people in the group will "bump into each other"

Facilitate informal exchange between groups. Informal information exchange between different organizational groups can be aided by designing the physical facilities to enhance interactions and by arranging the way the groups are situated within the facilities. Particular attention has to be paid to increasing the opportunities for people from different groups to encounter each other casually and in the normal course of the day. Among ways to increase the probabilities for chance encounters are: (1) a central space through which different groups have to pass, on their way to other parts of the organization and on leaving the building, (2) company eating places that bring people together, (3) multigroup coffee areas which also permit small groups to meet and interact, and (4) centralized services that bring people together from various areas.

By arranging office assignments with a view to their information-communication consequences, it is possible to change the frequency of exchanges between individuals, to encourage the development of new ideas, to lay the groundwork for new coherent organizational groupings, and to break off communication patterns when that is desired.

Facility rearrangements are a constant in organizational life, particularly in large firms. The thoughtful manager can take advantage of organizational moves, when they occur, to accomplish several objectives.

One way to increase communications between individuals is to locate them in the same office or in adjacent offices. Locating them near each other can also affect the ideas that are developed in the organization. I have experimented with the use of new office assignments after a move from one facility to another. The new assignments were used to accomplish several information-communication and organizational objectives. By locating people from different disciplines in close proximity, the degree of informal and social exchange was significantly increased, and a number of innovative ideas were proposed that drew upon the varied backgrounds of the professionals newly located near each other. Placing individuals in close proximity also prepared the ground for the formation of new organizational arrangements. In one case, the deliberate grouping of individuals from different organizations resulted in a voluntary proposal by them to form a group desired by management.

Sometimes it is organizationally desirable to break off communications between individuals or groups, and the design of facilities provides an excellent means to accomplish that end. For example, in an organization of professional engineers and geologists, the partner in charge of a regional office passed on the baton of management to a younger person but wanted to keep on doing professional work. The transfer of management was not working well because the professional staff kept turning to the former manager for advice and decisions. Taking advantage of the fact that people will walk a hundred feet on the same floor, but will not go up twelve steps to the next floor, the former manager's office was moved to a different floor, and the undesired pattern of communications was broken off.

Managements should study the flow and communications patterns in their organizations to identify and understand what affects the information-communication behavior that currently exist between groups. Awareness of the effects of current facilities, and of the arrangements of groups within those facilities, can lead to conscious "tuning" of the patterns of communications. For example, studies of college dormitories showed that the most popular person in the building had the room at the head of the stairs plus or minus one room. A manager who took over as CEO of a company experiencing a great deal of legal and organizational trauma deliberately located himself in the office facing the elevators that opened on the executive offices floor. Not even his secretary buffered him from whoever came or went by the elevator. He soon was accepted by the managers and professionals of the organization and harvested valuable exchanges early in his tenure which helped him turn the company around.

Task forces and special groups. Locate task forces or special groups that have a specific task and a given deadline within the same space. A common "bull pen" is the most effective physical arrangement for such a group. The "bull pen" arrangement allows for the greatest and richest exchange between the people in the room. Though no one prefers the "bull pen" to separate offices, the evidence is that it results in rich informal exchange among professionals.

Think spaces. There is also need for facilities where one cannot be interrupted and where exchanges are minimized. Think spaces are needed for limited but intense periods of work on a final report or publication or a design presentation, particularly where deadlines are involved. Data on how professionals spend their time show that they are interrupted every twenty to thirty minutes. To get a report done, a professional or manager "hides out" from the office, either at home or in some place that only a secretary or a close family member knows about. A few organizations recognize this need for protected spaces for limited periods and set facilities aside that can be reserved by a professional when necessary. Usually such facilities are made consciously inaccessible to others when in use. They have no telephones and are places where the professional can bring and leave materials during the time of occupation. Such facilities often are equipped with plenty of surfaces to spread out on (including cork or metal walls with magnets), drafting tables, computer terminals, and shelving.

Improve information transmission. Successful professional work is not just a function of the value of the solution to a problem, the elegance of a design, or the proof of an exciting hypothesis. Full success entails that the valuable solution be accepted, the elegant design be recognized and bought, and the proof be seen and accepted. Much of the value of good professional work can be lost through ineffective transmission of its results. A major problem for many professionals in larger organizations is to get others in the organization to be interested in, and accept, their efforts and outputs.

The manager can apply the data on information-communication behavior to improve the effectiveness of the transmission of information in activities such as proposal writing, data presentations, and dealing with clients, suppliers, and important third parties such as bankers and government officials. Transmission is successful when the results are seen, understood, accepted, and leave the recipient with a continuing good relationship with the sources of the information (a guarantee of positive future exchanges). For example, R & D people who develop frequent, informal exchanges with the company's marketing people are far more likely to see their work accepted (as well as avoid market disasters through what they learn from the marketing people). All the managerial actions suggested for increasing the flow of information in an organization apply to transmission to other organizations.

Where there are continuing exchanges. When continuing exchanges over time are anticipated, as in the case of relationships between different departments of a larger organization (e.g., R & D and marketing, advertising and production) or between professional organization and client, a manager should:

Establish and increase the number of face-to-face exchanges between people in the different groups
Encourage telephone communications
Provide opportunities for informal exchanges

For increased acceptance. The effects of source characteristics, such as credibility and attractiveness, on the acceptance of information should be designed into important formal and information transmission efforts. The effects of credibility are recognized in practice, consciously or unconsciously, by many: by writers, when they add an authority as co-author to a submitted manuscript, thereby raising the probability of favorable reviews by their peers and subsequent publication, and by organizations, when they add a major authority to a project proposal to raise the probability that the project will be accepted.

5

Technical Obsolescence, Burnout, and Staying Alive

THE EXPRESSIONS "professional obsolescence" and "technical obsolescence" are used to describe the state of knowledge and abilities of individuals. What is an obsolete or obsolescent person? According to the dictionary, something obsolete is no longer in use or is of a style or kind no longer in use. People are not obsolete. They are the most flexible resource available to us, and it does harm to consider them no longer to be of use or out of style unless we are referring to physical form: e.g., fat is out of style. What is at issue here is a state of knowledge and/or skills that affect an individual's ability to perform well in professional work.

There is no commonly accepted definition of professional and technical obsolescence. The many available definitions include the following: (1) ineffectiveness on the job, (2) lack of new knowledge or skills, (3) a failure to keep abreast of what is going on, and (4) lack of the knowledge and skill that may be required for future jobs.

All these definitions include the idea of a reduction in effective or efficient job performance over time due to discrepancies between job needs and professional capabilities. One view is that professional or managerial obsolescence takes place when the discrepancy between job needs and performance results from innovations in the field or when, for whatever reason, the skills and knowledge of the manager or professional are insufficient for the job (Burack & Patti, 1970). According to a second definition, professional obsolescence is the failure of a once-capable professional to achieve results currently expected of him or her. Another view holds that professional obsolescence is a reduction in technical effectiveness due to a lack of knowledge of new technologies and techniques developed since the individual's education (Dubin, 1972). Another view includes all of the foregoing along with the inability to perform future work as well (Kaufman, 1974). Consideration of the future implies that a professional may be doing an adequate job today but is obsolescent unless acquiring the knowledge that may be needed for future work.

The "lack of new knowledge or skills" definition assumes that, unless acquiring or in possession of new knowledge or skills, an individual is professionally obsolescent. Of course, many examples can be thought of where new methods and techniques have not proven out, and where there is a return to old methods that work well. The widespread concern with the Japanese "miracle" has led to the rediscovery of what was taught to the Japanese by Americans who no longer use those techniques. The Japanese use of quality control, worker participation, and production methods that minimize inventory are not new but, rather, represent the use and refinement of classical American industrial techniques that date back to the 1930s and 1940s.

Linked to the lack of new knowledge or skill is the failure to keep abreast of what is going on. In this vein, one suggested measure of professional obsolescence (or incompetence) borrowed from physics is the "half-life of knowledge," defined as "the time after completion of training when, because of new developments, practicing professionals have become roughly half as competent as they were upon graduation to meet the demands of their profession" (Dubin, 1972). Dubin estimated the half-life for psychologists to be ten to eleven years on the average, with a range of five to twenty years, and quoted estimates of other half-lifes: for physicians and engineers, for example, five years.

Plausible as it sounds, the "failure to keep abreast" definition of obsolescence raises serious problems. Keeping abreast of what, and going on where? How is half-life determined, and how is it related to ineffectiveness in the work place? The "where" things are going on that determines obsolescence in the failure-to-keep-abreast version is academia. Measures of this kind of obsolescence have been based on the numbers of publications that have appeared since training and on course offerings, additions, and deletions in the catalogs of five engineering colleges at five-year intervals (Zellikoff, 1969). Course offering changes were used to develop "erosion curves" of applicable knowledge an erosion curve is determined by the year of graduation and the subsequent change in courses.

The "failure to keep abreast" definition of obsolescence assumes that what is being published and taught by academics is necessarily applicable and crucial to professional performance. The assumption is open to question. There is serious doubt that the bulk of what is published is necessarily good and, if good, applicable. The rate of publication is more a product of the "publish or perish" syndrome that drives the more than 350,000 faculty members in American colleges and universities than it is of the expansion of knowledge. According to Dubin (1972), a professional would have to spend 20% of working time to keep abreast. Dubin also quotes a leading engineering psychologist who estimated that "a compulsive, well-versed engineering psychologist would have to read thirty to forty articles, books, theses, and technical reports every day of the year to merely keep abreast of the current literature." In other fields with higher rates of publication, the time demand would be greater. No working professional can possibly keep up with this outpouring of publications, nor does it seem to be necessary.

It would be difficult to defend the argument that course offerings are an index of applicable knowledge. In many of the most advanced fields practice is ahead of scholarship, and academics argue that it is necessary for them to consult with industry to keep up with their fields. A study of the ratings of scientists and engineers in an industrial laboratory (Oberg, 1960), found that those under thirty years of age (those with the most recent education) were rated as contributing least to their laboratory.

As was shown in Chapter 4 ("Managing Information"), professionals obtain most of their information from personal sources and through informal channels, not through the literature. A study that tracked the flow of information by means of radio, TV, newspapers, magazines, books, and point-to-point communications (i.e., first class mail, mailgram, facsimile, telex, and telephone), calculated that between 1960 and 1977 the number of words supplied to Americans grew at the rate of 8.9% per year, but that the words consumed went up only at the rate of 2.9% per year. The point-to-point media (person to person communications) were most productive, and the data show that people were willing to spend much more per-word-transmitted in these media (Poole, 1983). The productivity of person-to-person communications vs. print media would have been even more pronounced if the study had included the richest of all communications media—informal, face-to-face conversations.

All the measures of obsolescence used have elements of plausibility, but none hold up to serious examination. The concept of professional obsolescence is too vague. It is difficult to define what is to be measured, the dimensions to use, and the validity and reliability of the measures. How can we determine a standard of performance against which we will measure an individual? The definitions of professional obsolescence all include some statement about performance not being what it should be. How do we determine what it should be? How do we tease out the input of the individual from all of the other factors influencing productivity? What new knowledge should the professional have not to be obsolescent? How do we know which techniques and knowledge, of all that is churned out, are relevant and effective?

Managers assume that there is something to the notion of decrements of performance with time. They intuit that they can do something about preventing or ameliorating those decrements by taking some actions. When we stand back from the narrow focus imposed by the limited notions of "professional obsolescence," however, it is possible to discern a larger question that includes plateauing, burnout, and middle age crisis. We become aware of the more pervasive problems of adult growth, development, and aging. The more useful question becomes, how can we help both the professionals who work for us and ourselves as individuals stay intellectually and professionally alive throughout our working lives? Surely the answer is not to allot 20% or 50% of our time to a desperate ingestion of everything published in the fields of our interest.

POSSIBLE CAUSES OF OBSOLESCENCE

What might cause obsolescence? Is obsolescence inherent, a matter of time and age, of some inexorable accumulation of physiological, sociological, and psychological fat that cannot be avoided? Is obsolescence induced by physiolological deterioration? Is it genetic? Is it a result of social, psychological, or motivational factors that include burnout?

Age and Performance

Research shows little uniform deterioration with time, and, though many older workers stop developing, it is not possible to attribute obsolescence solely or primarily to aging. Some people stay professionally and intellectually alive and keep developing throughout their careers. As a consequence of the many myths about age and professional performance, inaccurate assumptions are made about older workers that lead to costly and harmful managerial practices. Only limited efforts are made to maintain the professional capabilities of the older worker, on the assumption that the effort is wasted. Older professionals are overlooked for the kinds of assignments that lead to growth and professional development.

One of the most widespread assumptions about age and performance is that peak intellectual and professional performance is achieved by about age thirty-five, with steady deterioration thereafter. The assumption has drawn much of its sustenance from studies using historical evidence on the "greats" of all time. A twenty-year study was made by Lehman (1953) of creative achievement by scientists (in both abstract and applied disciplines), philosophers, and composers. Lehman asked experts to identify the greatest achievements in their fields, and then plotted the age of the responsible individual at the time of his great achievement. He concluded that achievement peaked in the late thirties to early forties.

There are reasons to doubt whether the conclusion reached by Lehman is valid today. Lehman studied the greatest creators of all time, and therefore most of his subjects lived in times of short life expectancy. Mozart and Schubert died in their thirties: what would they have accomplished if they had lived longer? Beethoven, who lived into his fifties, composed his greatest works in the last years of his life. Another question is whether the accomplishments of the very great, those bordering on genius, are relevant to the work of the great bulk of professional and creative people. In fact, when Lehman studied a larger number of lesser contributions he found that their production continued over a far longer age span.

Cross-sectional studies of the productivity of scientists and engineers in relation to their age (Pelz & Andrews, 1976) found a saddle-shaped curve with two peaks of productivity, one in the mid-forties and one in the mid-fifties! The two-peaked curve is interesting in that there appears to be a sharp drop in productivity in the late forties followed by a sharp return to productivity. Research has shown there is no physiological basis for the drop. It is apparently the result of social and emotional factors,—what is now referred to as the mid-life crisis. At this age, a professional or manager has been working for over twenty years and suddenly realizes that a fiftieth birthday is looming. It is a time of taking account of what one has done, where one is, and where one is going. It is a very sobering and restless time in the lives of many professionals and managers, a time when many drop everything to "find themselves." The drop in productivity may be good evidence that the late forties is a critical time for many professional workers. Happily, according to the data, the drop in productivity passes (or else those who are seriously affected leave).

A study of age and the "relative value" of over nine hundred technical professional employees in an industrial laboratory (Oberg, 1960) also found a two-peaked curve, with the second peak occurring in the late fifties. In a first round of studies, using the laboratory's evaluation results, Oberg found the ages associated with highest relative value were thirty-six to forty years of age, followed by fifty-six to sixty years of age. The professionals under thirty years old received the lowest ratings. The first round was questioned because it included supervisors in the total population studied, and it was suggested that the supervisors would tend to raise the average age of those judged to have highest relative value. The data was reanalyzed, excluding supervisors, and as can be seen from Table 5–1, the age of those with the highest ratings went up instead of down: those fifty-six to sixty were first, followed by a tie between those fifty-one to fifty-five and those thirty-six to forty. There was a difference between the technical professionals in R & D and the engineers, with the most valued engineers tending to be older.

It is important to realize that most studies of age vs. performance, as measured by a variety of psychological instruments,

TABLE 5–1
Most Valued Professional by Age

	Most Valued	Next in Value
All professionals	36–40	56–60
Excluding managers	56–60	51–55 & 36–40
R & D professionals	31–35	36–40 & 51–55
Engineers	56–60 & 51–55	41–45 & 36–40

Source: From Oberg (1960).

are based on cross-sectional studies. It should be remembered that cross-sectional methods measure different age groups at the same point in time while longitudinal studies measure what happens to an age group at different periods through time. In study comparing age vs. performance, using a battery of psychological instruments which included both cross-sectional and longitudinal methods (Schaie & Strother, 1968), the longitudinal studies showed far less decrement in performance with age over time than did the cross-sectional studies.

The Schaie & Strother study demonstrates little decrement in basic intellectual capabilities with age, and suggests that the causes of technical obsolescence will be found elsewhere. In recent years, the records of performance of such great figures in the world of the arts as Picasso, Chagall, Jacques Lipchitz, Georgia O'Keeffe, and Pablo Casals have helped change the general perception of performance and age. A Japanese scholar has developed curves of human physical and intellectual capabilities that identify the different ages at which specific kinds of capabilities peak. He defines an envelope of curves bounded by an upper curve of those who function well and a lower curve of those whose capabilities decline early in life. On the higher performance curve of intellectual capabilities, memory is shown as peaking early, by the twenties. Mathematics peaks early, too, as everyone familiar with the world of mathematics would agree. Great mathematicians usually appear in their early twenties. One either is or is not a great mathematician, and thirty years of experience will not transform an average mathematician into a great one. The curve shows music as peaking early, too, and there is some evidence that music and mathematics are almost inborn talents. Engineering, management, architecture, and design peak in the mid-forties. The curve also shows that a quality labelled "judgment" peaks in the sixties and stays high until the eighties. Judgment might be defined as knowing where to put one's effort, where to make a stand, what is important, and what is not. In most professional fields experience makes a difference, and an intelligent, alert, older professional can give better performance than an intelligent, alert, younger professional.

Physiology and Obsolescence

Can professional obsolescence be linked to physiological changes? For almost every physiological and psychological variable (measured in large groups of people) the highest average value is found between ages twenty and thirty, with a steady, linear decline thereafter. What is masked by average results for large groups is the amount of variability around the averages (Fries & Crapo, 1981). When it comes to age vs. performance, there is a great deal of variability, demonstrating that chronological age is not a good measure of aging. Individuals age at very different rates.

The data are also influenced by the higher incidence of illness with age. Much of the functional decrement attributable to illness is hidden by the aggregate statistics. Attention has already been called to the inaccuracies introduced by the use of cross-sectional rather than longitudinal data. Some longitudinal data have shown actual improvements in performance with age (Nesselrode et al., 1972).

Because of the variability in human attributes with age, Fries and Crapo (1981) propose the notion of "plasticity," that the future capability for a given attribute is not fixed and inevitable but may be modified. They write, "We may anticipate success, [in human attribute] in some instances and lack of success in others. Given our present knowledge we cannot be certain of all the areas where improvement is impossible." They further suggest that positive changes can be effected by eliminating the variability caused by disease, taking advantage of favorable changes that are occurring to an entire age group, and/or improving the individual with time.

There is some intriguing evidence that the external environment may have a large role in determining whether brain cells are maintained during aging (Diamond, 1978). Some data suggest that mammalian brain development can result from environmental stimulation even in advanced age. It has been found, in experiments with laboratory animals, that when litter mates were separated into three different environments—standard, enriched and improverished—those raised in the rich environment had thicker and heavier cerebral cortexes (that part of the brain responsible for the highest brain functions) and showed more brain growth compared with those raised in the impoverished environments. This may indicate that the brain of humans can be maintained and even regenerated through physical and mental stimuli (Pelletier, 1981). What seems clear is that lively, rich environments can play an important role in maintaining the physiological capabilities related to intellectual, and thus professional, capacity.

Studies of performance vs. age and of the effects of the environment on the physiological capabilities associated with higher brain functions lead to a number of salient conclusions with regard to technical obsolescence and its management:

1. Though there appear to be some physiologically caused decrements in physical performance with age, such as muscle strength and motor speed, there is no convincing evidence of a physiologically necessary decrement in intellectual performance.
2. There is very wide individual variability when it comes to age and performance, and it is almost impossible to predict physiologically based individual capability solely on the basis of chronological age.
3. Illness is a major cause of decrements in performance with age, since there is a higher incidence of illness with age.
4. There appears to be a long-term, significant interaction between the kind of environment in which an individual lives and works and some of the work-related physiological capacities of that individual.

Sociological Explanations of Professional Obsolescence

Social pressures are serious contributors to professional obsolescence. One of the ironies of professional life is that success often leads to obsolescence, and the greater the professional success of the individual the greater the difficulty encountered in trying to do the things that keep one professionally alive. For example, a surgeon becomes noted because of knowledge, skills, and publications in his or her particular subfield of surgery (e.g., a particular cardiovascular procedure). Recognition brings with it many kinds of positive returns: invitations to speak at professional meetings, more demand for one's professional services, higher fees, promotions, and a large number of callers who provide the most flattering of feedback. For a research professional, success can mean the kind of power that comes with command of a laboratory, the budget and staff that goes with it, and election to prestigious positions in professional associations.

Once success has been achieved, many people find it socially difficult to do the things that keep them alive professionally. They perceive a risk to their professional status in undertaking something new and different that might not succeed. Many feel embarrassment in being seen taking a class to learn some new skill or technique, such as computer programming, (particularly when they are in a position to hire the possessors of such skills). The perceptions of risk and possible embarrassment are reinforced by the social environment and by actual threat of sanctions. One noted Nobel laureate informally confided to a group of listeners that every time he thought of trying something in a quite different field from his own, everyone would look at him with shocked surprise. The common response was, "But you can't do that! You're Dr. So-and-so, the Nobel laureate!"

In the organizational situation, there are many built-in incentives to avoid risks that go with doing the things that maintain intellectual growth. It is in the short-term interests of an organization to keep a successful professional doing what he or she has already been successful at, rather than to provide new and challenging opportunities. In preparing proposals for grants or research contracts, an organization claims distinction on the basis of the successful past performance of its best professionals, and, in effect, promises that those professionals will do the same kinds of things if funded. There is little competitive advantage in suggesting that someone will be used in a field in which he or she hasn't had extensive experience. Where a very competent professional is promoted into a managerial position, he or she often cannot develop professionally without an actual loss of position and status. In a research laboratory, the successful professional who is now director finds it almost impossible ever to get to a laboratory bench. The demands of administration, of going to meetings within the organization, of participating in conferences in interesting countries throughout the world, or of being chosen for special government panels—as well as the gratification to the ego—leave little time for the growth that can come only through doing the work of the profession.

Burnout

One possible root of technological obsolescence in some professionals is so-called burnout. "Burnout" has been used as an omnibus term to include everything from serious emotional difficulties arising from work of a highly traumatic nature, to simple boredom, to the loss of "idealism" experienced by social workers on their intitial encounter with the realities of working life. Realistically, the term "burnout"—that is, the loss of the capacity to function due to an overloading of one's emotional circuits—is applicable to very few professional activities and situations. Jobs that lead to burnout are those that regularly place a professional under extremes of emotional stress or demand. Burnout, in this sense, is a problem of maintaining human resources, and personal or managerial intervention is required if the individuals engaged in such activities are to be able to function through time or to remain in their professions.

There is evidence that nurses who work with the most extreme cases of mentally deficient children or with the dying do suffer from burnout and must be frequently rotated or replaced if they are to keep working. Other victims of burnout might include reporters on the police beat, health professionals working in emergency rooms, and police in combat. There are, of course, high-stress situations in every profession when there is work to be done under difficult conditions and tough deadlines. However, these pressures occur temporarily and are seldom frequent enough or of long enough duration to be a major professional problem.

Midcareer Crisis

A common phenomenon that can be termed "midlife transition" affects a large percentage of the U.S. population. Many refer to the midlife transition experience as the "midlife crisis," or, from the work viewpoint, the "midcareer crisis." Midlife transition, whether or not seen as a crisis, is a period of personal examination and appraisal of oneself and one's situation heightened by a realization of aging and mortality. The onset of the midlife transition phenomenon comes from many different sources: graying of hair, appearance of wrinkles, significant birthdays such as the fortieth or fiftieth, and the onset of grandparenthood. A special case is the mother and housewife whose children have left home and who experiences the "empty nest syndrome." Midlife transition is a turbulent experience in which the individual takes stock of where he or she has been and is going. The individual often experiences serious discords internally and externally.

One study of adult development (Levinson & Darrow, 1978) found that approximately 80% of the men studied experienced some form of midlife crisis (there were no women in the study). Few go through the period smoothly and without crisis. In some cases the response to this period is extreme. Some respond to midlife crises by "dropping out": they change careers, go back to school, join the ministry, get divorced and remarry, even commit suicide. Most go through the experience making many kinds of adjustments. Evidence of the crisis and recovery are found in the two-peak curves of performance of scientists and engineers described above. On average, for the professional worker, the "crisis" and subsequent decline in performance occur somewhere between the ages of forty-five and fifty-five.

Adjustment and recovery typically occurs within five to seven years.

Midlife transition becomes a problem for the manager of professionals when it becomes midlife crisis and affects the ability of an individual to work at full capacity. Awareness of this period of transition helps sensitize the manager to the problems being faced by the professionals going through the experience and prepares the manager to handle its effects on work and the organization. Management can take steps to minimize the negative effects of this tumultuous period of personal transition on both the individual and the firm. By work-related actions such as assignments, changes of function, opportunities for new experiences, and feedback, managers can minimize the drop in performance associated with midlife transition (keeping it from becoming a midlife crisis) and can help the professional who is going through the transition. On a more positive note, the fact that midlife transition is a period of personal evaluation and stock-taking makes it an ideal time to work with the individual to achieve major advances in personal professional development. The act of personal stock-taking makes it a time when the individual may be most open to change.

Summary

The maintenance of human resources is important in the management of professionals. The condition and future capabilities of its professionals must be a matter of concern to managers unless the organization has a life expectancy of one project. It is obvious that professionals are the key resource in professional work and their skills and knowledge determine whether an organization will get work and whether the work is successful.

The Age Discrimination in Employment Act of 1967 and long-term demographic trends have already determined that management will have no choice but to come to grips with the issue of older professionals. The professional work force will include a growing percentage of older professionals, and it is legally difficult to fire them. Thus, management has a vested interest in making sure that the younger professional becomes the productive older professional and that the older professional remains highly productive.

From a human point of view we must be concerned with keeping professionals productive throughout their working lifetime. Employers cannot ethically justify profiting from the most productive years of individuals and then getting rid of them. From a personal point of view every professional and manager has a vital interest in staying alive intellectually and professionally. If management does not take the initiative in professional development, the individual professional ought to take charge of his or her own personal and professional development. And whatever managers do for others with regard to staying alive professionally is something that they should be doing for themselves.

MAINTAINING HUMAN RESOURCES

Each professional worker represents a sizable investment by an organization. The hard, measurable costs of hiring and orienting a professional for an organization have been estimated to be on the order of $20,000–$30,000, and the hard costs fall short of realistic total costs. The hard costs don't include management time, the time of colleagues who help orient the newcomer to the organization, and all the other elements that go into a newcomer's learning curve. Over time, the total investment in a professional's competence in terms of experience, management, formal, and informal education is very large.

It is impossible to assign a cost figure to the special competencies required to work well in an organization. Even for the professional, skilled in communications and interpersonal relationships, it still takes at least a year to reach a full-tilt level of performance. Company-related skills are an amalgam of knowing who to talk to get things done, why things are done a certain way, what the social and political relationships that go beyond the organization chart are, and all that goes into what is now called "the corporate culture"—the social, business, and political values held strongly in the organization and the acceptable boundaries of social and work behavior.

The full replacement costs for a competent, experienced, long-term professional employee are incalculable. Despite the large investments made in professional workers, and despite the fact that they are the primary resource in professional activities, organizations let their human resources run down, become technically obsolete, or burn out. With equipment, organizations are very conscious of the investment made. Equipment is accounted for, carefully tended, maintained, oiled, polished, cleaned, and, where possible, updated. Preventive maintenance is practiced to keep equipment from faulty performance or breakdown. Management would quickly reprimand or replace someone who abused the equipment. Human resources are not given the same level of care and attention.

Organizations expend much effort on "personnel" or "human resources" with a view to evoking a higher current output, but only limited efforts are expended on the maintenance of capacity through time. Despite the abundance of training and development programs offered by organizations, they are seldom taken as seriously as equipment maintenance programs. There are no well-trained, well-equipped, round-the-clock human maintenance crews ready to respond to incipient problems. There are few instances of serious, data-based preventive maintenance efforts when it comes to the work-related (as opposed to emotional) needs of human resources. Organizations are ready to deal, in a repair sense, with such problems as drug addiction, alcoholism, and emotional breakdown, but much less ready to do repair on work capabilities. The work-related capability problems labeled "obsolescence," "plateauing," and "burnout" are handled by getting rid of the individuals, by counseling them through critical performance evaluations (and zero or small pay increases), or by avoidance. The plateaued senior professional is an embarrassment to management, and a cause of discomfort: "He's been here fifteen years, and he used to do very good work. What can we do with him?"

Dimensions of the Human Resource Maintenance Problem

The problem of maintenance of professional human resources is large and growing sharply in size and importance.
The problem has economic, legal, and personal dimensions.
The marketing of professional work is first a function of quality
and ability to deliver, and second, of costs. In professional activities, the capabilities of the professional workers make the difference between success and failure and determine the competitive
position of the organization. The capabilities, experience, and
reputations of the professional people in an organization determine whether it will even be considered for research and development, design, medical, and educational work. Costs become
an issue only when the price is beyond some given threshold.

Maintaining and improving the abilities of its professionals
can make a significant difference in the productivity of an organization. In large organizations, decrements in individual performance are often not noted until they are serious. An
aggregation of minor decrements can keep an organization from
realizing its optimum performance. Managements respond
slowly to decrements in the performance of their people. Since
professional work is not a matter of discrete, measurable, daily
output, it often takes time to realize that performance has been
going down.

The legal dimension has brought the maintenance of human
resources to a new level of serious consideration. Organizations
will have more older workers in their work forces, and they
will stay longer than in the past. Consequently, it makes sense
to ensure that professionals in the work force maintain and
improve their abilities throughout their careers. The Age Discrimination in Employment Act of 1967 which extended mandatory retirement in the private sector to age 70 as of 1979
has revolutionized industrial retirement policies. Today in the
United States, managements must realize that a large percentage of all workers will continue to work beyond age 65, the
percentage of the work force in the over-65 bracket is already
increasing rapidly. It can be tougher to justify firing someone
who is over 65 than someone who is a woman or in a minority

group. When it comes to professional workers all of the problems are amplified since professional workers opt to keep working more often than others. The percentage of professional workers over age 65 is going up more rapidly than the age of other workers, and it may be tougher legally to make a case for firing a professional than a blue-collar or white-collar worker.

The demographic trends in the United States are clear. In 1955, average life expectancy was 69.6 years of age. In 1980, life expectancy had gone up to 73.6 years of age (Hacker, 1983). Between 1968 and 1980, the total number of people over 65 years of age climbed from 16,559,580 to 25,544,133, a rise of 54.3%. By the year 2000, it is estimated that the over-65 group will represent about 20% of the population. The 65+ age group will number well over 45 million by 1990, and the number of people 65 or older who are eligible to work will rise to approximately 30,000,000.

Naturally, the death rate for older people is higher, and not all of them will want to continue working. However, even with regard to death rates and voluntary work rates, the numbers are changing in directions that mean more older workers, particularly professionals, will remain in the work force. Though the death rate for those over 65 is relatively high, it is dropping. Between 1970 and 1980, the death rate for those between 65 and 74 dropped from 37 to 30 per thousand, and the death rate for those between 65 and 69 was 24.6. There has been a general assumption that most workers, given the chance to retire, would happily opt out, and the statistics tend to support that idea. In 1960, 81% of men between 60 and 64 were in the labor force, and by 1979 it was only 62%. For women the equivalent numbers were 31% and 34%. Here, too, the numbers are changing.

The numbers representing those 65 and older in the labor force before 1980 do not reflect the effects of the Age Discrimination Act which began to apply in 1979, or of the cuts in Social Security benefits for early retirees, or of the tendency for people in higher occupational levels to want to continue working. A picture of the effect the opportunity to continue working has on decisions of the older worker can be obtained from the experiences of companies that suspended mandatory retirement before the act was passed (Thompson, 1979). Sears, Roebuck suspended mandatory retirement in 1978, and, to the surprise of management, 77% of the salaried and 60.6% of the hourly workers stayed on. In 1976 Polaroid suspended mandatory retirement, and by 1978 70% decided to continue working. Note that salaried employees stayed on at a higher rate than hourly workers. There is also some indication that more productive people opt to stay on. In 1979, Polaroid's corporate retirement administrator observed that retirement is a very self-selective process. Those with health or performance problems wanted to leave. Those who were productive were likely to stay, and their absentee rate was almost half the corporate average. A survey of 3,800 top executives of major companies who had retired between 1961 and 1976 found that half continued to work: 17% at paying jobs, 11% at paid volunteer jobs, and 22% at nonpaying volunteer jobs (Wikstrom, 1978).

The human dimension has several aspects. The worker who has plateaued, to whom work is not a positive experience anymore, is a burden to the organization, has stopped growing as an individual, and is often a problem for his or her family. The plateaued worker stops contributing to others in the organization, and becomes isolated from the professional exchanges flowing through the informal social-professional circles in and outside the organization. The negative effects are cumulative and compounded. The less the individual is included in professional exchanges, the less he or she contributes, the fewer the exchanges and so on. The plateaued individual often has a negative effect on the expectations of newcomers, and tends to be the cynical counterpoint to every effort to do something new in the organization. Perhaps one of the most poignant problems facing a manager of professionals is the plateaued individual. Few start out on a plateau. The majority of workers begin with high hopes and expectations. Somewhere along the line, the expectations and hopes disappear for the plateaued worker. It is a challenge for management to keep workers from plateauing, and to renew the growth of those who have plateaued.

The phenomenon labeled "burnout" is a special aspect of the human resources maintenance problem. Burnout refers to a process in which the professional's attitudes and behavior change in negative ways in response to job stress (Cherniss, 1980). Much has been written about stress and its causes, effects, and management. There is evidence that unmanaged stress can have deleterious effects on health, and certainly health affects performance. The term "burnout" has been used widely to describe a variety of phenomena including boredom, middle-age crisis, and serious emotional exhaustion that results from working in highly stressful or depressing jobs. The subject is included here because many of the managerial considerations and actions that apply to technological obsolescence pertain to the non-physchopathological aspects of burnout.

Maintenance of professional capabilities is not just a concern for organizations that hire professionals. It is also a personal question for the individual professional and manager. Each of us is faced with the problem of keeping alive professionally and intellectually, and of finding ways to maintain a personal interest in the world of ideas and work.

What the Manager Can Do About Professional Obsolescence

Definitions of professional obsolescence vary, and some make little sense, but the underlying idea of a need to maintain professional effectiveness is sound. Serious questions are raised by the available evidence about inherent decrements of performance with age or about the physiological basis for obsolescence. The results of many studies show that a substantial amount of what we call professional obsolescence may be socially induced and managable. It is reasonable to suggest that there are many things that managements can do to prevent or even reverse what is called professional obsolescence.

In all managerial functions there are elements, from hiring and firing to retirement, that can be used to achieve and maintain the capabilities of an organization's professionals. Much of what maintains professional capabilities throughout a working career is identical with what is required to achieve high performance in the short run. A management that is aware of what is needed and what is possible for maintenance of professional capabilities throughout a working career can design its functions to serve both the short run and the long run simultaneously.

First, management must take an overall viewpoint not based on the assumption that performance declines inexorably with age and that older workers are to be tolerated, not used. Management can provide (1) good hiring that includes consideration of the long run, (2) appropriate motivation, reward, and incentive structures that reinforce work behaviors leading to high performance in the long run, (3) policies, planning, and procedures that provide diversity, (4) an environment that is lively and enriching, and (5) health maintenance programs and incentives that help assure continued high performance (and lower insurance costs).

Hiring. Management can start by hiring the kinds of people that are least likely to become professionally obsolete. Some of the clues to who is least likely to become obsolete have already been given in our discussions of hiring and information-communication behavior:

1. *Performance persists.* Individuals who are high performers tend to remain high performers, and high-performing individuals tend to take care of their own professional development. The best indication that someone will not become professionally obsolete is a past record of continuing high performance over time. In addition, a record of good personal responses to life events strongly indicate an ability to adjust to changes. Individuals who are healthy emotionally tend to remain so through life, and "adjust their personalities and values to reflect changes throughout the life cycle," (Casady, 1975).

2. *Generalists outlast specialists.* The odds are in favor of the competent generalist (with at least one area of special competence) over the competent specialist when it comes to remaining professionally useful over time. Professional obsolescence comes most disastrously when a field changes radically. Specialists can always be used as consultants, and as the profession

changes so can your repertoire of consultants. The generalist will most easily adjust to a shift in a profession.

3. *High communicators are more likely to remain current in their profession than others.* The high communicator reads more and reads more widely than others, and is constantly in communication with others in a wide variety of social-professional networks. The high communicator functions by being aware, and keeping others aware, of what is going on in his or her fields of interest.

A picture of what the individual should be like in the last part of a professional career helps us put hiring and subsequent human resource maintenance activities into perspective. By characterizing the capable, productive, lively, older individual it is possible to obtain a model to work toward with others and for oneself. Think of the most lively older professional (or just older person) you can remember: what characterized that individual? In characterizing the competent older professional you probably will include most of the following in your list:

1. *A future orientation:* looking forward to what is going to happen rather than to the past
2. *Optimism:* a positive feeling about making things work rather than a firm conviction that nothing will work
3. *Curiosity:* a strong interest in many things and in new things, and a curiosity expressed both by reading and talking to many people
4. *Humor:* an ability to laugh at things including oneself
5. *Energy and activity:* a high level of energy, and probably good health
6. *Diversity:* working and interested in a wide range of things

It would be worthwhile, at the time of hiring, to look at a potential hire and try to visualize that person in midcareer and in late career. Can that individual be seen as having, or being likely to gain the characteristics associated with the productive older professional?

The characteristics most desirable in any hire are those that have the highest probability of assuring long-term development: good past performance, a positive, optimistic outlook on life, a broad-based set of professional interests, and positive information-communication habits.

Motivation, rewards, and incentives. The formal and informal personnel feedback systems should deliberately reinforce activities that maintain professional vitality. The formal systems should be designed to reward risk-taking (or at least not to penalize the taking of risks), especially among younger professionals. If failed efforts are penalized severely, the organization will lose those it should be keeping, and reinforce the propensity to avoid new approaches among those who remain. Individuals should be reinforced in their efforts to try fields or techniques new to them.

Positive reinforcement should also be given for the information-communication behavior that enhances the individual and the organization: reading, attending conferences, taking courses, and transmitting information to others. The incentive system should include incentives that reward good professional performance with development opportunities such as study trips, courses (perhaps a chance to get an advanced degree), personal subscriptions to professional journals, professional society dues, and trips to professional conferences.

The informal feedback system is even more important than the formal system. The formal system can make explicit what the organization values. A formal review system can explicitly give points for innovative behavior or for desirable information-communication behavior. However, it is management, especially the first-line manager, that is most effective in determining how the formal system works operationally. It is the first-line manager who provides the vital, daily feedback which most affects work behavior. Making the first-line manager aware of an overall organizational interest in the long-term development of its professionals is the first step, and can be accomplished by making the maintenance function a key part of the manager's formal and informal evaluation and incentive system. Typically, first-line managers tend to restrict themselves to a short-term perspective on performance except when it comes to promotions, and it takes explicit and consistent emphasis by top management to change this perspective.

Even without the prodding of higher management and the formal evaluation system for managers, the thoughtful manager can provide informal feedback that encourages the younger professional to try new things, to read, to explore new ideas. By judicious use of work assignments, the manager can diversify the experiences of all the professionals for whom he or she is responsible. Sometimes, in providing diverse work assignments for the professionals, a manager must consciously take the risk that someone else who has been doing the kind of work assigned for a long time might do it better, on the grounds that the longer term effects will be better for both professionals.

The youngest professionals should be encouraged to develop at least one or more areas of special competence, but the professionals in their thirties should be encouraged to broaden their field of professional interests. It is critical to help the professional who is in the thirties develop a desire and ability for self-direction and self-confidence in undertaking professional risks. If professionals have not developed those abilities and feelings by the time they reach their forties, it is very difficult, if not impossible, to develop them at that time.

From a maintenance viewpoint, performance evaluation is a monitoring system for professional obsolescence that should be used to trigger managerial actions. High performers should be provided support for what they are already doing to maintain their own professional capabilities: a budget for development, an unlimited publications budget, a portion of self-determined time. The persistent low performers should be moved. If they have always been low performers they should be fired and provided with outplacement counseling. The low performer who has performed well in the past is worth taking some time to examine. In some cases, the decline in performance may be due to something in the individual's personal life that has nothing to do with work. In other cases, it may be simply a case of boredom or midlife transition. If the latter is true, low performance may be overcome by moving the individual to a different group, giving that person a new and very different assignment, or shifting him or her to an entirely different kind of function (e.g., from basic to applied research, from operational activities to analysis, from design to testing).

It is the middle performer who should receive the most maintenance effort. The middle performer has the highest propensity to shift in level of performance, and the shift can be upward or downward. The focus should be on helping those evaluated as middle performers to develop a long-term outlook on their own development. Those in their thirties should be encouraged to undertake a program of courses or to obtain an advanced degree. Most attention should be paid to the individuals who have been with the organization for three or more years. They are most likely to stay, and an investment in them is most likely to be retained by the organization.

An enriching environment. As was already pointed out, on the basis of animal experiments, an enriched environment may have positive effects on the development of higher brain functions. Extrapolating to the work situation, it can reasonably be claimed that an enriched work environment is important to the maintenance and growth of professionals. Management can enrich the work environment in many ways.

The work environment is the sum total of the physical, social, and cultural elements in the work situation to which an individual is responsive. The environment includes formal elements such as the organization's policies, administrative systems and procedures, and the organization's formal organization structure. The informal elements include the organization's culture and its informal organization. An organization's culture affects the patterns of behavior of the people in the organization, and determines the way things are done. The informal organization includes the relationships between people which fall outside the formal organization chart, and which influence what gets done and the way it gets done within the organization. Management has direct control of the formal elements in the work environment, and can have a significant influence on some of the informal elements.

It is important to develop an organizational climate that will enhance the self-confidence of the professionals and their willingness and ability to take chances professionally. Policies and procedures that penalize risk, that do not include the professional in the decision-making process, and that make it difficult to get support for anything new and different will drive away the high performers, prevent the development of risk-takers among the younger professionals, and attract and retain those who are threatened by change.

Management policies should include consideration of the long-run development of professional workers, and can be expressed in the organization's administrative systems and procedures. The most important area of policy and procedure should be concerned with encouraging and institutionalizing diversity. Diversity is achieved for the individual by diverse assignments, by having more than one project to work on at a time, by being assigned more than one function to perform, by frequent contact with many kinds of professionals, by travel, by an occasional move to a different group and location, and by a mix or alternation of administration and professional work. Procedurally, management can assure that diversity is encouraged, even required, and certainly not penalized. Some examples of ways to encourage risk-taking (new and diverse experiences) have already been discussed. Many others can be developed in areas such as job rotation, intracorporate moves, and transfers that are thoughtful rather than ham-handed.

The individual manager can do much to influence the informal elements in the office culture by the feedback provided to individuals, by the assignments made, by the people an individual is assigned to work with, by physical location of individuals, and by personal example. The personal example of managers is a primary source informing an individual about the culture of an organization. The manager who is seen reading, taking courses, attending conferences, trying out new things, and taking risks is the strongest signal the individual professional can receive. The top manager who "walks the plant" and who takes a favorable interest in new ideas can increase risk-taking in the organization, and also help the individuals to do those things that lead to personal development.

Health. Health may be the critical *sine qua non* for maintaining an individual's professional ability in the later years of a career. The most important cause of decrements in performance of the older worker is a decline in health. An organization that formally undertakes to enhance the health of its workers has taken a big step toward maintaining professional capabilities for the long run (as well as minimizing its health-related insurance burden). Fortunately, there is a widespread and growing involvement of Americans with health, and encouraging health-related programs is easier today than it once was.

Management should take active steps to encourage health maintenance and enhancement activities by its professional staff. The same kinds of incentives that have been applied to educational programs can be used: partial or complete payment of health programs, intensive health programs, incentives for not smoking and controlling weight, and providing company health facilities.

6

Creativity

A HIGH PREMIUM is placed on creativity in all the professions. It is a compliment to be called a creative scientist, lawyer, advertising person, professor, manager, or market researcher. In the design professions such as architecture, engineering, industrial design, and in the plastic arts, creativity is a prime differentiator between very good and ordinary work. Even in professions that deliver services, like the health professions, it is a compliment to be called a creative surgeon or diagnostician. Only in accounting, and a few other fields, is the term "creative" one of criticism, and only when it refers to someone who finds ways to "creatively" fix the books. Many top managements complain that they need more creativity in their organizations and specify it as something desired in a candidate for hire.

> The reasonable man adapts himself to the world, the unreasonable man adapts the world to himself, therefore, all progress depends on the unreasonable man.
>
> —George Bernard Shaw

The high value placed on creativity throughout society comes from a desire for something akin to magic. Creativity is seen as a special human power that will dissolve difficult problems, generate spectacular ideas and products, break new intellectual ground, and transform lackluster organizations into lively ones. In the popular view a creative person is one who comes up with new and different ideas, designs, theories, and works of art in ways that are not amenable to explanation.

Creativity has fascinated humans from the earliest beginnings of history. It has always been seen as something mysterious, irrational, spontaneous, intuitive. In early history, creativity was openly treated like a form of magic. At times, creativity was seen as divine, partaking of the work of the Creator. At other times, it was seen as superhuman, supernatural, and satanic, and appropriately feared. Today, after almost a hundred years of research on the subject, creativity is still seen by the majority as an infrequent, irregularly distributed, and mysterious human power. For the most part creativity and the creative person are viewed as good for society. The current worldwide infatuation with high technology is a manifestation of the positive, popular view of creativity and the closely associated terms, invention and innovation. Creativity is seen as a means for saving countries from unemployment and cities from stagnation. Corporate executives often see it as a means to increase productivity and profitability.

WHAT IS CREATIVITY?

References to creativity can be found in ancient legends, but systematic research on the subject did not begin until Sir Francis Galton undertook his studies of genius and human faculties in the latter half of the nineteenth century. Since Galton, several lines of research have been pursued on aspects of exceptional human intellectual or cognitive abilities, including creativity and intelligence, without producing general agreement on what is meant by creativity, how to measure it, or how to elicit or develop it.

Creativity has been defined in relation to various frames of reference: as a process, as a product, and as a set of human characteristics. The dictionary views creativity as the power or ability to create, to originate, or to produce. In dictionary definitions, creativity carries implications of originality and productivity. In the broad literature that discusses creativity, the term overlaps (and is often used interchangeably with) terms such as "inventiveness," "innovativeness," "productive thinking," and the act of "discovery." The literature includes contributions from psychology, philosophy, sociology, anthropology, the history of science and technology, the history of thought, economics, biography, and from the specific fields in which creativity plays a conspicuous role, such as the plastic and performing arts, scientific and engineering fields, management, and medicine.

Almost all the literature concerned with creativity differentiates the creative from the noncreative in terms of product. Considerations of creativity, particularly from the perspective of managers, must be concerned with product. A few psychologists treat creativity from the viewpoint of process and/or or the meaning of the process to the individual engaged in it. However, the latter approach precludes differentiating between two exercises of creativity.

Two individuals may have a personal experience validly identified as "creative," but one may result in a product with no redeeming features, and the other result in something beautiful, useful, and elegant. Under the influence of psychedelic drugs, a person may experience vivid, original, beautiful visions, and consider the experience as "creative." However, unless those visions result in some tangible work of art, cure, invention, design, or concept, they do not enter the world of recognized creativity, nor are they of concern to anyone beyond the individual who experienced them. The creative experience that does not result in a product is in the same class as the sound of the tree falling in the forest that no one hears.

The experiential view of creativity is also misleading in implying that all creative work results from personally dramatic experiences, including a heightened state of feeling, and that creativity cannot proceed without that feeling. In an interview, John Kenneth Galbraith, the economist and prolific author, commented that there was no difference in the quality of what he produced when he felt "inspired" and when he was just working at writing. Galbraith also commented on the fragility of academic colleagues who waited for inspiration to strike and who produced little or nothing.

In the literature concerned with creativity and creative thinking, the majority of definitions include the criteria of novelty and utility. The definitions insist on "newness," "novelty," "originality":

"new combinations of ideas and things" (Edel, 1967)

"a new association of existing elements" (Bailey, 1978)

"newness or novelty" (Rothenberg & Hausman, 1976)

"the forming of associative elements into new combinations" (Mednick, 1976)

"a response that is novel or at least statistically infrequent" (MacKinnon, 1968)

"the production of an idea, concept, creation, or discovery that is new or original to its creator" (Gregory, 1967)

There are problems with using "originality" as a criterion in the definition. If someone creates something without knowing it has already been created by someone else, can that individual be creative? The answer is, yes. There have been cases of simultaneous invention by individuals who knew nothing of each other's work. The inventions are evidence of the creativity of each of the individuals. Though one inventor may be credited with the discovery, it does not take away from the magnitude or quality of the creative effort achieved by the other.

Originality refers to something statistically infrequent. The schizophrenic who babbles incoherent sentences may be expressing something original, in the sense of its being statistically infrequent, but no one would call the babble creative. "Thus, 7,363,474 is quite an original answer to the problem 'How much is 12 + 12?' However, it is only when . . . this answer is useful that we can also call it creative" (Mednick, 1976). The chances of an original idea being useful, and thereby creative, is small.

Often managements place high hopes on creativity-enhancing programs without realizing that generating a large number of original ideas will lead to very few useful ones. A hypothetical example (from Bourne et al., 1971) may make the point. If only one out of five thousand original ideas meets the criteria for creativity, and an individual produces 20 original ideas in a typical working period, the odds are 1/250 that one of the ideas will be creative. If, by great effort, it is possible to double that individual's production of original ideas (a massive increase), the odds for generating a creative idea are still only 1/125.

Value is the second major criterion for judging creativity. Value is expressed as "utility," "satisfaction," "acceptance," "meeting requirements," "meaningfulness." Creativity is an activity with social implications, since utility implies value to someone in addition to the creator. The role of social utility in creativity is pointed out by many scholars in the field of creativity:

> "although the literal definition of the term creation does not necessarily include the attribute of value . . . the term is almost invariably used to convey value either tacitly or explicitly" (Rothenberg & Hausman, 1976)

> "useful or satisfying to its creator or someone else in some period of time" (Gregory, 1967)

> "satisfy some expressed or implied human need" (Taylor, 1961)

> "acceptable as tenable or useful or satisfying [to] a group in some point of time" (Stein, 1963)

References to time are included in definitions to take into account creative products not accepted or seen to have value for decades or even centuries after they appear. History is full of examples of works of art, music, inventions, and scientific discoveries not recognized or even noticed when first exposed to others. Some definitions make the point that humans do not create something out of nothing, and include in the concept of creativity the association or combination of existing things and ideas—an important notion when considering what it takes to do something creative.

Creativity, Invention, and Innovation

"Innovation," "invention," and "creativity" are often used interchangeably, particularly in everyday language. Among scholars in the field of creativity, "innovation" is used to define the process by which a new product or idea is introduced into use or practice. Innovation sometimes refers only to the first use of a new thing or idea. In this sense, discussions of innovation are concerned with the recognition, first use, or diffusion of an innovation, and take into account such things as entrepreneurship and marketing.

It is convenient to use "invention" to refer to the process that generates an idea, develops it, and brings it into practice. In this sense of the word, creativity is then the first step in the invention process. As Edison said, "Invention is 5% inspiration and 95% perspiration." Creativity is what Edison called "inspiration," the generation of an original, useful idea, the critical first step in the process. Invention is the process of selection of the idea to be worked on and its detailed development into producible, usable form. Innovation is the process by which the invention is first brought into use by an individual, company, or agency.

Differentiating creativity, invention, and innovation help us to see the differences in the required process elements more clearly. Creativity requires the ability to reach out to widely separated components, and to synthesize them. The creative effort does best by generating as many useful, new ideas as possible from which to select one or two to develop. The rest of the overall invention process consists of selecting the idea(s) to develop, requires convergent thinking and the ability to discard irrelevant ideas, and it includes analysis as opposed to synthesis. The rest of the invention process consists of detailed development of the idea(s) into producable, workable form, a continuous (often tedious) effort which includes the solution of a myriad of design problems, each of which may entail repeating the selection process many times at a micro level. The invention process also includes tests or trials of all the detailed parts as well as the whole, and many repetitions of the efforts.

THE WHO AND HOW OF CREATIVITY: THROUGH THE PRISM OF RESEARCH

In trying to evoke and develop creativity in an organization, managers are interested in such questions as: Can creative people be identified for the purpose of hiring? Are there valid and reliable tests that can predict who will be creative? Can creativity be developed or enhanced in employees? Are there creativity techniques that can be taught to employees that will increase creativity within the organization? What kinds of management actions help or retard creativity? What kinds of environments enhance or deter creativity? What differentiates the creative organization from those that aren't creative? Researchers on creativity have generated data that provide some answers to these managerial questions.

The questions guiding creativity research have been: Who is creative? What is the creative process? What influences the creative process? Answers to the research questions have been sought by identifying creations and their creators, by studying the characteristics of both, by inquiring into the way the creators went about their tasks, and by examining the external factors that influenced creativity. Research into questions about the creative person has been primarily carried out by psychologists, but has also attracted the interest of educators and scientists from a variety of fields who have been curious about creative people in general or creative people in a particular field. Research into questions about the creativity process has also been primarily undertaken by psychologists interested in the psychology of thinking, and also by sociologists interested in social and environmental influences on the creative process, by philosophers, and by engineers, artists, and scientists interested in teaching the process to others or adopting it for personal use.

All this research has led to the development of tests that attempt to identify creative people, techniques for enhancing creativity, and a number of findings concerning managerial and organizational factors that appear to influence the presence and quality of creativity.

The Creative Individual

Is everyone creative? When the creative individual is discussed there is often a mistaken implication that creativity is a special gift, shared by few. However, all functioning humans are creative to some extent and in some activity. To get through a single week, perhaps even a single day, of our lives each person is required to draw upon and usefully associate a multitude of previously unrelated ideas, things, and ways of acting. Think of all of the ideas published in popular magazine or newspaper columns, such as "Hints From Heloise," in which everyday people demonstrate their creativity, and remember Shapero's Second Law, "No matter how you design a system, humans make it work anyway."

Everyone is creative, but there are individuals who are demonstrably more creative than others. Managers can look to studies of creative individuals to see what characteristics they display, and the way they go about their work, to learn how to identify such people and facilitate their creativeness. In addition, the data on creative individuals help illustrate how to raise the creative level of all employees through the way they are managed, the environment they work in, and the human development activities provided.

Studies of creative individuals have been predominantly studies of professionals. The professionals studied have included scientists, architects, writers, artists, managers, mathematicians, engineers, and inventors. From the studies a composite profile of the creative individual has emerged, with some variations that reflect intrinsic differences between the professions. For example, writers are found to be more psychology-oriented, while scientists and engineers are found to prefer working with things and abstractions to working with people. Creative managers are found to be more power-oriented, practically a requirement in the profession. Creative scientists are found to have higher IQs than creative people in other professions, a reflection on the entry requirements for science. On the other hand, creative scientists perform less well than artists and writers on tests for divergent thinking, one characteristic highly associated with creativity.

From the beginnings of research on creativity, highly creative individuals have been distinguished from less creative people by their intellectual and personal characteristics. Many researchers in the field agree on several of these characteristics, though there are differences of opinion in explaining their meaning. Despite the degree of agreement, a cautionary note should be sounded. The characteristics of highly creative people have been identified after they have demonstrated creativity. There has been little success in predicting that someone who has never been creative before will be creative, on the basis of the identified characteristics alone. Prediction is weakest when based on personality characteristics. "The strength of the association between creativity and the identified personality characteristics is modest" (Parloff & Datta, 1967). There may be more predictive value in intellectual characteristics, but here too the record is not impressive. It must be remembered that it takes a high order of motivation and straightforward (not necessarily creative) intellectual capabilities to create.

Intellectual characteristics. The list of intellectual characteristics identified with highly creative individuals can be clustered under the general headings of fluency, originality, flexibility, tolerance of ambiguity, playfulness, and IQ. It is difficult, of course, to make a neat separation between the intellectual characteristics identified in the literature and those characterized as personality characteristics. Some characteristics such as "nonconformity" are cited both in terms of intellect and personality since there are scholars in the field who find that high creatives may be nonconformist in their intellectual and professional activities but not socially.

Fluency entails the ability to generate a large number of different ideas rapidly (Guilford, 1967). Creativity is the ability to come up with useful ideas, and the highly creative person is someone who has a rich flow of ideas. Fluency is associated with originality.

Originality is the quality of generating "unusual, atypical (therefore more probably new) answers to questions, responses to situation, interpretations of events" (Steiner, 1965). The combination of fluency and originality almost read like a definition of creative activity: the rapid generation of a large number of original (preferably useful) ideas.

Flexibility is the ability to move from one frame of reference and one method of approach to another. It is the ability to produce a great variety of ideas and to solve problems by using conventional or unconventional methods (Guilford, 1967). Flexibility can also be interpreted to include intellectual *nonconformity*. The highly creative person does not readily accept intellectual authorities, and is much more likely than less creative people to question conventional wisdom. Both fluency and flexibility are associated with broad interests and exposure to many ideas. The highly creative person tends to read widely, and continuously expands his or her interests and circle of acquaintances, seeking new experiences and traveling.

Tolerance of ambiguity is the ability to live, perform, and be comfortable with situations in which the questions aren't clearly defined, the methods are unfamiliar, the resources are not all in hand, and the rules are not in order. It is the ability to commit oneself to solve a problem without quite knowing how to go about it. Tolerance of ambiguity is manifested by some apparently contradictory characteristics identified with creative people: (1) an interest in contradictions along with a desire to bring order, (2) a strong drive to finish a problem, but a resistance to finishing in the latter stages of solution, and (3) a tendency to defer judgment, a liking for complexity in problems, and a drive for simplicity. A closer look at the apparent contradictions suggests that they are not as opposed as they appear at first glance. The creative person wants to create form out of chaos, simplicity out of complexity, and resists closure as the time for solution approaches because of the new possibilities revealed by the process of creation. The high creative evaluates ideas on the basis of content rather than source, and follows the idea where it leads. The high creative prefers risks that lie between the sure thing (no risk) and the lottery (high risk), and is happiest where the individual plays a part in overcoming the risk.

Playfulness and humor are hallmarks of the high creative. The high creative likes to play with ideas, enjoys combining them in unlikely ways. There is a relationship between humor and creativity. Both require that you see things out of the usual pattern. In this regard the high creative and the humorist are akin. Koestler (1964), in his masterpiece on creativity, devotes his first four chapters to the subject of humor. Koestler's description of the pattern underlying humor holds true for all creativity: "[Humor involves] perceiving a situation or event in two habitually incompatible associative contexts. This causes an abrupt transfer of the train of thought from one matrix to another governed by a different logic." The creative person is at ease with fantasy, and has the ability to regress easily into it. However, the ability to fantasize is combined with an ability to switch back to a high level of rationality (Crosby, 1968). Both flexibility and playfulness result in behavior that may appear impulsive, with quick shifts of focus and direction.

IQ, as scored on tests, has little correlation with creativity. It takes a fairly high IQ to enter a profession, but beyond that creativity and IQ are unrelated.

Left-brain, right-brain functions and differences have received much attention, particularly in the popular literature. Much research and interest have focussed in the functions and roles of the lateral halves of the brain, especially with relation to creativity. Evidence suggests that each half of the brain may house different kinds of capabilities and activities. The left brain appears to be dominant in handling language, classifying objects into standard categories, and in selecting individual objects from large mixes of objects. The right brain appears to be dominant in dealing with shapes, forms, and spatial relationships, and in recognizing patterns. Indications (as yet, not fully demonstrated) are that the left brain is the seat of analytical thinking, and the right brain is the seat of synthetic, integrative thinking. Most of the thinking identified with creativity are attributed to the right hemisphere of the brain. Spatial visualization and spatial thinking, integration, intuition, and emotion are all considered to be functions of the right hemisphere. Creativity is seen as the association or combination of widely separated items, an act of synthesizing dependent on pattern recognition and intuition, and therefore a right-brain function.

It is, therefore, believed by many that high creatives are far more right-brain–oriented than others.

The left-brain, right-brain subject has to be treated with caution (Gardner, 1982). The data are insufficient as yet to come to the sweeping conclusions being made about the brain hemisphere location of various kinds of thinking. There is also very little known about how the two hemispheres interact, something that appears vital to carrying out any function attributed to either hemisphere itself.

Personality characteristics. Researchers have characterized high creatives by a host of qualities that can be roughly described as: strong work motivation, independent, nonconformist, high energy.

Strong work motivation characterizes the highly creative person. High creatives are motivated by problems and the work at hand. They show strong curiosity and tend to be positive, enthusiastic, and optimistic about the work they are doing and the problems they are undertaking. High creatives are intrigued and captured by problems, and are more likely to be motivated by the appeal of a problem than by an appeal based on the needs of the organization. It is hard to think of someone consistently generating creative solutions without a strong interest in the problems being addressed and a positive or optimistic feeling about the chances for solution. They get more immersed in the project than others, and are apt to work longer and harder without any external pressures or incentives (Steiner, 1965). They are more likely to express a positive interest in the intrinsic challenge of the job than in such extrinsic incentives as salary and status.

Independence and autonomy are attributed to high creatives by all writers on the subject. High creatives have their own standards and are less concerned with what others think or of making a good impression on others when it comes to their work. Along with an independent, internal set of standards goes a strong sense of self-acceptance that is often seen by others as self-assertiveness. High creatives are strongly self-disciplined and display self-confidence in attacking new and unfamiliar problems. In the discussion of the high creatives' tolerance of ambiguity it was pointed out that they are able to commit themselves to a problem without knowing yet how to solve it. The high creative is at the opposite pole from the person whose immediate response is, "It won't work! It can't be done."

Often, to the chagrin of managers and co-workers, high creatives tend to think more in terms of their profession than of the organization. They have been described as more "cosmopolitan" than their colleagues. "Cosmopolitan" is used as the opposite of "provincial": meaning that the high creatives are more at ease in a larger variety of contexts and organizations than others. Again, it is almost axiomatic that creating something new requires independence of thought and an ability to swim against the tide.

Nonconformity, both intellectually and personally, appears to be a central characteristic of high creatives. Part of the nonconformist characterization stems from the high creative's unconcern with making a good impression on others. They tend to belong to fewer organizations than others in their profession. High creatives often see themselves as "different."

Nonconformity raises two issues. Is bizarre behavior the hallmark of the highly creative person? How can nonconformity coexist with self-discipline? Not many people who are bizarre are judged to be creative, and not many creative people act in bizarre ways. The nonconformity identified with highly creative people does not mean nonconformity in all aspects of life. (Also, highly creative people are not creative in all aspects of their lives.) Creative people are nonconformist in their ideas and work, but not necessarily in their social lives. Creative scientists are usually not social nonconformists. Adolescents identified as high creatives in science were found to exercise self-discipline and to be reasonably circumspect in dealings with others (Parloff & Datta, 1967).

Nonconformity and self-discipline are not necessarily antagonists. Creative people are strongly goal-oriented, and to achieve their goals they must exercise much self-discipline. High creatives are known to resist closure as they continue to see new possibilities as their work unfolds, though typically they also feel a strong desire to finish the work they start.

Creativity is a social activity in the sense that its results must be appreciated by someone besides the creator. To be judged creative, an idea, invention, design, book, or work of art must meet the test of acceptance by others at some period of time. In professional fields that depend on working with others and where acceptance of the product depends on others, social nonconformity can prevent the creation from full acceptance in the marketplace. There is an historic tradition in literature, music, and the plastic arts of creative people who are social nonconformists. These are fields where the creative person works alone and is often not recognized or appreciated in his or her lifetime. In other professions, such as science, engineering, architecture, and medicine, one is almost always required to work with colleagues and clients to realize one's creation, and social nonconformity can get in the way.

Nevertheless, creative professionals have characteristics, and often behave in ways, that do not conform with the norms of behavior in most large, bureaucratic organizations. They are nonconformist, they are playful, they are independent. In a study of highly creative vs. high IQ students it was found that both parents and teachers preferred the high IQ students to the high creatives, because they were more apt to want to please parents and teachers. The high creatives, with their humor, independence, nonconformity, and playfulness tended to make parents and teachers uneasy. In organizational life, the intelligent, but conforming, professional keeps management happy, does a good job, and doesn't rock the boat. The high creatives among the employees will tend to make most managers a bit uncomfortable. They will tend to be irreverent and often will be the sources of jokes about the organization and management. They will be irreverent towards company procedures, and will be subject to the charge of not showing the proper amount of "loyalty" (Getzels & Jackson, 1962).

High energy also characterizes the high creative. Several researchers depict the high creative as having great drive, and as being "quick." Whether the perceived high levels of energy result from great motivation or physiological inheritance is not clear. One manifestation of the high creative's level of energy is a tendency to work on several projects at once.

Predicting Creativity

From the beginning, much research on creativity has focussed on developing ways of predicting who will demonstrate high creativity in the future. One approach, based on biographical and autobiographical studies of individuals with demonstrated high creativity, attempts to develop predictive profiles. Included among the profile methods is factor analysis. Other attempts have produced psychometric instruments to measure intellectual capabilities considered by the researcher as central to creativity. Most of the latter have measured divergent thinking. Despite several decades of research effort on creativity and highly creative individuals, there is as yet no profile or test that reliably predicts who will be highly creative in the future. Efforts to develop tests to predict later creativity in students have borne little result. Longitudinal studies of the predictive strength of divergent-thinking tests given to students have been disappointing (Howieson, 1981; Kogan, 1974). So far, the only good indication that an individual will be highly creative in the future has been demonstrated high creativity in the past. (See box on Edison's test.)

The Environment for Creativity

Two aspects of the environment for creativity have been examined by researchers: (1) the kinds of familial and educational environments in childhood that lead to creativity in adulthood, and (2) the kinds of immediate, organizational, and physical environments associated with high creativity. The effect of childhood environments in subsequent creativity is of special interest to educators and psychologists (and concerned parents), though of little utility for managers. One finding worth noting, however, was that high creatives, unlike those with high IQs, came from families in which parents put little stress on grades (Getzels & Jackson, 1962). It should also be noted, however, that many of the prescriptions for encouraging creative development in children are at odds with the way creative geniuses in the past were raised.

The manager of professionals is concerned with organiza-

THOMAS EDISON'S TEST FOR APPLICANTS
FOR JOBS IN HIS LABORATORY

A small controversy was created in 1921 by the publication of questions used by Thomas Edison as a test of applicants for positions in his laboratory. According to reports in the *New York Times*, the information about the test was provided by two young men who had taken the test and flunked, but who demonstrated phenomenal memories by reconstructing 146 questions which Edison refused to provide. At one testing of six hundred applicants only twenty-seven were marked eligible, and according to Edison the rest failed, "most of them miserably." Edison was also quoted to the effect that "college men are amazingly ignorant." The *Times* articles raised a flurry of responses in *Harper's Magazine, The Literary Digest,* and *Current Opinion,* which reported the results of research on answers to the questions showing learned disagreements about the answers to the questions and questioned the validity of the questionnaire as a means for identifying inventive people.

According to the *Times* sources and experts, some of Edison's questions and answers were the following:

What city and country produce the finest china?
Some said Limoges, France, some said Sevres, France, some said Dresden, Germany, and some said Copenhagen, Denmark.

tional environments associated with high creativity and how they might be generated. Most of the organizational characteristics that appear to enhance creativity relate to the characteristics attributed to highly creative individuals (Steiner, 1965). For example, since nonconformity in both thought and action characterizes high creatives, the organization that is tolerant of a large variety of deviance from the norm is more likely to enhance creativity. It is not surprising to find many "high tech" companies, architectural firms, advertising organizations, and academic faculties are marked by unconventional dress and little rigidity concerning hours of work.

What country consumed the most tea before the war?
   (World War I) Russia.
Where do we get prunes from?
   Prunes are grown in the Santa Clara Valley and elsewhere.
Who was Bessemer and what did he do?
   An English engineer. He invented the process for making
   steel by taking the carbon out of molten iron by the air-
   blast.

The questions included many about famous historical figures, about
physical and economic geography, about science, and about inventions:

Where is Korea?
From where do we import figs?
Who was Bolivar?
Who was Plutarch?
What is the speed of sound?
What causes the tides?
Who invented the cotton gin?
How is window glass made?
What is porcelain?

Many characteristics of creative organizations (Steiner,
1965) are identical with those recommended in other chapters.
They include the following:

Open channels of communications are maintained.
Contacts with outside sources are encouraged.
Nonspecialists are assigned to problems.
Ideas are evaluated on their merits rather than on the status
   of their originator.
Management encourages experiments with new ideas rather
   than making "rational" prejudgments.

Decentralization is practiced.
Much autonomy is allowed professional employees.
Management is tolerant of risk-taking.
The organization is not run tightly or rigidly.
Participative decision making is encouraged.
Employees have fun.

THE PROCESS OF CREATING

Each individual develops a unique approach to the act of creation. Biographies of creative geniuses are replete with descriptions of seemingly ludicrous conditions insisted upon by great creators. "Schiller seems to have depended on the smell of decomposing apples which he habitually kept concealed in his desk! . . . Kipling reports . . . [an] inability to write creatively with a lead pencil. . . . [He] seemed to demand the blackest ink, all blue-blacks being 'an abomination' to his creative tendencies. . . . At certain precise times of the day Kant worked in bed. There he . . . had some intellectual dependence upon the tactile stimulation provided by the blankets, which were arranged round him in a highly original way invented by himself" (McKellar, 1957).

In spite of the apparent uniqueness of the creative process in each individual and the idiosyncratic patterns followed by many creative individuals, studies of the process are in fair agreement that it follows a recognizable overall pattern. The creative process has been variously described, but most descriptions include a series of steps, varying in number, that can be subsumed within the following four steps: (1) preparation, (2) incubation, (3) illumination, and (4) verification.

Preparation

The creative process begins with a problem perceived or experienced. Whenever humans have a problem, and don't know how to solve it by direct action, they resort to thinking, problem-solving, and creativity. The problems that lead to creative responses arise from many sources. They can be thrust upon one or assigned from the outside, be perceived as a threat or opportunity, be encountered, or be sought out because humans are dreaming, restless creatures who enjoy the creative process. Once a problem is perceived, the creative process begins.

Popular writings on creativity feature the dramatic insight, the lightning-like flash of recognition leading to a creative solution. However, research shows that the conscious "creative" moment comes only after intensive preparation and a period of subconscious incubation. Louis Pasteur put it succinctly: "Chance only favors the prepared mind." Helmholz, the great physiologist, described his own creative process: "It was always necessary, first of all, that I should have turned my problem over on all sides to such an extent that I had all its angles and complexities 'in my head' and could run through them freely without writing" (McKellar, 1957). In a study of highly productive inventors, Rossman (1964) found that they all started the process by "soaking themselves in the problem." Though Rossman reports that some inventors reviewed all previous efforts to solve the problem and others avoided being influenced by previous attempts, all spent time thoroughly exploring the problem to be solved.

The preparation process can include literature searches, talking to many people about aspects of the problem, experimentation, and doodling. Sometimes the preparation process can appear as unplanned, unfocused meandering through a variety of materials. McKellar (1957) considers it as almost a form of "overlearning" to the point where some of the materials become "automatic" in one's consciousness. The gathering of information is a critical part of the process in which the individual examines the materials critically, but not negatively. The creative process requires discriminating criticism that does not reject, but builds upon the materials examined.

Incubation

Incubation is a process that goes on below the level of consciousness. It cannot be commanded. Incubation appears to be a gestation period in which the process goes on subsconsciously, and it works best when the individual is inactive with regard to the problem or working on something else. A passage of time, vital to the process, varies with the problem and individual (McKellar, 1957). The philosopher Nietzsche spoke of a period of eighteen months, and the poetess Amy Lowell spoke of six months. It can be a period of frustration for the individual working against a deadline, for it cannot be pushed or rushed. It is a period when apparently nothing is happening.

One soaks oneself in the problem and then waits. The passage of time is often accomplished by sleep. It is as if sleep provides the time and the opportunity to abandon consciousness of the problem and let the unconscious work. Some great creative discoveries have surfaced in sleep. Kekulé, discoverer of the benzene ring, one of the most important and original discoveries in organic chemistry, realized his discovery as the result of a dream of the image of a snake that seized hold of its own tail. Many of Descartes' basic notions of analytical geometry formed in his dreams. Everyone has had the experience of "fighting" a problem to an impasse, and having the solution suddenly crystallize while visiting with friends or discussing other things. The need for a period of incubation may explain why professionals who work on more than one project at a time are more productive than others. Having more than one project permits a person to switch to another project when apparently at an impasse. Switching from one project to another permits the first project to incubate until it is ready, while one is still doing something productive.

The incubation process is recognized but not understood. One plausible explanation is that it is a period in which the mind tests different asociations, matches different frames of reference and different conceptual elements to see if they make sense. This explantion fits with the most accepted view of creativity as a process of association.

Probably the most widely held psychological conception is that creativity is the ability to call up and make new and useful combinations out of divergent bits of stored information (Guilford, 1964). The more creative the individual the greater the ability to synthesize remote bits of information. The likelihood of a solution being creative is a function of the number and uncommoness of associative elements an individual brings together (Mednick, 1962). The latter notion has been incorporated into a test for creative ability, The Remote Associations test (Mednick & Mednick, 1964). The test taker is asked to "make sense" out of each of thirty sets of three, not obviously related, terms by providing a fourth term related to them (e.g., the fourth term related to "cookies," "sixteen," and "heart" would be "sweet"). Another associationist view is Koestler's "bisociation of matrices," expressed by the metaphor of creativity as a "dumping together on the floor the contents of different drawers in one's mind" (Koestler, 1964).

Illumination

The Gestalt psychologists refer to illumination as the "aha!" phenomenon. It is that sudden insight, that flash of understanding, in which the solution appears. The mathematician Polya describes it as entering an unfamiliar room in the dark, and stumbling around, falling over pieces of furniture, looking for the light switch. When the switch is found and activated, everything falls into place. All historic examples of the incubation process end with that moment of illumination.

Verification

After the exhilaration of illumination comes the tedious, time-consuming stage of verification. The creative idea must pass the tests of validity, reality, utility, realizability, costs, time, and acceptance in the marketplace.

CREATIVITY FROM THE VIEWPOINT OF THE MANAGER

Can anything systematic be done to increase creativity in individuals and in an organization? Does management really want creativity and the somewhat less controlled conditions necessary to foster it?

To individuals, more creativity carries an implication of special, personally gratifying experiences. To managers, more creativity means new ideas, inventions, and solutions that will do wonderful things for the organization in the marketplace. Few, however, have thought through the consequences of having more creative people and of allowing the conditions that enhance creative behavior in their organizations.

Can Anything Be Done to Increase Creativity?

Trying to answer the converse of the question, "Can anything be done to increase creativity?" quickly illustrates how much is generally known about conditions for creativity. Pose the question "Can anything be done to kill creativity in an individual or an organization?" and the mind immediately fills with answers:

Discourage and penalize risk-taking.
Discourage and ridicule new ideas.
Reject and discourage attempts to try unusual methods.
Make sure all communications follow formal organizational
    lines and all employees cover themselves.
Discourage reading and communications with people out-
    side the immediate organization.
Discourage nonconformity of any kind.
Discourage joking and humor.
Provide no recognition.
Provide no resources.

We easily intuit what it takes to minimize creative behavior, which suggests that it must be possible to improve creativity or, at least, to minimize barriers to creativity. The available information strongly indicates that it is possible to improve one's own creativity and the creativity of employees. It is possible to increase the creative activities and products of an organization. Increasing creativity in an organization is achievable, but it takes a lot more effort than preventing it from occurring. Continuity and stability are important attributes in society, and, of necessity, the dice are loaded against divergence and change.

Does Management Really Want to Live with More Creativity in the Organization?

Highly creative people are attracted by the work, by the problem being worked on, which is good from an organizational viewpoint, but they don't respond in satisfactory ways to the political or organizational constraints that are involved in every problem. Creative people are nonconformists. They are jokers. They have little reverence for authority or procedures. They are short on apparent "loyalty" to the organizations they work for. They don't respond to the kinds of incentives that stir others. They are not moved by status. High creatives don't seem to care about what others think, and they don't easily become part of a general consensus. (Could a preference for consensus management be why the Japanese have recently expressed concern about a lack of creativity in Japan?) In short, creative people can make most managers very uncomfortable. As was stated above teachers and even parents were far more comfortable with students and children with high IQs than with those who were highly creative.

A case can be always made for creativity, but managers should carefully and honestly think about whether they truly need more creativity and can live with it. If successful at hiring and retaining high creatives, and at generating the conditions needed to keep them creative, management may be creating conditions that make it difficult for its own natural style of doing things. New methods, processes and products can be purchased, copied, and stolen. According to one ironic maxim, it doesn't pay to be first—pioneers get killed. Some years ago, the head of a metal machining company producing thousands of metal fasteners picked through his catalog and fondly indicated product after product that had been invented by other companies. "You know," he said, "we don't know anything about managing creative people, but we're very, very good at designing around other people's designs. What we're really competent at is production and marketing, and we beat the hell out of the creative companies. I can't wait for their next products." Cynical? Perhaps, but it highlights the questions raised here. Many can benefit from the creativity of a few, and there are industries, companies, and fields where creativity is far less needed than in others.

On the Road to More Creativity

If desired, creativity can be consciously and systematically enhanced in an organization through hiring, motivation, organization, and management actions.

Hiring. The number of highly creative people in an organization can be increased by a hiring policy that deliberately attempts to identify, locate, and hire them. The only valid and reliable way to identify individuals with a high probability of future creative performance is through evidence of past creative performance. The more recent and continuous the past creative performance, the more likely there will be future creative performance.

It is the convention in some professional fields to come to an employment interview with evidence of past creative performance. Architects, artists, advertising professionals, writers, composers, and reporters come to an interview with portfolios of their work. Even where portfolio evidence is presented, questions remain in the mind of the interviewer. A newspaper editor may wonder whether the folio of articles submitted by a candidate for a position as reporter represents the abilities of the reporter or of his or her editor.

Where examples of a professional's work are not as easily demonstrated as in the arts and architecture, the task of determining past creative performance is harder. It is difficult to tease out evidence of the individual creative contributions of an engineer or scientist who has worked on a project that employed scores or hundreds of professionals. How can the creative performance of a teacher or accountant be ascertained? One way to tackle the problem is to put the questions directly to the individual: "What are the most creative things you have done on the job in the past three years? What are the most creative things you have ever done?" Similar questions about the individual's work can be asked of others who are familiar with it. In some fields patents, in others publications, may serve the purpose, though they should be examined for their content.

Tests, profiles of traits, and checklists are neither valid nor reliable. No available test can determine who will perform creatively in the future with any reliability. (One may be tempted to follow the example of the author who tried to hire on the basis of the apparent relationship between a good sense of humor and creativity. The rationale was, "If they don't turn out to be creative, at least they'll be a barrel of laughs.")

Motivation. Creative behavior can be maintained and enhanced through incentives that reward creative output and encourage risk-taking, and the use of new methods, processes, and materials. For those who are already highly creative, incentives can maintain and encourage their creative efforts and help retain them in the organization. For other professionals, incentives and positive feedback from management can encourage them to overcome some of the natural blocks to creativity and to take more risks and be more curious. As with any other desired behavior, feedback from management, the performance evaluation system, and the example of management can help stimulate creativity. If a manager smiles on "far out" ideas when they are ventured, lets them be tried (even when he or she is personally sure they won't work), and will even express some extravagant ideas himself, others may feel freer to think and act creatively.

Providing the necessaries. The availability of resources for initial creative efforts is a powerful indicator of management support for creative activities. The resources required to give an idea a preliminary investigation are seldom of any magnitude. Direct provision of resources, or turning a blind and benevolent eye on the inevitable "bootlegging" of an unauthorized project, both serve the purpose of support for creative experimentation. Providing resources for preliminary explorations of ideas without requiring exhaustive justification is a form of intellectual overhead and should be treated as such, formally or informally. (Remember that time is one of the most important resources required for creative activities.)

Some boost to creativity can be obtained through educational programs, though management should be wary of "patented" techniques. All creativity-enhancing techniques have some limited value in terms of stirring up new ideas for a short time. An inherent limitation in almost all of the techniques is that they purport to provide *the* way to the generation of creative ideas or to problem solving. The overall process follows a broad general pattern, but individuals must find their own personal approach.

Managing. Managers should assign tough deadlines but stay out of the operating details of a project. There is no conflict between a deadline and creativity. Creative people resist closure because they see new possibilities as the project unfolds. For all the complaints, deadlines are necessary. Without deadlines few creative projects would ever finish.

Both productivity and creativity can be enhanced by assigning more than one project to a professional. Not all the projects have to be of equal weight, or size, or value. The ability to switch to a second project and let the first project incubate in the subconscious is important to creativity. With only one project and a tough deadline, there is a tendency to try to force the project at times when it can't be forced. Having other projects provides a legitimate (forgivable) and productive way to back off from a stymied project when a pause is needed.

At the beginning of a project, managers might ask for two distinctly different solutions to a problem, two design approaches, two different experimental treatments. This is best done at the conceptual design stage before it is necessary to commit large amounts of time or resources to elaborate the solution.

New projects need fresh, unchanneled thinking. Managers might make up project groups to include people of different backgrounds, and refrain from always assigning projects to the individuals who have done that kind of work before and are apparently most suited to it.

Each professional's assignments should provide diversity for that individual. And highly productive groups of five or more years duration should be made more diverse through the addition of new people and by making certain that the individuals in the group get occasional assignments to work with other groups.

Organization. Organizational mechanisms to assure that new ideas don't get turned down for the wrong reasons (such as middle-management cautiousness) are important. One company set up a new products committee to which any employee, and not just professionals, could submit ideas. The committee, made up of senior scientists, product development people, and a patent lawyer, investigated and discussed each idea and wrote up a decision stating why the idea was accepted, rejected, or recommended for more research. By taking a positive and encouraging stance the company developed a strong flow of ideas from throughout the organization.

There should be a legitimate (nonthreatening) means for taking an idea up the management line if it is rejected by first-line management. The means may be a new product committee, of the type described above, or a procedure for periodic review of ideas people feel strongly about. After many attempts to correlate creativity with personal characteristics, GE found that a key variable was the ability not to be dissuaded from their intuitions. The former director of technical systems and materials Jerome Suran believes that high creatives are stubborn types, "because you don't get past the first level of management in a big company unless you feel strongly about your ideas" (Cullem, 1981).

A periodic review of organizational procedures and forms, with a view to identifying and removing those that cannot pass a test of necessity, is often a good idea. Too many required administrative procedures and forms sop up time and energy and impede creative activity. Procedures and forms are pervasive forces for conformity, and the more there are, the less space and time is left for nonconforming, creative thought and effort. Professional organizations should follow the role that for every procedure or form that is added, at least one should be removed.

A Little Bit of Theory About Motivation

THEORIES ABOUT WORK MOTIVATION provide frameworks that can help a manager understand the kinds of personnel actions and incentives that might be appropriate at different times.

McGREGOR'S THEORY X AND THEORY Y

McGregor pointed out the belief systems of a manager with regard to subordinates has an effect on the behavior of those subordinates. He illustrated his theory with two opposite management belief systems he labeled Theory X and Theory Y.

Theory X is typical of approaches to management current in factories at the turn of the century. Theory X represents an authoritarian viewpoint characterized by the following assumptions about humans:

1. The average human has an inherent dislike of work, and will avoid it if possible.

2. Because of an inherent dislike of work, most people have to be coerced, controlled, directed, and threatened with punishment to get them to put forth adequate effort to achieve organizational goals.
3. The average person prefers to be directed, wishes to avoid responsibility, has relatively little ambition, and wants security above all.

Theory Y is characterized by a very different set of assumptions about humans:

1. The expenditure of physical and mental effort in work is as natural as play or rest.
2. External control and the threat of punishment are not the only means for bringing about effort toward organizational objectives. Humans will exercise self-direction and self-control in the service of objectives to which they are committed.
3. Commitment to objectives is a function of the rewards associated with achievement.
4. The average human learns, under proper conditions, not only to accept but to seek responsibility.
5. The capacity to exercise a relatively high degree of imagination, ingenuity, and creativity in the solution of organizational problems is widely, not narrowly, distributed in the population.
6. Under the conditions of modern industrial life, the intellectual potentialities of the average human being are only partially used.

A Theory X management depends heavily on direction from above, detailed procedures for doing work, and does not permit much decision-making responsibility among employees. Theory X management is characterized by conformity, mistrust, and antagonism, and depends heavily on the carrot-and-stick approach to motivation.

A Theory Y management takes a far more participative approach. Theory Y management is marked by delegation of authority, increasing variety of activities and responsibilities, and by efforts to improve the free flow of communications within the organization. Theory Y puts responsibility for the work performance of employees squarely on the shoulders of management. If employees are lazy, uncreative, difficult to deal with, it is the responsbility of management.

MASLOW'S HIERARCHY OF NEEDS

Maslow's theory postulates that humans have basic needs and are motivated to act to satisfy those needs. Once people satisfy a given need, it will no longer have motivating power until it is once again unsatisfied. Further, Maslow holds that there is a basic needs hierarchy, and that each lower set of needs in the hierarchy must be satisfied before the next set will act as a motivator. When someone is unsatisfied at the physiological level, higher order levels of need are not as important. Someone suffering from hunger will not be motivated by incentives based on recognition. Maslow's hierarchy of basic human needs starting from the most basic are:

1. Physiological needs: hunger, thirst, air, shelter, sex
2. Safety needs: security, freedom from threats, a minimum level of predictability
3. Social needs: friendship, acceptance by peers, affection
4. Esteem needs: respect, recognition beyond peer acceptance, status, prestige
5. Self-actualization: self-fulfillment, realization of one's full potential, and growth

In the work situation physiological needs include a salary and basic working conditions. Safety needs include job security, fringe benefits such as insurance and medical coverage, and regular salary increases. Social needs include personal professional relationships, the compatibility of one's work group, and treatment by one's supervisor. Esteem needs concern job titles, recognition by one's supervisor and peers, promotion, adequate pay compared to others, merit pay increases, and awards. Self-actualization needs include the chance to express creativity and to try challenging new kinds of work.

Maslow's theory provides a useful way to look at practical

aspects of employee motivation, and at the kinds of incentives to be considered for different occupational levels and different individuals.

The hierarchy of needs suggests a progression of incentives effective at different stages of a professional career. To the newly graduated professional, safety needs are important. The young professional will tend to be more concerned with salary and housing. In hard economic times there will be a stronger interest in getting some assurance about job security. It is important to understand this at the time of hiring, and to provide the kinds of responses that reflect this understanding.

With time, safety needs are satisfied. Love or social needs come to the fore. The professional is integrated into the organization and establishes personal and professional ties with colleagues on the job. The approval and friendship of colleagues are needed, and the alert manager recognizes the need for compatible working groups. The quality of supervision is an important ingredient in satisfying the social needs of the professional.

As the individual develops professionally through time, the need for esteem replaces the need for social acceptance. Recognition of professional achievement becomes very important. Promotions, awards, and merit pay increases are the incentives that are most effective at this level. The opportunity to participate in professional organizations with the attendant election to positions of responsibility is an appropriate incentive, as is formal recognition by the organization. It is useful for management to establish awards for professional activities given by peers and management.

Perhaps the most difficult level for management to deal with is that of self-actualization. This is the level where the professional feels a need to learn and try new experiences. Self-actualization needs are most prominent at the height of the career of a successful professional who has established a reputation for expertise in particular areas and has been promoted to a position of responsibility level. It is difficult for both the individual and management to encourage ventures into new fields. For the individual there is risk, though the need for something different is strongly felt. Management faces the possibility of foregoing a known professional output. It is important for management to institutionalize ways to allow its most proven and valuable professionals to try something new.

THE TWO-FACTOR THEORY OF HERZBERG AND ASSOCIATES

Herzberg's theory states that there are two separate states of employee feeling: one that goes from strong dissatisfaction to no dissatisfaction, and one that goes from nonsatisfaction to strong satisfaction. The two states are not continuous and are assymetrical. Dissatisfaction is not the opposite of satisfaction. The opposite of satisfaction is nonsatisfaction, and the opposite of dissatisfaction is nondissatisfaction.

Removal of whatever factors cause dissatisfaction shifts the employee to a condition of no dissatisfaction, but it does not lead to satisfaction. Herzberg refers to the actions to remove dissatisfiers as "hygiene" and calls dissatisfiers "hygiene factors": necessary, like brushing teeth, they do not lead to satisfaction. Another set of factors contributes to satisfaction, and Herzberg designates them as "motivators." Dissatisfiers or demotivators have to be taken into account and removed before motivators can take full effect.

Demotivators include the following in descending order of importance: company policy and administration, supervision and relationships with supervisors, work conditions, salary, relationships with peers, personal life, relationships with subordinates, status, and security. Of course, the situation is not just black and white. According to Herzberg's studies, the "demotivators" account for 69% of job dissatisfaction and only 19% of job satisfaction.

Motivators or satisfiers include the following in descending order of importance: achievement, recognition, the work itself, responsibility, advancement, and growth. The absence of motivators can contribute to dissatisfaction as well. Being deprived of a chance for achievement, for recognition for responsibility, or for advancement are causes for dissatisfaction and are demotivating. Nevertheless, according to Herzberg, the "motivators" account for 81% of job satisfaction and 31% of dissatisfaction.

Ask any group of professionals (or managers) to cite the most satisfying and most dissatisfying work experiences of the last six months. The largest number of dissatisfers will be concerned with company policies and administration, ranging from the way the company assigns offices and parking places and handles expense vouchers, to its policies on promotion. Professionals are also often sensitive to items considered incompatible with their status, such as a requirement to punch a time clock, a rigid monitoring of working hours, with no allowance for individual schedules of work, or over-bureaucratic policies on obtaining technical books.

Most satisfying experiences have to do with achievements: "I brought the project in on time in spite of an inadequate budget" or "I cracked a problem that everyone thought couldn't be done." Recognition is a frequent source of satisfaction, as is pleasure in the work itself.

The theory suggests that before you can develop an effective approach to motivating the employee, you must first take care of the hygiene factors. Efforts to motivate will not work or work well if company policies and administration, supervision, work conditions, salary, and security are bad or insufficient. It would be useful to audit the demotivators in one's organization before embarking on an ambitious program of incentives.

Items that demotivate should not be considered incentives. An increase in health benefits will be gladly accepted but will not motivate. (It is unlikely that a professional would boast to a colleague at a professional meeting about the "great" health plan in his organization.) A program for motivating professional employees must use incentives that give the individual a chance for achievement, recognition, interesting work, responsibility, advancement (which is another form of recognition), and personal growth. Enhancement of the motivators in the work situation will generate satisfaction and positive motivation.

A Spectrum of Techniques for Overcoming Perceptual Barriers to Creativity

TECHNIQUES to overcome perceptual barriers to creativity are designed to force individuals to change the way they perceive a problem and its elements, to shift the elements into different frames of reference, or to stretch the abilities to associate diverse elements.

ANALOGIES

Historically, the most prevalent and most powerful creativity "technique" is the use of analogies. An analogy is a resemblance in form or function between two things that are essentially different. A current widely used analogy is that of the computer as a brain. When the computer is considered as a brain we attribute to it, and therefore design into it, brainlike functions.

Mathematics

Some recommend that mathematics be used instead of verbal analogies. Mathematics is the queen of analogies. When an equation or a mathematical model is constructed, it is intended to be a mathematical analogue of some physical, behavioral, or social phenomena. In science or engineering, the equation $y = ax + b$ represents a linear relationship between two physical, social, or behaviorial entities, y, and x. It is more convenient to manipulate the equation than the entities and thus to "create" new perceptions of what might be understood about or done with those entities.

Physical and Biological Analogies

Probably the first analogies used by humans were physical and biological analogies. Observing nature, primitive humans observed the turtle and noted that its shell provided it with protection. The thought must have occurred that analogous protection could be provided for humans: in a creative flash the shield was invented, possibly using the shell of the turtle.

CHANGING THE FRAME OF REFERENCE

By changing the frame of reference in which a problem has been stated, an individual is able to see the problem in a different light, gain new insights, and see new elements and potential associations.

Lateral Thinking

De Bono (1970) differentiates two kinds of thinking, "vertical thinking" and "lateral thinking." Vertical thinking takes a known pattern and extends and develops it. Lateral thinking tries to restructure the pattern by putting its parts together in different ways. Lateral thinking is not so much a technique as a way of thinking that goes about deliberately seeking other ways to state the problem, or to restructure the patterns. It is a way of trying to release information that might be hidden by the normal ways problems are stated.

Synectics

"Synectics" is a technique that uses analogies and metaphors in a systematic way to change the frame of reference in which the problem is perceived (Gordon (1961). The initial problem is restated and looked at variously through the use of analogies and metaphors. The kinds of analogies used include an effort personally to identify with the problem. The personal analogy approach is one in which the individual tries to project himself or herself into the midst of the problem.

Forced Associations

A number of techniques build upon the idea of the association of unlikely elements, and upon the great power of association present in all humans. The techniques vary from ways of deliberately associating selected and structured elements to ways of stimulating creativity by making deliberate random associations.

Matrices

A two-dimensional or three-dimensional matrix using problem and solution attributes as its headings is a convenient tool for examining each intersection of columns and rows, one at a time. By examining each of the intersections in the matrix, the individual is forced to consider a great number of associations that suggest problem and solution possibilities that would not otherwise be thought of. One approach to the use of matrices for creativity purposes is that of Zwicky (1969), the noted astrophysicist, who called his matrix the "morphological manifold" or the "morphological box." Zwicky's morphological matrix used such problem attributes as materials, functions, and media as headings for rows and columns, and then examined the intersections to see what they suggested.

Random Associations

The associative capabilities of the human mind are so great that, bringing two randomly selected elements together, most people can make sense of them. Creativity techniques using random associations are good ways of breaking the perceptual set of one's mind and stretching one's imaginative horizon. One of the simplest ways of using random associations is to find a word randomly, using any book or a dictionary, and to then associate that word with the problem being addressed.

OVERCOMING SOCIAL AND EMOTIONAL BLOCKS

Beginning with adolescence, the individual feels social pressure to conform with accepted norms of thought and action. Some authorities believe that all children start out with a high potential for creativity, but that much of the potential is suppressed in adolescence, a period of great conformity. Consequently, a major barrier to creativity is the pressure to conform and the individual's fear of appearing a fool in front of supervisors and collegues. A number of creativity techniques are designed to overcome such social and emotional blocks as well as to break perceptual habits.

Brainstorming

The best known of the creativity techniques used to overcome social and emotional barriers is known as brainstorming. Brainstorming is based on four operating rules (Osborne, 1963; Stein, 1975): (1) criticism is ruled out, (2) freewheeling is welcomed, (3) quantity is desirable, and (4) combination and improvement are sought. The operating rules are designed to encourage deferment of judgment—to encourage maximum stretching of the imagination by delaying analytical, judgmental braking on the mind, and to make sure that individuals are encouraged to express "crazy" ideas without fear of negative social judgment. Quantity is encouraged on the assumption that it will breed quality, by eventually simply getting beyond the conventional through sheer force of numbers.

Brainstorming is conducted in group sessions, with a leader who is charged with keeping the session moving along by questions, encouragement, and by stopping any criticisms. Participants are encouraged to build on each other's ideas, but they are stopped short if they criticize. Records of the ideas are kept by a secretary or taped.

Guidelines for Creative Problem Solving

1. Soak yourself in the problem. Read, review, examine, and analyze any material you can find on the problem. Talk to people who know about it. Look at the problem from every side. Do not accept authority uncritically; question the premises. Insist on finding a way to solve the problem, rejecting any conclusion that there is no way to solve it.

As a manager, always challenge the judgment that "it can't be done." One successful manager listens to all the reasons the section can give as to why something won't work, then counters: "I agree it can't be done, but if we had to do it or be shot, what could we do?" That always changes the atmosphere and turns the group to finding ways to attack the problem rather than judge it. Provide your people with all the information you can, erring on the side of overload. Encourage them to contact a wide variety of sources for information and to soak themselves in the problem.

2. Play with the problem. Stay loose and flexible when considering the problem. Try out different assumptions; imagine that one of the conditions affecting the problem is removed, and see where the problem leads now. Approach the problem from different directions and turn it inside out. Assume different environments. Mentally shift the positions of various parts of the problem spatially and temporally. Change the order of events or the situation.

As a manager, encourage your people to explore the problem from every conceivable viewpoint. Through discussion and questioning, suggest "wild" approaches in the early stages of a project.

3. Suspend judgment. Don't draw early conclusions, which will lock you in and hamper your creative freedom. Do not become fixated on a particular part of the problem definition, losing sight of the larger ramifications. Avoid settling on an early partial or total solution, but stay open to new information and possibilities not yet considered. As solutions occur to you, write them down in a notebook and deliberately set them on a back burner until later in the project. Get them out of your mind.

As a manager, remember that you represent deadlines and budgets, and your people will tend to believe you expect early solutions from them. Help them to suspend judgment by keeping the pressure off and encouraging them to write down and defer their solutions until later.

4. Come up with at least two solutions. When you decide to produce two solutions, you are sure to keep thinking about the problem instead of fixating on one idea. Studies have shown that second solutions tend to be more creative. In one experiment, the request for a second solution increased the number of "creative" solutions from 16 to 52 percent. A further request for a third solution pushed the subjects to the limit, but still resulted in a 25 percent increase in very good, creative solutions (Hyman and Anderson, 1965).

As a manager, call for two distinct solutions to the problem, not necessarily worked out in detail, but substantially different. In most cases, all the anxieties and rigidities of the professional go into the first solution, whereas the second is more free-flowing. A group asked for ways of delivering high-quality education for less money, for example, will come up with a first solution calling for cutting costs, increasing tuition, and putting facilities to money-making uses outside of teaching. Second solutions will then involve engaging academics who are not research-oriented but good teachers to teach double loads for more money and (in lieu of student loans) investing in students in expectation of a percentage of their first five years' earnings (which would extend a university's concern with its products in a positive way).

5. *What do you do when you're stuck?* Try a variety of ways of picturing the problem and the solution: from verbal description to graphics to abstractions. Many creative scientists, mathematicians, and writers get a new perspective on problems by making sketches and diagrams.

Try your problem on outsiders. When you discuss your problem with others, you see it differently because you have to put it into terms intelligible to them. Their answers may be less important than your own presentation, but their unexpected questions may bring new areas of your brain into play.

Take a break. Give your subconscious a chance to work. When you're really stumped, go on to something else for a while. Creative problem solving is a ripening process, remember, so you can't force it. Working on it around the clock will only exhaust you.

As a manager, make yourself available as one of the people on whom to try out problems. Ask the problem solver to "draw you a picture" to help you understand the problem. When a person becomes too intense and is making no progress, give that person some short different assignment, to give the subconscious a chance to work.

Bibliography

Chapter 1. HIRING

AZEVEDO, R. E. "Scientists, Engineers and the Job Search Process." *California Management Review* 17, no. 2 (Winter 1974).

BASSETT, G. A. *A Study of Factors Associated with Turnover of Exempt Personnel.* Crotonville, N. Y.: Behavioral Research Service, General Electric Co., 1967.

BREAUGH, J. A. "Relationship between Recruiting Sources and Employee Performance, Absenteeism and Work Attitudes." *Academy of Management Journal* 24, no. 1 (1981).

CAMPBELL, J. P., M. D. DUNNETTE, E. E. LAWLER III, and K. E. WEICK, JR. *Managerial Behavior, Performance, and Effectiveness.* New York: McGraw-Hill, 1970.

CASCIO, W. F. "Accuracy of Verifiable Biographical Information Blank Responses." *Journal of Applied Psychology* 60 (1975).

DRAHEIM, K., R. HOWELL, and A. SHAPERO. *The Development of a Potential Defense R & D Complex: A Study of Minneapolis–St. Paul.* Menlo Park, Calif.: Stanford Research Institute, 1966.

DRAKE, L. R., H. R. KAPLAN, and R. A. STONE. "Organizational Performance as a Function of Recruitment Criteria and Effectiveness." *Personnel Journal* 5, no. 52 (October 1973).

FARRIS, G. F. "A Predictive Study of Turnover." *Personnel Psychology* 24 (Summer 1971).

HALL, D. T., and I. F. C. HALL. "What's New in Career Management." *Organizational Dynamics* 5 (Summer 1976).

HAMMOND, G., and J. KERN. *Teaching Comprehensive Medical Care.* Cambridge, Mass.: Harvard University Press, 1959.

HARRELL, T. W., and M. S. HARRELL. *Predictors of Business Manager Success at 10 Years Out of MBA.* Technical Report no. 10. Stanford, Calif.: Graduate School of Business, Stanford University, May 1976.

HOWELL, R. P., M. GORFINKEL, and D. BENT. *Individual Characteristics Significant to Salary Levels of Engineers and Scientists.* Menlo Park, Calif.: Stanford Research Institute, 1966.

JARRELL, D. W. "An Evaluation of Recruitment Sources for R & D." *Research Management* (March 1974).

JINDAL, G. R., and C. H. SANDBERG. "What It Costs to Hire a Professional." *Research Management* (July 1978).

LANDY, F. J., and D. A. TRUMBO. *Psychology of Work Behavior.* Rev. ed. Homewood, Ill.: Dorsey Press, 1980.

LEVENSON, H. "Distinctions within the Concept of Internal-External Control: Development of a New Scale." *Proceedings of the 80th Annual Convention of the American Psychological Association* (1972).

LIVINGSTON, J. S. "Myth of the Well-Educated Manager." *Harvard Business Review* 49, no. 1 (January–February 1971).

MARTIN, D. D., W. J. KEARNEY, and G. D. HOLDEFER. "The Decision to Hire: A Comparison of Selection Tools." *Business Perspectives,* Southern Illinois University (Spring 1971).

MARTIN, R. A., and J. PACHERES. "Good Scholars Not Always the Best." *Business Week,* February 1962, 24.

MEYER, H., and S. CUOMO. *Who Leaves? A Study of Background Characteristics of Engineers Associated with Turnover.* Crotonville, N. Y.: Behavioral Research Service, General Electric Co. 1962.

MOSEL, J. N., and H. W. GOHEEN. "The Validity of the Employment Recommendation Questionnaire in Personnel Selection." *Personnel Psychology* 12 (1959).

PORTER, L. W., and R. M. STEERS. "Organizational Work and Personal

Factors in Employee Turnover and Absenteeism." *Psychological Bulletin* 8, no. 2 (1973).

POSNER, B. Z. "Comparing Recruiter, Students, and Faculty Perceptions of Important Applicant and Job Characteristics." *Personnel Psychology* 34, no. 2 (1981).

PRICE, J. L. *The Study of Turnover.* Ames, Iowa: Iowa State University Press, 1977.

PRICE, R. L., P. H. THOMPSON, and G. W. DALTON. "A Longitudinal Study of Technological Obsolescence." *Research Management* 18, no. 6 (November 1975).

ROTTER, J. B. "Generalized Expectancies for Internal vs. External Control of Reinforcement." *Psychological Monographs* 80 (1966).

SCHICK, G. J., and B. F. KUNNECKE. "Do High Grades, Top Schools, or an Advanced Degree Lead to Job Security and Extraordinary Salary Progression?" *Interfaces* 11, no. 6 (December 1981).

SCHNEIDER, B. *Staffing Organizations.* Palisades, Calif.: Goodyear Publishing, 1976.

SHAPERO, A. "The Decision to Hire." *Chemtech* (February 1977).

————, D. M. HUFFMAN, and A. M. CHAMMAH. *The Effective Use of Scientific and Technical Information in Industrial and Non-Profit Settings.* Austin: University of Texas at Austin, 1978.

————, R. HOWELL, and J. R. TOMBAUGH. *The Structure and Dynamics of the Defense R & D Industry: The Los Angeles and Boston Complexes.* Menlo Park, Calif.: Stanford Research Institute, 1965.

SHETTY, Y. K., and N. S. PEERY. "Are Top Executives Transferable Across Companies?" *Business Horizons* 19, no. 3. (1976).

WILLIAMS, F. J., and T. W. HARRELL. "Predicting Success in Business." *Journal of Applied Psychology* 48 (1964).

Chapter 2. MOTIVATION

ALBANESE, R., and D. D. VAN FLEET. *Organizational Behavior.* New York: Dryden Press, 1983.

ARONOFF, C. "The Rise of the Behavioral Perspective in Selected General Management Textbooks: An Empirical Investigation through Content Analysis." *Academy of Management Journal* 18, no. 4 (December 1975).

BRIM, O. G., JR. "Socialization Through the Life Cycle." In *Socializa-*

tion After Childhood, edited by O. G. Brim, Jr., and S. Wheeler. New York: John Wiley and Sons, 1966.

DEWHIRST, H. D. "The Socialization of the Young Professional: A Study of Changes in the Career Values of Engineers and Scientists During the First Five Years of Employment." Ph.D. diss., University of Texas at Austin, 1970.

GELLERMAN, S. W. *Management by Motivation*. New York: American Management Association, 1968.

HERBERT, T. T. *Dimensions of Organizational Behavior*. 2d ed. New York: Macmillan, 1981.

HERZBERG, F., B. MAUSNER, and B. SNYDERMAN. *The Motivation to Work*. 2d ed. New York: John Wiley and Sons, 1959.

JONES, M. R., ed. *Nebraska Symposium on Motivation*. Lincoln: University of Nebraska Press, 1955.

LANDY, F. J., and D. A. TRUMBO. *Psychology of Work Behavior*. Rev. ed. Homewood, Illinois: The Dorsey Press, 1980.

McGREGOR, D. *The Human Side of Enterprise*. New York: McGraw-Hill, 1960.

MASLOW, A. H. *Motivation and Personality*. 2d ed. New York: Harper and Row, 1970.

PELZ, F. M., and D. C. ANDREWS. *Scientists in Organizations*. Rev. ed. Ann Arbor: University of Michigan Press, 1976.

ROGERS, R. E., and R. H. McINTIRE. *Organization and Management Theory*. New York: John Wiley and Sons, 1983.

STEERS, R. M., and L. W. PORTER. *Motivation and Work Behavior*. 3d ed. New York: McGraw-Hill, 1983.

SZILYAGI, A. D., JR., and M. J. WALLACE. *Organizational Behavior and Performance*. 3d ed. Santa Monica, Calif.: Goodyear Publishing, 1983.

Chapter 3. PERFORMANCE EVALUATION

Appraising Management Performance: Current Practices and Future Direction. New York: Conference Board, no. 723, 1977.

DRUCKER, P. *The Practice of Management*. New York: Harper and Bros., 1954.

GORDON, G., and S. MARQUIS. "Effect of Differing Administrative Authority on Scientific Innovation." Working Paper no. 4, Graduate School of Business, University of Chicago, 1963.

IVANCEVICH, J. M. "Changes in Performance in a Management by Objectives Program." *Administrative Science Quarterly* 19 (1974).

KANE, J. S. and E. E. LAWLER, III. "Performance Appraisal Effectiveness: Its Assessment and Determinants." In *Research in Organizational Behavior,* edited by B. M. Staw. Greenwich, Conn.: JAI Press, 1979.

KONDRASUK, J. N. "Studies in MBO Effectiveness." *Academy of Management Review* 6, no. 3 (1981).

KRANTZ, I. W. "Evaluating the Technical Employee: Results Approach." *Personnel* (January–February 1964).

LANDY, F. J., J. L. BARNES, J. CLEVELAND, and K. MURPHY. "Attitudes Toward Performance Appraisal." University Park, Pa.: Penn State Report Series, 1978.

LANDY, F. J., and D. A. TRUMBO. *Psychology of Work Behavior.* Rev. ed. Homewood, Ill.: Dorsey Press, 1980.

LOCKE, E. A. "Toward a Theory of Task Motivation and Incentives." *Organizational Behavior and Human Performance.* May 1968.

MEYER, H. H., E. KAY, and J. R. P. FRENCH, JR. "Split Roles in Performance Appraisal." *Harvard Business Review* (January–February 1965).

ODIORNE, G. S. *Management by Objectives.* New York: Pitman, 1965.

PELZ, D. C., and F. M. ANDREWS. *Scientists in Organizations: Productive Climates for Research and Development.* Rev. ed. Ann Arbor: University of Michigan Press, 1976.

SZILYAGYI, A. D., JR., and M. J. WALLACE, JR. *Organizational Behavior and Performance.* 2d ed. Santa Monica: Goodyear Publishing Company, 1980.

WEXLEY, K. N., and G. A. YUKL. *Organizational Behavior and Personnel Psychology.* Homewood, Ill.: Richard D. Irwin, 1977.

WIKSTROM, W. S. "Managing by and with Objectives." *Studies in Personnel Policy,* no. 212. New York: National Industrial Conference Board, 1968.

Chapter 4. MANAGING INFORMATION

ALLEN, T. J., "Managing the Flow of Scientific and Technological Information." Ph.D. diss., Massachusetts Institute of Technology, 1966.

————. *Managing the Flow of Technology: Technology Transfer and the Dissemination of Technological Information within the R & D Organization*. Cambridge: MIT Press, 1977.

ALLEN, T. J., D. M. S. LEE, and M. L. TUSHMAN. "R & D Performance as a Function of Internal Communications, Project Management, and the Nature of the Work." *IEEE Transactions of Engineering Management* (February 1980).

BERNAL, J. D. "The Transmission of Scientific Information." *The Proceedings of the International Conference on Scientific Information, Part 1.* Washington, D.C. (1959).

BERSCHEID, E., and E. H. WALSTER. *Interpersonal Attraction*. Reading, Pa.: Addison-Wesley Publishing, 1969.

BODENSTEINER, W. D. "Information Channel Utilization Under Varying Research and Development Project Conditions." Ph.D. diss., University of Texas at Austin, 1970.

CHADWICK-JONES, J. K. *Social Exchange Theory*. London: Academic Press, 1976.

COMPTON, B. E. "Scientific Communication." In *Handbook of Communication*, edited by I. de Sola Pool and W. Schramm. Chicago: Rand McNally College Publishing, 1973.

CRANE, D. *Invisible Colleges*. Chicago: University of Chicago Press, 1972.

GOLDHAR, J. D. "An Exploratory Study of Technological Innovation." D.B.A. diss., George Washington University, 1971.

GOLDMARK, P. C. *Maverick Inventor: My Turbulent Years*. New York: E. P. Dutton, 1973.

GROSS, A. E., and J. G. LATANE. "Receiving Help, Reciprocation and Interpersonal Attraction." *Journal of Applied Social Psychology* (July-September 1974).

HODGE, D. M., and G. H. NELSON. *Biological Laboratories Communication*. Fort Detrick, Frederick, Md.: U.S. Biological Laboratories, 1965.

HOLLAND, W. E. "Intra- and Inter-organizational Communications Behavior of Scientists and Engineers with High Information Potential." Ph.D. diss., University of Texas at Austin, 1970.

JENNY, H. K., and W. J. UNDERWOOD. *Engineering Information Survey Results*. New York: RCA, 1978.

KOESTLER, A. *The Act of Creation*. New York: Macmillan, 1964.

LIN, N. *The Study of Human Communications*. Indianapolis, Ind.: Bobbs-Merrill, 1973.

McGuire, W. J. "The Nature of Attitudes and Attitude Change." In *The Handbook of Social Psychology*, Vol. 3. 2d ed., edited by G. Lindzey and E. Aronson. Reading, Mass.: Addison-Wesley, 1969.

————. "Persuasion, Resistance, and Attitude Change." In *Handbook of Communication*, Chicago: Rand McNally College Publishing, 1973.

Menzel, H. *The Flow of Information among Scientists: Report.* New York: Bureau of Applied Research, Columbia University, 1958.

————. "The Information Needs of Current Scientific Research." *Library Quarterly* 34 (January 1964).

Myers, L. A., Jr., and D. M. Huffman. "Information Systems in Research and Development: Global Gatekeepers versus Specialist Gatekeepers." Austin, Texas, *Department of Management Working Paper*, no. 81/82–4–31 (July 1982).

Milgram, S. "The Small World Problem." *Psychology Today*, January 1967.

Parker, E. B., D. A. Lingwood, and W. J. Paisley. *Communication and Research Productivity in an Interdisciplinary Behavioral Science Research Area.* Stanford: Institute for Communication Research, Stanford University, 1968.

Pelz, D. C., and F. M. Andrews. *Scientists in Organizations: Productive Climates for Research and Development.* Rev. ed. Ann Arbor: University of Michigan Press, 1976.

Price, D. J. de Solla. *Little Science, Big Science.* New York: Columbia University Press, 1963.

Shapero, A., D. M. Huffman, and A. M. Chammah. *The Effective Use of Scientific and Technical Information in Industrial and Non-Profit Settings: A Study of Managerial Interventions.* Austin: University of Texas, 1978.

Vorwerk, E. G. *Time Usage by Municipal Managers: An Exploratory Study.* Ph.D. diss., University of Texas at Austin, 1979.

Chapter 5.   TECHNICAL OBSOLESCENCE, BURNOUT, AND STAYING ALIVE

Burack, E. H., and G. C. Pati. "Technology and Managerial Obsolescence." *MSU Business Topics* 18, no. 2 (Michigan State University, 1970).

Casady, M. "If You're Active and Savvy at 30, You'll Be Warm and Witty at 70." *Psychology Today*, November 1975.

CHERNISS, C. *Professional Burnout in Human Service Organizations.* New York: Praeger, 1980.

DIAMOND, M. C. "The Aging Brain: Some Enlightening and Optimistic Results." *American Scientist* 66 (January–February 1978).

DUBIN, S. S. "Obsolescence or Lifelong Education: A Choice for the Professional." *American Psychologist,* May 1972.

FRIES, J. F. and L. M. CRAPO. *Vitality and Aging.* San Francisco: W. H. Freeman, 1981.

HACKER, A., ed. *U.S.: A Statistical Portrait of the American People.* New York: The Viking Press, 1983.

KAUFMAN, H. G. *Obsolescence and Professional Career Development.* New York: AMACOM, 1974.

LEHMAN, H. C. *Age and Achievement.* Princeton, N. J.: Princeton University Press, 1953.

LEVINSON, D. J., and C. N. DARROW. *The Seasons of a Man's Life.* New York: Knopf, 1978.

NESSELRODE, J. F., K. W. SCHAIE, and P. B. BALTES. "Ontogenetic and Generational Components of Structural and Quantitative Change in Adult Behavior." *Journal of Gerontology,* no. 27 (1972).

OBERG, W. "Age and Achievement and the Technical Man." *Personnel Psychology* 13 (Summer 1960).

PELLETIER, K. R. *Longevity.* New York: Delacorte Press/Seymour Lawrence, 1981.

PELZ, D. C., and F. M. ANDREWS. *Scientists in Organizations.* 2d ed. Ann Arbor: University of Michigan Press, 1976.

POOL, I. DE SOLA. "Tracking the Flow of Information." *Science* 12 (August 1983).

SCHAIE, K. W., and C. R. STROTHER. "A Cross-Sequential Study of Age Changes in Cognitive Behavior." *Psychological Bulletin* 70, no. 6 (1968).

THOMPSON, D. B. "Aging Workers: Experienced or Exhausted." *Industry Week,* July 9, 1979.

WICKSTROM, W. S. "The Productive Years of Former Managers." Conference Board Report no. 747. New York: The Conference Board, 1978.

ZELLIKOFF, S. B. "On the Obsolescence and Retraining of Engineering Personnel." *Training and Development Journal* (May 1969).

Chapter 6. CREATIVITY

BAILEY, R. L. *Disciplined Creativity for Engineers.* Ann Arbor: Ann Arbor Science, 1978.

BARRON, F. "The Psychology of Creativity." In *The Creativity Question,* edited by A. Rothenberg and C. R. Hausman. Durham, N.C.: Duke University Press, 1976.

BOURNE, L. E., JR., B. R. EKSTRAND, and R. L. DOMINOWSKI. *The Psychology of Thinking.* Englewood Cliffs, N.J.: Prentice-Hall, 1971.

CROSBY, A. *Creativity and Performance in Industrial Organizations.* London: Tavistock, 1968.

CULLEM, T. "Stimulating Creativity." *Electronic Engineering Times,* July 20, 1981.

DE BONO, E. *Lateral Thinking.* New York: Harper & Row, 1970.

EDEL, D. H. *Introduction to Creative Design.* Englewood Cliffs, N.J.: Prentice-Hall, 1967.

GARDNER, J. *Art, Mind and Brain.* New York: Basic Books, 1982.

GETZELS, J. W., and P. W. JACKSON. *Creativity and Intelligence.* New York: John Wiley and Sons, 1962.

GORDON, W. J. J. *Synectics.* New York: Harper, 1961.

GREGORY, C. E. *The Management of Intelligence.* New York: McGraw-Hill, 1967.

GUILFORD, J. P. *The Nature of Human Intelligence.* New York: McGraw-Hill, 1967.

HOWIESON, N. "A Longitudinal Study of Creativity: 1965–1975." *Journal of Creative Behavior* 15, no. 2 (April–June 1981).

HYMAN, R., and B. ANDERSON. "Solving Problems." *International Science and Technology* (September 1965).

KOESTLER, A. *The Act of Creation.* New York: Macmillan, 1964.

KOGAN, N., and E. PANKOVE. "Long Term Predictive Validity of Divergent Thinking Tests. Some negative evidence." *Journal of Educational Psychology* 66, no. 6 (1974).

MACKINNON, D. W. "Identification and Development of Creative Personnel." *Personnel Administration* (January–February 1968).

MCKELLAR, P. *Imagination and Thinking.* New York: Basic Books, 1957.

MEDNICK, S. A. "The Associative Basis of the Creative Process." *Psychology Review,* 69, no. 3 (1962).

———. "The Associative Basis of the Creative Process." In *The Creativ-*

ity Question, edited by A. Rothenberg and C. R. Hausman. Durham: N.C.: Duke University Press, 1976.

Mednick, S. A., and M. T. Mednick. *Remote Associates Test.* Boston: Houghton Mifflin, 1964.

Osborn, A. F. *Applied Imagination.* New York: Scribner, 1963.

Parloff, M. B., L. Datta, M. Kleman, and J. H. Handlon. "Personality Characteristics Which Differentiate Creative Male Adolescents and Adults." NIMH Creativity Reports, 1967.

Prentky, R. A. *Creativity and Psychopathology.* New York: Praeger, 1980.

Rossman, J. *Industrial Creativity.* New Hyde Park, N.Y.: University Books, 1964.

Rothenberg, A., and C. R. Hausman, eds. *The Creativity Question.* Durham, N.C.: Duke University Press, 1976.

Stein, M. I. *Stimulating Creativity,* Vol. 2. New York: Academic Press, 1975.

————. "A Transactional Approach to Creativity." In *Scientific Creativity: Its Recognition and Development,* edited by C. W. Taylor and F. Barron. New York: John Wiley and Sons, 1963.

Steiner, G. A. "Introduction." In *The Creative Organization,* edited by G. A. Steiner. Chicago: University of Chicago Press, 1965.

Taylor, Jack W. *How to Create New Ideas.* Englewood Cliffs, N.J.: Prentice-Hall, 1961.

Zwicky, F. *Discovery, Invention, Research: Through the Morphological Approach.* New York: Macmillan, 1969.

APPENDIX B

De Bono, E. *Lateral Thinking.* New York: Harper & Row, 1970.

APPENDIX C

Hyman, R., and B. Anderson. "Solving Problems." *International Science and Technology* (1965).

Index